Get the ebook FREE!

To get a free PDF copy of this book (sold separately for $29.99) purchase the print book and register it at the Manning website following the instructions inside this insert.

That's it!

Thanks from Manning!

Team Foundation Server 2008 in Action

JAMIL AZHER

MANNING

Greenwich
(74° w. long.)

For online information and ordering of this and other Manning books, please visit www.manning.com. The publisher offers discounts on this book when ordered in quantity. For more information, please contact

Special Sales Department
Manning Publications Co.
Sound View Court 3B   fax: (609) 877-8256
Greenwich, CT 06830   email: orders@manning.com

Manning Publications Co.
Sound View Court 3B
Greenwich, CT 06830

Development Editor Jeff Bleiel
Copyeditor: Benjamin Berg
Typesetter: Gordan Salinovic
Cover designer: Leslie Haimes
Proofreader: Katie Tennant

ISBN 1933988592
Printed in the United States of America
2 3 4 5 6 7 8 9 10 – MAL – 13 12 11 10 09

To my father, Azher Ali, and my mother, Sakina Azher,
who taught me that life's greatest accomplishments
are those that are in the service of humanity

contents

10 Using workflow with TFS 268

preface

Ever since I started writing software code—over two decades ago, but it feels like just the other day—I've wondered whether I'm doing it the "right" way. I still haven't figured out what the right way is—but I'm sure that I've done software development in plenty of wrong ways.

When I created my first BASIC program for a college project many years ago, it was a long list of "spaghetti code" hundreds of lines long, with no separation of concerns. (Although object-oriented or service-oriented programming didn't exist in those days, I could've used subroutines to mitigate the problem.) After a disastrous outcome, I quickly learned the value of solving complex problems by weaving together simple pieces.

When I started to write code for a living, I didn't think to ask clients for written requirements and acceptance criteria. I did months of wasted work assuming that I understood their stated, though undocumented, business needs. I found out that despite good intentions, misunderstandings can occur when objectives aren't specified and expectations aren't recorded.

When I started to manage globally distributed teams, I learned that simply reviewing status reports carries no assurance that projects are on track. I realized that visibility has to come from the state of the software and not from a report that someone writes based on conversations with developers. The tricky part, of course, was to be able to create a mechanism so that software state can be defined, measured, and monitored.

When I began working on enterprise projects, I underestimated the difficulty associated with integrating disparate systems and managing complex deployments in outsourced datacenters. The problems became more acute when organizational boundaries needed to be crossed. I learned about the complexity of modern IT environments and how optimistic assumptions about integration and deployment can lead to execution failures and even expensive lawsuits.

Let's face it. Software development has never been easy and is not getting any easier. The technology learning curve is getting steeper; the requirements for security, interoperability, and availability are increasingly stringent; and project teams are becoming dispersed in multiple locations and time zones. While the tools have improved significantly over time, so has complexity. As a professional software developer, I don't feel that my job is easier than what it was a decade ago. There are now more wrong ways to develop software development than ever before.

This leads us back to the original question. What is the right way to do software development? There's no shortage of methodologies and technologies from which to choose. As a community, we've made significant progress based on accumulated experience. But independent studies show that the overall success rate for software projects remains stuck between 30 and 35 percent (projects that are completed on time, within budget, and meet requirements).

Perhaps there's no universal right way to do software development. Perhaps it's situation-specific. Perhaps it depends on project type, skill level, team structure, motivation, organizational culture, experience, and deadlines. This is what I've come to believe. Although we could define a small set of universal "rights" (for example, making code secure) and "wrongs" (shipping code without testing), many of the good and bad practices are context-specific. And some aren't. The art of project management is defining what makes sense in your environment.

This realization has led me to think about adopting a flexible application lifecycle management (ALM) platform instead of trying to find a silver bullet. While I think that the right strategy is situation-specific, once you define what's right for a given situation, you need an infrastructure to implement it.

I don't know of many organizations that can easily create a horizontal ALM platform. Instead, people buy or download individual tools for various pieces of the ALM solution. (The few integrated toolsets available in the market have traditionally been too expensive or too inflexible.) For a long time, I used these individual tools, but always found it difficult to weave them together on an end-to-end basis. Many of the products worked fine as point solutions, but covering the entire software development lifecycle using disparate tools isn't an easy undertaking. Nor is it efficient.

One day in 2004, I heard about a product called Visual Studio Team System (VSTS) from Microsoft. The server piece of VSTS is called Team Foundation Server (TFS). This is the component responsible for the platform's ALM capabilities. What impressed me right away was the system's integrated functionalities—covering the entire software lifecycle. The next welcome feature was its customizability. From that day on, I've spent many exhausting days and sleepless nights tinkering with TFS, talking to customers, and thinking about how the product can be used to solve real-life problems.

I wanted to share my observations by writing a book. I wanted to write based on real-life challenges—the learning that comes from the collective experience of the community of software professionals. I tried to capture that knowledge from one-on-one interviews, newsgroup postings, user group meetings, and experimentations with the product.

TFS is an ambitious product. Like any large product, many of its operational, programmable, and extensible features aren't self-evident. Moreover, customizations and workarounds are sometimes needed to meet specific needs. I wanted to write a book that provided this kind of actionable information to the practitioners.

To me, TFS was a compelling story that had to be told.

I wanted to tell that story.

acknowledgments

A book project is rarely a solo undertaking. The insights of many defined and enriched the material presented here. Writing a book is like running a marathon. And having a great team makes all the difference.

Many thanks to my editor Michael Stephens and Manning publisher Marjan Bace for defining the vision and making the project a reality.

Thanks to development editor Jeff Bleiel for making the chapters user-friendly. I am grateful to copyeditor Benjamin Berg and to technical proofreader Robert Horvick for catching errors and offering suggestions that made the content more readable and relevant. Thanks to project editor Mary Piergies for keeping the endeavor on track and to Karen Tegtmeyer for coordinating the reviews. Thanks to proofreader Katie Tennant for her extraordinary patience as we went back and forth on changes. The Manning team was a pleasure to work with and I'm grateful for their professional support.

My heartfelt thanks to reviewers Buck Hodges, Michael Ruminer, Benjamin Day, Steven Borg, Martin Woodward, Willy-Peter Schaub, Dave Corun, Eric Swanson, Christian Siegers, Derik Whittaker, David Barkol, Alpana Prasad, and many others for their input and feedback. Without their guidance and mentorship, the book would not be what it is today. Thanks to the technical team at Orion Informatics—Shafqat Ahmed, Zakir Hossain, Omar Raihan, Manojit Paul, Rabiul Islam, and Farzana Samad—for ensuring the accuracy of the code.

Finally, my love and gratitude to my dear wife Rokeya Khan for tolerating the late nights, mood swings, and abrogation of family responsibilities. How could I not also thank my young sons, Nasif and Zarif, for believing that someday I'll tear myself from the computer and show them the magical place where the earth meets the sky!

about this book

This book is about the science of creating software. More and more organizations are demanding that instead of being a mysterious activity practiced by a smart but unsocial group of people, software development should become a transparent business process that produces reliable outcomes. Software has become too important in the modern world to leave its creation to chance and faith.

Transparency generates trust. Communication improves productivity. Collaboration decreases execution risks. These are time-honored tenets that work when undertaking any team activity. Software development is no different. But implementing this knowledge in everyday software development activities isn't easy, given how diverse the stakeholders are and how dispersed the teams are. It requires a platform that facilitates transparency, collaboration, and communication without any special effort by the practitioners involved. After all, people on the project teams already have too many other issues to think about.

This book teaches you how to use TFS to implement a consistent, reliable, and repeatable software development process. You'll learn how the platform works out of the box as well as how to customize it. You'll understand some of the limitations as well as the possibilities. You'll realize that software development doesn't have to be based on luck and last-minute heroics. You can construct, instrument, and institute a process that produces better outcomes. TFS gives you that power.

Audience

This book is intended for ALM practitioners in the field. It contains actionable information for program and project managers looking to set up their preferred development processes and to monitor execution status. There's information for developers interested in optimally configuring source code repositories and build systems. There's guidance for database professionals attempting to better integrate their work with the rest of the development activities. And there's material for IT administrators thinking about deploying the platform in managed data centers in a secure, scalable, and highly available manner.

The goal of the TFS platform is to integrate the myriad stakeholders in the extended development team.

The book is for people who are trying to make it happen.

Roadmap

Chapter 1 starts with a brief background on the evolution of software development methodologies. We then learn how TFS fits into the overall application lifecycle management (ALM) landscape and what the platform's key features are. We review the major functional areas to get a conceptual understanding of how the system works as a whole.

Chapter 2 describes the changes in TFS 2008. TFS 2008 offers important enhancements in build and version control. These changes improve performance, scalability, and flexibility.

Chapter 3 talks about the database management capabilities of TFS. Despite the ubiquitous presence of databases in software development efforts, database professionals have traditionally had to operate outside the mainstream development processes. We learn how TFS can integrate database management in the core development process.

Chapter 4 reviews the underlying principles of effective source code management. We learn how to undertake parallel development using various branching models. We also learn how to maintain shared code and coordinate the work of distributed feature teams.

Chapter 5 talks about version control policies. Policies are important because they provide consistent guidance regarding what's acceptable in a given development process. In this chapter, we learn about access control as well as check-in policies.

Chapter 6 introduces the concept of merging. Given the complexities of real-life merge operations, effective tool support is essential for productivity and safety. We also learn about the TFS event engine and how it can be used to coordinate code maintenance actions of distributed teams.

Chapter 7 is about creating reliable builds. We learn about the core concepts in Team Build and explore its inner workings. We then apply this knowledge to create different kinds of builds. We also create a service that creates test builds before committing changes to the main repository.

Chapter 8 delves into the details of setting up an automated system for versioning assemblies. This is important because without an effective versioning mechanism, you end up in chaos when deploying build binaries. We learn about versioning Windows as well as web applications.

Chapter 9 focuses on the operational aspects of TFS. We learn how to deploy TFS for scalability and availability, how to weigh relevant factors when organizing team projects, and how to create and expose key performance indicators (KPIs) for monitoring project health.

Chapter 10 switches gears and talks about TFS within the context of larger business processes. We explore how TFS can be integrated in a broader organizational workflow. The benefits of a workflow-based system include built-in support for long-running activities, better resource management, and tracking features.

Code conventions and downloads

All source code in listings or in text is in a `fixed-width font like this` to separate it from ordinary text. Code annotations accompany many of the listings, highlighting important concepts. In some cases, numbered bullets link to explanations that follow the listing.

The complete example code for the book can be downloaded from the Manning web site at www.manning.com/azher or www.manning.com/TeamFoundationServerin-Action. You'll find source code and other supporting artifacts there.

Author Online

The purchase of *Team Foundation Server in Action* includes free access to a private forum run by Manning Publications where you can make comments about the book, ask technical questions, and receive help from the author and other users. You can access and subscribe to the forum at www.manning.com/azher or www.manning.com/TeamFoundationServerinAction. This page provides information on how to get on the forum once you are registered, what kind of help is available, and the rules of conduct in the forum.

Manning's commitment to our readers is to provide a venue where a meaningful dialogue among individual readers and between readers and author can take place. It's not a commitment to any specific amount of participation on the part of the author, whose contribution to the book's forum remains voluntary (and unpaid). We suggest you try asking the author some challenging questions, lest his interest stray!

The Author Online forum and the archives of previous discussions will be accessible from the publisher's website as long as the book is in print.

About the title

By combining introductions, overviews, and how-to examples, the *In Action* books are designed to help learning and remembering. According to research in cognitive science, the things people remember are things they discover during self-motivated exploration.

Although no one at Manning is a cognitive scientist, we are convinced that for learning to become permanent it must pass through stages of exploration, play, and, interestingly, retelling of what is being learned. People understand and remember new things, which is to say they master them, only after actively exploring them. Humans learn *in action*. An essential part of an *In Action* guide is that it is example-driven. It encourages the reader to try things out, to play with new code, and explore new ideas.

There is another, more mundane, reason for the title of this book: our readers are busy. They use books to do a job or to solve a problem. They need books that allow them to jump in and jump out easily and learn just what they want just when they want it. They need books that aid them *in action*. The books in this series are designed for such readers.

About the cover illustration

The figure on the cover of *Team Foundation Server in Action* is captioned "A Friend of the Artist." The illustration is taken from a French book, *Encyclopedie des Voyages* by J. G. St. Saveur, published in Paris in the 19th century. The diversity of the drawings in the Encyclopedie speaks vividly of the uniqueness and individuality of the world's towns and provinces and of its citizens less than 200 years ago. This was a time when dress codes identified people uniquely as belonging to a certain locality or country or profession or station in life, and that were easily recognizable by others.

Dress codes have changed since then and the diversity and distinctions by region and class, so rich at the time, have faded away. It is now often hard to tell the inhabitant of one continent from another. Perhaps, trying to view it optimistically, we have traded a cultural and visual diversity for a more varied personal life. Or a more varied and interesting intellectual and technical life.

We at Manning celebrate the inventiveness, the initiative, and the fun of the computer business with book covers based on the rich diversity of regional life two centuries ago brought back to life by the pictures from this collection.

Part 1

Exploring Team Foundation Server

In part 1 of the book, we take a broad look at some of the salient features of Team Foundation Server (TFS). We learn how TFS fits into the overall application lifecycle management (ALM) process, what the major features are, how the platform is architected, and how it can be extended.

We also review the changes introduced in TFS 2008—such as major enhancements in Team Build, incremental improvements in Team Foundation version control, and integration of Visual Studio Team System 2008 Database Edition.

Since our goal is to obtain a general understanding of how TFS works, the material in part 1 is mostly introductory in nature. We cover a lot of ground and aim to develop a broad understanding of the major functionalities in TFS.

TFS and the practice
of software development

Visual Studio Team System 2008 (VSTS) is Microsoft's application lifecycle management (ALM) platform for managing the end-to-end software development process. It's a vast product with wide-ranging capabilities. VSTS first debuted in 2005, with incremental improvements added in 2008, and contains both general purpose as well as role-based capabilities. The platform can be extended as needed. Given how geographically distributed, technically complex, and strategically important enterprise software projects have become, I feel that VSTS deserves a careful look with regard to solving real-life development challenges. The days are gone when you could hope to develop enterprise software, with acceptable quality and within a reasonable timeframe, without effective tool support.

This book is about improving your software projects by leveraging the capabilities of the Microsoft ALM platform. In this book, we learn how to resolve various

3

practical issues by applying the system's native capabilities, as well as by augmenting them via customizations.

As practitioners in the information technology (IT) industry, we all know that software development isn't easy. Why this is so has been extensively debated since the industry was born. Despite the advent of myriad development methodologies, infrastructure tools, and careful project management, most projects still run behind schedule and over budget. A recent study showed that only 35 percent of software projects can be categorized as successful (completed on time, within budget, and met user requirements).

Of course, this situation isn't unique to the IT industry. We see unexpected delays and cost overruns when large-scale projects are undertaken in many other sectors, such as construction, transportation, and life sciences. Perhaps the complex and volatile nature of the real world makes it impossible for humans to make perfect predictions. Nevertheless, unless we constantly strive to improve our estimation and execution processes—with the understanding that perfection is a goal, not a yardstick to beat people with—progress, however incremental, will become impossible. Chaos comes easy.

While I don't know of an absolute "right" way to do software development, I do feel that outcomes can be improved by focusing on the basics. Industry studies have shown that key success factors include executive support, effective communication between stakeholders, good architecture, skilled team members, incremental development, extensive testing, requirement stability, and the ability to dynamically adjust course based on changing realities. There are no surprises here. Therefore, the question becomes not so much whether we *know* what the best practices are as much as how best to *practice* them on a day-to-day basis. Of course, you need to deal with some issues (such as obtaining and retaining skilled resources) in an administrative manner. For others, it's critical that you select an ALM platform that can mitigate execution risks and promote adoption of good practices. VSTS is such a platform.

The client portion of VSTS is segmented along various roles—architects, developers, testers, and database professionals (see figure 1.1). If you're interested in *all* client-side features, you can purchase Visual Studio Team System 2008 Team Suite, which combines the full range of capabilities. Stakeholders who need to participate in the lifecycle but don't want to install the Visual Studio *IDE (integrated development environment)* can use the Visual Studio Team System Web Access 2008 Power Tool (TSWA). TSWA enables you to access TFS using only a web browser.

Visual Studio Team System 2008 Team Foundation Server (TFS) is the server-based portion of VSTS. TFS offers core features such as process definition and instantiation, work item tracking, source code management, project portal, build management, reporting, and so on.

In this chapter, we review the high-level features of TFS. You'll learn about the following:

- *How TFS fits into the software development process*—Brief background on development practices and how TFS fits into the overall context
- *Technical architecture of TFS*—How TFS is structured, and the major services and components in each tier.
- *Major features*—Work item tracking, version control, team build, project portal, and reports

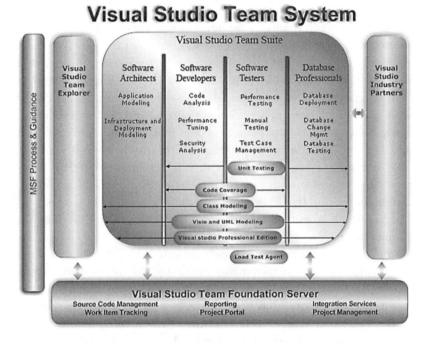

Figure 1.1   VSTS consists of TFS and several role-based client products.

1.1   Background on software development processes

The practice of software development has evolved considerably in the last 50 years. When early computer programs were written in the 1950s and 1960s, engineers mostly followed a *code and fix* approach to solve business problems. This ad hoc process soon became untenable for large-scale development projects. In the 1970s, the *waterfall* model, emphasizing up-front design and meticulous planning, was proposed as a way to reduce execution risk. The waterfall model had an enormous impact on software engineering and continues to be followed in many organizations today.

In the 1990s, the IT industry went through seismic changes. The primary drivers were business- as well as technology-related. With the introduction of personal computers in the 1980s, computing power increased dramatically, while the associated hardware and software costs went down. Global communication was revolutionized with the advent of the World Wide Web in the 1990s. Businesses became geographically unfettered and 24/7 service availability became routine. The new world demanded rapid software delivery in the face of constantly changing business realities.

As a result of these transformations in the 1990s, software projects increased in complexity while simultaneously demanding drastic cuts in implementation time. The requirements for security, availability, interoperability, scalability, and performance became much greater than they were in the 1970s or 1980s. Furthermore, development teams became distributed globally and started working asynchronously—significantly increasing the chances of miscommunication and mismanagement.

Beyond the waterfall, new software development methodologies were proposed to meet the requirements of the brave new world. *Iterative* processes, emphasizing incremental delivery of value, were proposed in the 1990s. Iterative processes such as the Microsoft Solutions Framework (MSF), Rational Unified Process (RUP), and others essentially suggested mini waterfall-based cycles—the development period was divided into iterations that incrementally enriched a core set of key functionalities.

In early 2000, *agile* processes were proposed in an attempt to further reduce development time and increase productivity. Agile processes, such as extreme programming (XP), Scrum, Crystal, and feature-driven development (FDD), advocate high-fidelity communication (mostly face to face). They also significantly reduce documentation, eliminate big up-front planning and design work, advocate testing as an integrated part of development, and relentlessly emphasize creating working software that meets immediate needs.

However, despite the prevalence of so many methodologies, the industry-wide success rate for software projects remains low. Why has the project success rate not improved in the last decade? We've already discussed many reasons, but in my opinion, one of the main reasons has been the lack of widely available, cost-effective, and *integrated* toolsets to implement a chosen process on an end-to-end basis. Although, in theory, a process may sound great, if you don't have the right infrastructure to realize it, the discussion remains largely academic.

Microsoft's entry in the ALM market opens up new possibilities. The Microsoft Solutions Framework (MSF) provides a process framework where you can plug in your chosen process. VSTS ships with two built-in process templates—MSF for Agile Software Development and MSF for CMMI Process Improvement. You can add other third-party process templates (such as RUP or Scrum) or create a custom process.

TFS provides the infrastructure needed to support enterprise-wide processes across distributed organizations. The artifacts, policies, and workflows defined in the process are available to the entire team via TFS. TFS also provides the metrics and reports needed to gain visibility regarding project status, trends, and roadblocks. The ultimate goal is to provide a "friction-free" environment where the infrastructure enhances collaboration, productivity, and quality.

1.2   *TFS architecture*

TFS is based on a distributed architecture. The product consists of three logical tiers (see figure 1.2). They are discussed in sections 1.2.1 through 1.2.3.

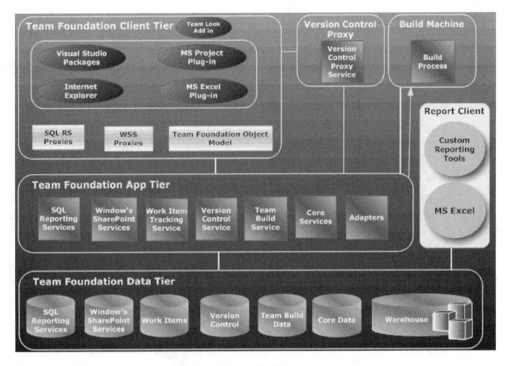

Figure 1.2 TFS is based on a logical three-tier architecture.

1.2.1   *Client tier*

The client tier consists of components that interact with the user. It includes Team Explorer, add-ins for Microsoft Excel and Microsoft Project, command-line tools, and third-party VSIP (Visual Studio Industry Partners) packages. Components in the client tier communicate with the application tier via a set of APIs defined in the Team Foundation object model.

1.2.2   *Application tier*

The application tier consists of a number of web services that provide access to core system services. The services are grouped in two categories—data services (work item tracking, source control, build management) and integration services (security, registration, events, linking, classification). Additionally, the application tier hosts the SharePoint-based portal and SSRS (SQL Server Reporting Services)–based reports.

1.2.3   *Data tier*

The data tier consists of operational databases, a data warehouse, and an Analysis Services (OLAP) cube. This tier stores persistent data related to work items, source code, builds, team projects, security, activities, notifications, and so on.

1.3   *Major features*

The features offered by TFS can be divided in five categories (see figure 1.3). They are discussed in sections 1.3.1 through 1.3.5.

Figure 1.3   TFS offers five major features.

1.3.1   *Work item tracking*

The work item tracking (WIT) system enables you to create, modify, copy, and query work items. In TFS, the term *work item* denotes an item that you want to track during the development process. Work items include bugs, tasks, scenarios, requirements, change requests, and so on. The work item types that are available in a team project are defined in the corresponding process template. You can also create custom work item types in addition to the built-in ones.

A work item type definition contains field definitions, form layout information, and state transition rules. Work item type definitions are stored in XML files associated with process templates. You can use the Process Template Editor included in the TFS Power Tools to graphically edit the work item types (download TFS Power Tools from http://msdn2.microsoft.com/en-us/tfs2008/bb980963.aspx).

Work items can be queried using a SQL-like query syntax called *Work Item Query Language (WIQL)*. The VSTS IDE includes a graphical query editor for creating and executing queries. You can also create and execute WIQL queries from custom program code using the TFS object model.

The work item form (see figure 1.4) is fully customizable. You can change the look and feel by creating new tabs, adding or removing form fields, and inserting custom

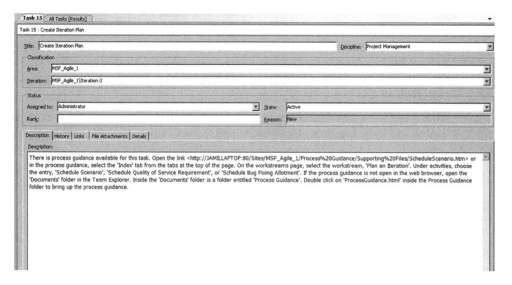

Figure 1.4   Work item tracking enables you to monitor execution status of requirements, functional specs, tasks, bugs, and more.

controls. Work items can be linked to one other (support for hierarchically linked work items is coming in the next version), can contain attachments, and also have an audit log showing the change history.

Work items can be bidirectionally synchronized with Excel and Project for consumption by stakeholders who may use these products for data entry and project management. You can also use the TFS object model to synchronize work items with other products as needed (such as your enterprise project management system).

1.3.2 *Version control*

Team Foundation version control (TFVC) provides the capability to store files in a central repository, along with their version information (see figure 1.5). Effective support for managing and evolving source files is critical for implementing an ALM platform that helps, not hinders, the development process. Arguably, the most important asset in your development effort is the source code itself. You need a flexible and reliable system for developers to store code files, secure them, retrieve them as needed, isolate concurrent development efforts, and attach metadata to each check-in.

TFVC provides reliable change management via atomic check-ins. When you check in a set of changes as part of a single changeset, either *all* changes will be committed to the repository or *none* will be committed. This transactional check-in behavior ensures that the codebase remains in a consistent state at all times. You don't have to worry about a partial update breaking the internal consistency of the codebase.

TFVC supports check-in policies that help protect the integrity of the codebase. Check-in policies help ensure that the code being checked in meets appropriate quality criteria. The quality criteria may include passing static code analysis, associating check-ins with work items, and so on. You can also create custom check-in policies and implement your own change control criteria. If a developer checks in code by overriding a policy, TFVC can send out an email alert containing the reason. The policy override information is also recorded in the data warehouse, allowing the creation of reports to track the action.

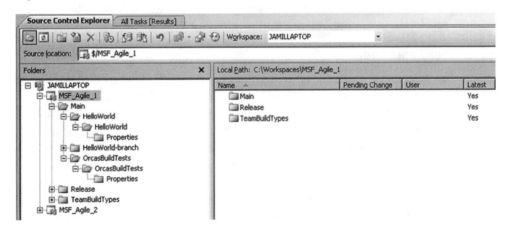

Figure 1.5 **Version control provides a central repository for source code and other artifacts.**

TFVC makes it possible for developers to create shelvesets. Shelvesets are used to store pending version control changes, associated work-item links, and comments on the server without performing a check-in operation. Developers can use shelvesets to back up changes before starting a new task, to easily share changes between multiple developers, or to perform code reviews.

TFVC offers low-overhead branching and merging capabilities to facilitate parallel development. Branching allows a collection of files to evolve on two independent paths, or branches. Branching creates a parent-child relationship between the two collections of files, such that changes made on one side of the relationship don't affect the other until an effort is made to merge the changes from one branch to another. Branching is commonly used at various milestones within the development lifecycle. During the development phase, multiple child branches can be used to allow teams to develop features in isolation before merging back to a common parent branch. When the product ships, a "release" branch can be created so that product maintenance is done in isolation from the next version's development. After release, branching can be used to create service packs and patches to support the product.

Merging is used to integrate code between branches. TVFC enables you to easily merge code that's located in related branches (branches that are related via parent-child relationships). Although less straightforward, TFVC allows you to merge code between unrelated branches using a *baseless* merge. Typically, all changesets up to a particular point are included in a merge. However, TFVC also supports *cherry pick* merges, where you can specify certain changesets to be included in the merge. You can also view merge candidates, review merge histories, detect and resolve merge conflicts, and roll back merges.

When you put it all together, you'll find that TFVC provides a scalable enterprise-class infrastructure for supporting your code management needs. Using third-party products, you can use TFVC within other IDEs and operating systems. Whether you follow an agile or a more formal development methodology, you'll find that TFVC provides strong support during all phases of the software lifecycle—including development, testing, release, and maintenance.

1.3.3 Build automation

An automated build system that empowers you to build early and often is crucial for success. In addition to simply compiling the source files, a good build system generates tracking and quality information for each build. The tracking information should include which files were changed, which bugs were fixed, which features were implemented, who launched the build, and so on. The quality information should include which build verification tests (BVTs) ran successfully, what kind of code coverage was achieved, and the like.

Team Build provides an out-of-the-box integrated infrastructure for managing automated builds. Under the covers, Team Build uses the MSBuild engine to generate assemblies. However, Team Build adds a host of other features that facilitate traceability, collaboration, and quality. For example, Team Build generates a unique number for each build, downloads source code from TFVC, associates appropriate work items with the build, performs static code analysis, executes BVTs, generates code coverage information, and pushes the generated binaries to designated drop locations. You also get a build report showing the changesets that were included in the build, the work items that were resolved, relevant quality and timing information, and other metadata associated with the build (see figure 1.6).

You can customize the build process in several ways. You can create custom MSBuild tasks that can fine-tune the build process using the full power of your chosen programming language. These tasks can be invoked at specific points during the build process. Team Build specifically provides customizable targets that you can override for extending the build process. Additionally, Team Build provides a number of properties that you can configure to customize the build process.

In addition to streamlining the build execution process, Team Build provides a number of features that facilitate build management. You can specify which kinds of binaries to retain in the drop location and for how long, when to trigger builds (Team Build supports *continuous integration* builds and rolling builds as well as scheduled builds), which build machine to use for executing builds, which directories to use for downloading the source files and for generating the output binaries, and so on. Appropriate team members can also indicate the quality and QA status of each build (such as Initial Test Passed, UAT Passed, Ready for Deployment, and so forth). Team Build can also generate notifications when a build is completed or when a build quality is changed.

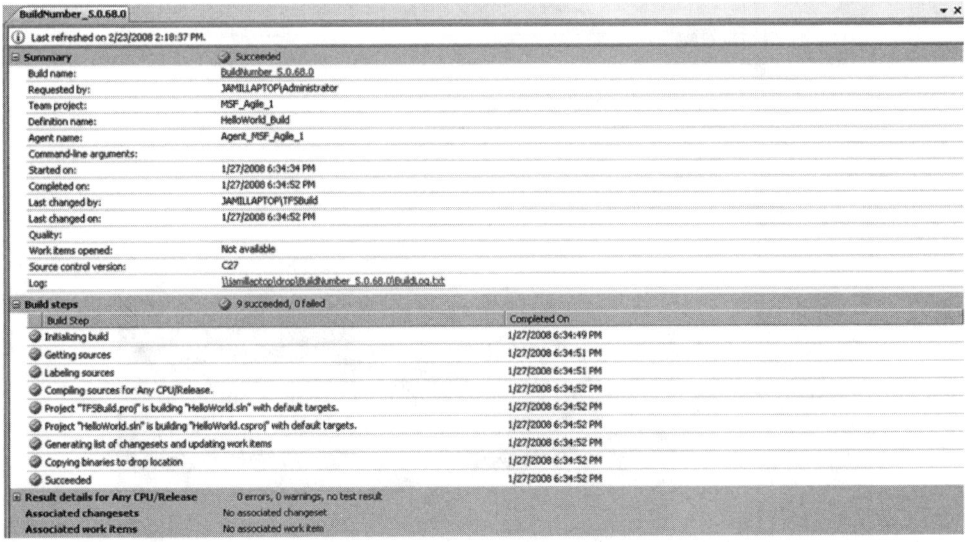

Figure 1.6   Team Build offers a full-featured build creation and management infrastructure.

1.3.4   *Project portal*

Effective communication between stakeholders is a key enabler of success in any software development effort. Without effective communication, requirements get misconstrued, priorities get misaligned, and resources get misplaced. When working with distributed or offshore teams, the need for effective communication is magnified many times. In any software project, you must ensure smooth information flow and augment it with effective metrics.

TFS facilitates information exchange by creating a SharePoint-based project portal for each team project (see figure 1.7). The project portal serves as the focal point for all stakeholders, across departmental boundaries. The portal hosts shared documents, reports, and key performance indicators (KPIs), threaded discussions, announcements, process guidance information, meeting workspaces, custom links, and whatever else you might consider appropriate for promoting collaboration. Anybody can access the project portal and obtain relevant information using just a web browser from anywhere in the world—without installing Visual Studio, acquiring VSTS licenses, or worrying about firewalls. In addition to offering timely information, the portal provides a sense of community, continuity, and context. The project portal can also serve as an executive dashboard for members of the executive team.

TFS supports project portals based on Windows SharePoint Services 3.0, Microsoft Office SharePoint Server 2007, and Windows SharePoint Services 2.0. The default project portal is created during the creation of a team project. You can customize the portal using the standard customization options available in SharePoint.

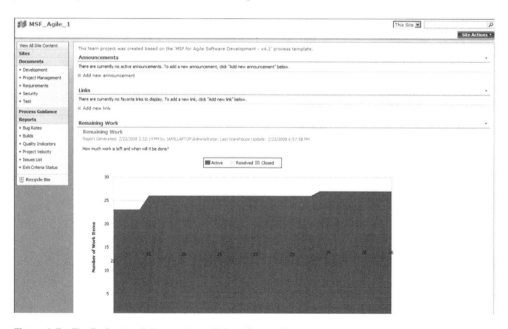

Figure 1.7   The Project portal promotes collaboration and transparency.

You can change the look and feel of the portal using SharePoint Designer, as well as create custom web parts and add them to the portal. You can create custom reports and perform additional analysis. You can also create custom workflows associated with shared documents. The default document libraries and their contents can be customized by modifying the WssTasks.xml file associated with the process template. The site template itself can also be customized so that new portals are based on your custom design.

1.3.5 Reporting

Reports enable you to keep your finger on the pulse of your development project. You can view information in near–real-time regarding critical aspects of project health—bug rates, velocity, test results, regressions, remaining work, build results, work items, and so on (see figure 1.8). Additionally, you can create custom reports and KPIs to better understand progress, identify bottlenecks, detect trends, and predict outcomes. Effective project management is impossible unless you have access to accurate data and can easily analyze the information using your preferred representational formats (views).

TFS reports are based on SQL Server Reporting Services (SSRS). You can use the included reports out of the box, modify them, or create new ones using Visual Studio Report Designer. Your custom reports can be included in the process template so that the new reports are automatically included in new team projects (which are created based on the modified process template). For wide distribution, reports can be placed

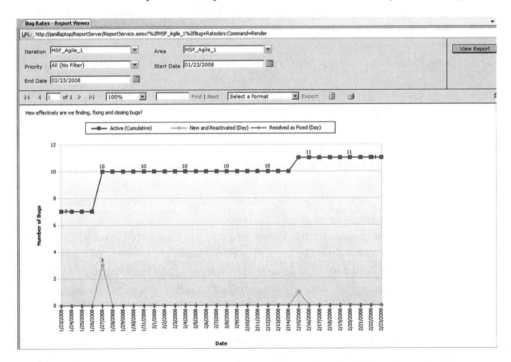

Figure 1.8   Predefined and custom reports help you understand trends, bottlenecks, and performance.

in the SharePoint-based project portal, in addition to being accessible from Team Explorer. For ad hoc reporting purposes, you can use Excel (or other third-party tools) to slice and dice the underlying data.

Reports access the data stored in back-end relational and Analysis Services databases. The TFS data repository consists of a number of operational databases (not used for reporting), a relational data warehouse, and an Analysis Services database (OLAP cube). At regular intervals, the content and the schema of the data warehouse as well as the cube are refreshed based on the data in the operational databases. This approach provides flexibility and performance.

The Analysis Services database contains a cube named Team System that is most often used in reports to display aggregate information. The cube contains several measure groups (such as code churn, test result, and current work item) and dimensions (such as date, team project, and build quality). For ease of navigation, and to provide focused context, the cube is logically subdivided into a number of categories called *perspectives* (such as build, current work item, and test result). Like any other Analysis Services cube, you can enhance the Team System cube as needed to meet your unique needs. For example, you can add KPIs, change the format of the cube, partition the data, and so on.

1.4   *Summary*

In this chapter, we learned how TFS fits within the general context of software engineering. We reviewed the platform's high-level architecture and studied its major subsystems. We saw that TFS enables you to implement your chosen development methodology on an enterprise scale. The product provides a robust ALM infrastructure, consisting of work item tracking, version control, build automation, project portal, and reporting. TFS also interoperates with other products in the enterprise ecosystem, such as third-party requirement gathering tools (for example, CaliberRM), third-party IDEs (such as Eclipse), as well as Microsoft Office products. You can customize TFS as well as extend its out-of-the-box features using the object model APIs. You can also listen to TFS events, and leverage other extensibility points.

In the next chapter, we review the specific improvements that have taken place in TFS 2008. Despite an impressive array of features in TFS 2005, there was room for improvement, especially in the build subsystem. We review the changes and show you how to take advantage of the enhancements.

The rest of the book drills down into real-life issues that arise when applying TFS in the field. As practitioners in the industry, we know that there can be no one-size-fits-all approach. In order to be able to successfully use any horizontal ALM platform within the enterprise, we must have the assurance that the system meets the general needs of security, reliability, scalability, auditability, interoperability, and performance. Not only that, but it also must expose well-designed extensibility points that can be utilized to meet the unique needs of the organization. Furthermore, the platform should have a familiar user interface as well as internal consistency to facilitate easy adoption.

Lastly, the product should be a well-behaved enterprise citizen, for painless hosting, operation, and maintenance in enterprise IT facilities. This implies that the platform should leverage as many existing IT assets as possible (such as databases, portals, reporting services, and so on) for ease of administration as well as to lower cost of ownership. TFS meets many of these enterprise requirements.

Although there's definite room for improvement in TFS (and we study some of those aspects in detail in the following chapters), we believe that TFS offers a compelling solution for mitigating many common lifecycle concerns. You can start using TFS today to improve your software development process.

1.5 References

"Standish Group Report: There's Less Development Chaos Today." *SD Times*. March 15, 2008. http://www.sdtimes.com/content/article.aspx?ArticleID=30247

Exploring the
changes in TFS 2008

This chapter covers

- Architecture of Team Build
- Creating and managing builds
- New functionalities in version control

Visual Studio 2005 Team Foundation Server (TFS 2005) was a version one product. As such, it had certain deficiencies that are typically inherent in the first generation of such an ambitious system. Visual Studio 2008 Team Foundation Server (TFS 2008) delivers improvements in several areas, such as enhanced features in Team Build and Team Foundation version control (TFVC), better performance and scalability, more flexible system configuration, simplified installation, and support for SharePoint Server 2007 and Microsoft SQL Server 2008.

Although the changes are generally incremental in nature, they add up to make TFS 2008 a more reliable, usable, and extendable product.

This chapter discusses some of the new features available in TFS 2008. We look at some of the important changes that are likely to impact your software development process. Specifically, we focus on the improvements made in Team Build and Team Foundation version control. The material in this chapter is introductory in nature.

In this chapter, you'll learn about the following:

- *Topology and configuration of build agents and Team Build service*—A build agent represents an instance of the Team Build service that can generate builds. Learn how to create build agents and configure various properties (such as security, build directory, and communication port) to suit your build environment.

- *How to create new build definitions and queue builds*—A build definition contains metadata (such as solutions to build, tests to run, drop management policies, and so on) regarding a build. At runtime, a build definition is handed over to a build agent for execution. A build agent can execute a single build definition per team project at a time. Additional build requests are queued. You can prioritize these builds as well as remove them from the queue. You can also stop or pause builds that are in progress. Learn how to create continuous integration (CI builds), rolling builds, and scheduled builds.

- *How to execute parallel builds*—Executing builds in parallel (building configurations and solutions simultaneously) on multi-processor or multi-core machines can speed up the build process significantly for large projects. Learn how to configure Team Build to support parallel builds and what takes place behind the scenes.

- *How to use the Build Explorer*—The Build Explorer serves as the build management dashboard. You can view the status of queued and completed builds, set priorities, start and stop builds, manage build agents, and filter the displayed list using various criteria.

- *How to manage build qualities*—Build qualities indicate the status of a build after evaluation by the Software Quality Assurance (SQA) group, or by the Central Build group, depending upon how the roles in your organization are structured. You can now customize the available build qualities in Team Build. Learn how to define build qualities and assign them to individual builds.

- *How to generate incremental builds*—Downloading only the modified source files and building only the corresponding binaries can significantly speed up the build process for large projects. Learn how to use the new properties offered by Team Build and perform incremental builds.

- *How to use the Team Build object model*—The new object model for Team Build exposes many more ways to interact with the build system. Learn about the main interfaces and classes. Create sample programs to discover real-time status of build agents, queue builds, and to find a build given a work item number.

- *How to get the latest version on check-out*—Team Foundation version control now offers the capability to automatically download the latest version when you check out a file for editing. Learn about the pros and cons of this approach and how to turn it on or off.

- *How to work with files in offline mode*—Visual Studio 2008 offers built-in support for manipulating source files in offline mode when Team Foundation Server 2008 isn't available. Learn how to use the offline feature and how to synchronize the modified files with TFVC once TFS 2008 is available again.
- *How to compare folders*—You can now compare folders (in addition to files) in TFVC. Both local and server folders can be selected for comparison. Learn how to use this feature and configure various options foroptimum results.
- *How to use annotations*—Annotations enable you to see the change history of a file on a line-by-line basis. This information is helpful for understanding the evolution of a file at a fine-grained level. Learn how to determine who changed what and when.

2.1   Team Build

Team Build has gone through significant changes in TFS 2008. The changes involve how builds are set up as well as the internal structure of the Team Build targets file. In this section, we look at the major changes and how they affect the way you use Team Build.

2.1.1   Topology and security

The most important topology change in Team Build involves using Windows Communication Foundation (WCF) web services to talk to the build agent (the build machine) from the application tier machine (see figure 2.1). The application tier machine in TFS 2005 used .NET remoting to talk to the build machine, whereas the application tier machine in TFS 2008 uses WCF. The WCF service is hosted in a managed Windows service in the build machine. Consequently, Internet Information Server (IIS) is not required to be installed on the build computer.

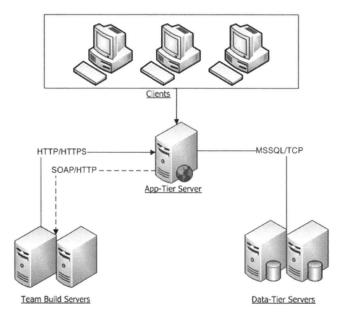

Figure 2.1   TFS 2008 uses WCF web services to communicate with build agents.

The Team Build service is implemented in an assembly named TFSBuildService.exe located in the %ProgramFiles%\Microsoft Visual Studio 9.0\Common7\IDE\Private-Assemblies folder. Within this assembly, a class named `Microsoft.TeamFoundation.Build.Agent.BuildServiceManager` (inherited from `System.ServiceProcess.ServiceBase`) implements the Windows service. In the `OnStart` method (inherited from the `ServiceBase` class), an instance of the `System.ServiceModel.ServiceHost` class is created for hosting the WCF service. The main class for implementing the WCF service is called `Microsoft.TeamFoundation.Build.Agent.AgentService`. This class implements the WCF service contract and exposes key methods for starting and stopping builds, getting information about in-progress builds, and so on (see figure 2.2).

You can configure the build agent to use a secure HTTPS communication channel as well as require a client certificate. You can also select the authentication protocol to be used, such as NTLM (the default), Kerberos, and so forth. To further limit access, you can specify a single user account that's allowed to communicate with the build agent.

The security settings are specified in the TFSBuildService.exe.config file, located in the %ProgramFiles%\Microsoft Visual Studio 9.0\Common7\IDE\PrivateAssemblies folder. When using HTTPS, also make sure that the Require Secure Channel (HTTPS) check box is selected in the Build Agent Properties dialog box (see figure 2.3). To learn about how to set up build agents to require HTTPS, visit http://msdn2.microsoft.com/en-us/library/bb778431(VS.90).aspx.

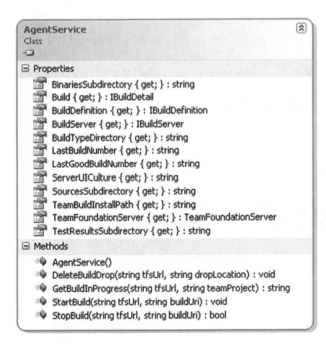

Figure 2.2 The `AgentService` class contains high-level methods and properties for managing the build process.

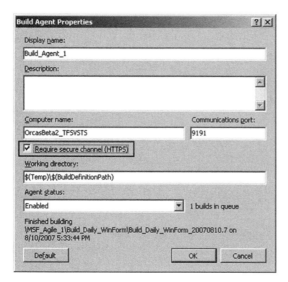

Figure 2.3   You can use HTTPS to secure communications with build agents.

2.1.2   *Build agents and team projects*

In TFS 2008, the notion of a build machine has been abstracted to some degree. Conceptually, a build agent represents a service that can create builds. The long-term goal is to eventually have a pool of build agents, each publishing information about supported team projects as well as other operational metadata. The published information will enable you to select a build agent to generate a particular build, based on current conditions and performance characteristics.

In TFS 2008, build agents are scoped to team projects. In the Build menu, if you click Manage Build Agents, the Manage Build Agents dialog box appears, displaying only the build agents that belong to the currently selected team project (see figure 2.4). This means that if you want to create builds for different team projects on the same build machine, you need to define a separate build agent for each team project. This behavior is inconvenient and counterintuitive, and is expected to be changed in a future version.

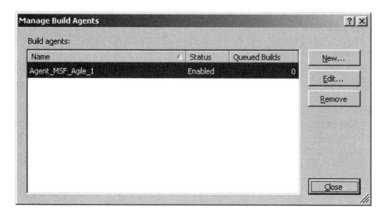

Figure 2.4   The Manage Build Agents dialog box enables you to create, update, and delete build agents.

Although typically a single build agent runs on a given build machine, you can manually configure multiple build agents to run on the same machine (listening on different ports). A typical scenario might be to use the same physical build machine to accept build requests from multiple TFS servers.

2.1.3 *Understanding the structure of the build directory*

In TFS 2005, you could specify the build directory when launching a build. In TFS 2008, the build directory path is a property associated with a build agent (see figure 2.3 displayed earlier), and can't be specified at runtime.

In TFS 2008, the default directory path associated with a build agent is $(Temp)\$(BuildDefinitionPath). The $(Temp) variable represents the temp directory associated with the account under which the Team Build service is running (for example, C:\Documents and Settings\TFSBuild\Local Settings\Temp on my machine). The $(BuildDefinitionPath) variable expands to <TeamProject_Name>\ <BuildDefinition_Name>. For example, if the team project name is MSF_Agile_1 and the build definition name is Nightly_Build, then $(BuildDefinitionPath) will expand to MSF_Agile_1\ Nightly_Build.

If you're concerned about the length of the path, you can use the $(Build-DefinitionId) variable instead of $(BuildDefinitionPath). $(BuildDefinitionId) expands to an integer associated with the build definition. You can also use environment variables to represent the path, or simply hard-code it.

Under the path defined by $(Temp)\$(BuildDefinitionPath), Team Build creates the following three subdirectories (see figure 2.5):

- *Sources*—Contains the source files downloaded from TFVC
- *Binaries*—Contains the generated binaries
- *BuildTypes*—Contains the TFSBuild.proj file, the TFSBuild.rsp file, and build log

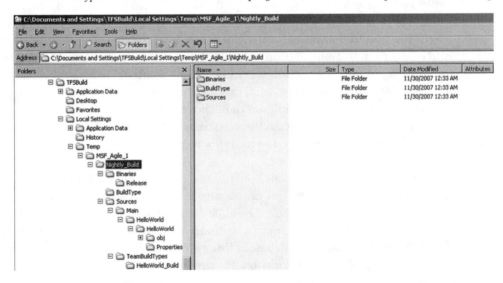

Figure 2.5   The Build directory contains various subdirectories for downloaded source files and generated build binaries.

If you want to change the names of the Sources and Binaries subdirectories, you can modify the `SourcesSubdirectory` and `BinariesSubdirectory` keys, respectively, in the TFSBuildService.exe.config file (located in the %ProgramFiles%\Microsoft Visual Studio 9.0\Common7\IDE\PrivateAssemblies folder). You can also specify the subdirectory for storing test results (not displayed in figure 2.5) using the `TestResultsSubdirectory` key.

Understanding the structure of the build directory is important in various scenarios. For example, if you encounter the 260-character limit in Windows for file paths, you can use the techniques described earlier to shorten the path of the build directory. (For more information regarding the 260-character limit, visit http://msdn2.microsoft.com/en-us/library/aa365247.aspx.) Furthermore, if you create multiple build agents (for processing builds from the same team project or for processing builds from multiple TFS servers) on the same machine, you need to specify different build directories to prevent potential conflicts.

2.1.4   *Creating a new build definition*

Build definitions in TFS 2008 replace the old build types of TFS 2005. A build type in TFS 2005 was represented by three files—TFSBuild.proj, TFSBuild.rsp, and WorkspaceMappings.xml. These files were located in the $/<Team Project>/TeamBuildTypes/ <Build_Type> folder in TFVC. A build definition in TFS 2008 encapsulates more information (such as retention policies and triggers) and can be queued for execution. The MSBuild project-related data for a build definition is still stored in the TFVC repository (in TFSBuild.proj and TFSBuild.rsp files located in your chosen TFVC folder). But other information associated with a build definition is stored in the TFSBuild database (for example, workspace mapping information is stored in tbl_WorkSpaceMapping table, drop location is stored in tbl_BuildDefinition, build agent information is stored in tbl_BuildAgent, and so on). Unlike build types in TFS 2005, you get a user interface in TFS 2008 to edit some of the information associated with a build definition, which you access by right-clicking the build definition and selecting Edit Build Definition from the context menu. However, the MSBuild project-related information still has to be edited manually by checking out the TFSBuild.proj and/or TFSBuild.rsp files, making changes, and checking them back in.

To create a new build definition, right-click the Builds node in Team Explorer and click New Build Definition from the context menu. The Build Definition dialog box has six tabs oriented vertically. Let us review the functionality of each tab.

THE GENERAL TAB

The General tab (see figure 2.6) contains the name of the build definition as well as an optional description. You can deactivate a build definition by selecting the Disable This Build Definition check box. The ability to disable a build definition is useful, for example, when you want to temporarily disable a scheduled or continuous integration build definition while the codebase is being fixed. (You wouldn't want broken builds to be piling up based on a faulty codebase.) But if there are builds that are already

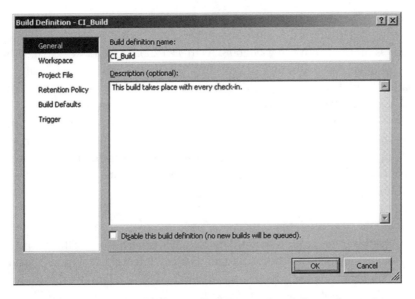

Figure 2.6 Use the General tab to specify the name, description, and current availability of the build definition.

queued or running, those won't be affected when the Disable This Build Definition check box is selected.

THE WORKSPACE TAB

The Workspace tab (see figure 2.7) allows you to construct a *build workspace*. A build workspace maps TFVC folders to local folders. The local folders reside under the root

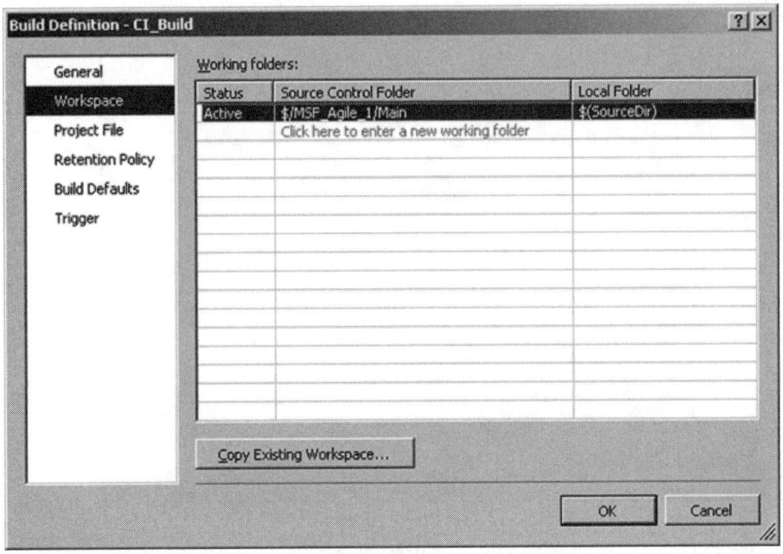

Figure 2.7 Use the Workspace tab to map TFVC folders to local folders.

build directory specified for the build agent. Unlike TFS 2005, you can't specify the build directory at runtime. If you've used TFS 2005, you'll find that defining build workspaces is more intuitive in TFS 2008. As in TFS 2005, a build workspace filters the solutions available for generating builds. Build workspaces also filter the files that are downloaded from TFVC during a build (as in TFS 2005, only the files located in the specified server folders are downloaded). Furthermore, as in TFS 2005, build workspaces limit the changesets associated with a build by labeling only the files that belong to the specified server folders. However, unlike TFS 2005, build workspaces in TFS 2008 allow you to select code from multiple team projects. Instead of creating a workspace from scratch, you can copy an existing workspace from TFVC by clicking Copy Existing Workspace.

THE PROJECT FILE TAB

The Project File tab (see figure 2.8) enables you to create a new TFSBuild.proj file or select an existing one. Note that unlike TFS 2005, where the TFSBuild.proj file was required to be located in the $/<Team Project>/TeamBuildTypes/<Build_Type> folder, in TFS 2008, this file can be in any folder in TFVC. This allows you to branch and merge the TFSBuild.proj file along with the corresponding source files. If a TFS-Build.proj file hasn't been selected, a Create button appears in the Project File tab. Click Create to construct a new TFSBuild.proj file. This action displays the MSBuild Project File Creation Wizard (see figure 2.9). This wizard is similar to the one available in TFS 2005 for creating build types. You can select the solutions to build (order the solutions based upon dependencies), specify the build verification tests to run, collect code analysis data, and so on.

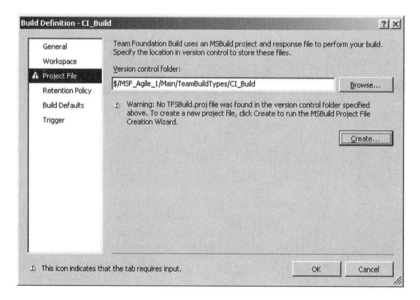

Figure 2.8   Use the Project File tab to select an existing MSBuild project file or to create a new one.

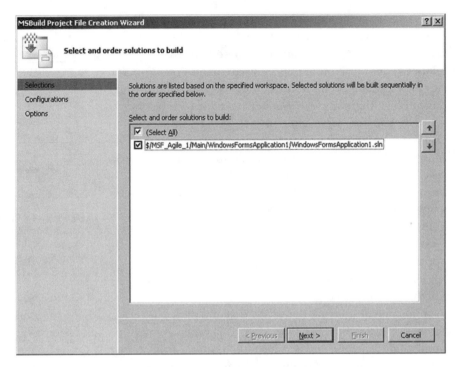

Figure 2.9 Use the MSBuild Project File Creation Wizard to generate an MSBuild project file based on your selections.

THE RETENTION POLICY TAB

The Retention Policy tab (see figure 2.10) helps you manage the binaries in the drop location. For each build outcome, you can specify whether to keep old build binaries,

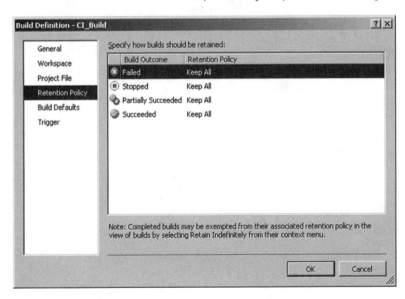

Figure 2.10 Use the Retention Policy tab to indicate automated drop management choices.

and how many versions should be kept. Although you can't specify custom retention policies in TFS 2008, the out-of-the-box retention policies help automate routine housekeeping tasks related to optimization of build storage space. Retention policies are especially useful in the context of continuous integration builds, where a great number of build binaries may be generated in an active codeline, to avoid proliferation of unneeded builds in the filesystem.

If you don't want a particular build to be governed by the specified retention policies, you can make exceptions on a case-by-case basis. Select the build using Build Explorer, right-click a build to display the context menu, and select Retain Indefinitely (see figure 2.11). Later on, if you want the build to be maintained as per the retention policies, you can turn the option off again.

Figure 2.11 Choose Retain Indefinitely to exempt a build from the retention policies.

THE BUILD DEFAULTS TAB

The Build Defaults tab (see figure 2.12) lets you specify the default build agent and the drop location. To create a new build agent, click New. This displays the Build Agent Properties dialog box (see figure 2.3, displayed previously). A build agent represents a single build machine and accepts build requests from a single TFS server. Many of the properties related to a build agent can be customized by modifying the TFSBuild-Service.exe.config file located in the %ProgramFiles%\Microsoft Visual Studio 9.0\Common7\IDE\PrivateAssemblies folder.

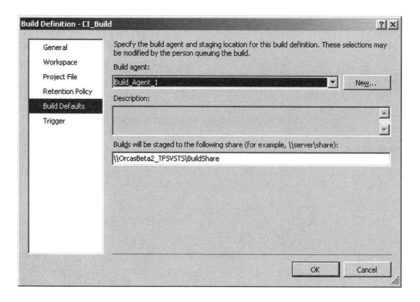

Figure 2.12 Use the Build Defaults tab to specify the default build agent and the drop location.

THE TRIGGER TAB

The Trigger tab (see figure 2.13) allows you to select the timing of builds. TFS 2008 supports continuous integration (CI builds) by launching automatic builds whenever a check-in takes place in TFVC (TFS 2005 doesn't have built-in support for CI builds). You can generate a build upon every check-in or accumulate check-ins until the previous build is completed (this is called a *rolling build*). When selecting rolling builds, you can also choose to initiate builds at certain intervals, limiting the number of builds that are created each day.

If you select Accumulate Check-ins Until the Prior Build Finishes and specify a delay time, Team Build will only launch builds at specified intervals (assuming there are outstanding check-ins). However, the first check-in will trigger a build immediately; the delay will kick in from the second check-in onward.

You can also generate builds based on a schedule (select the Build Every Week on the Following Days option and make appropriate selections). The scheduled build feature enables you to create daily or nightly builds.

When creating builds, Team Build is smart enough to consider only those check-ins that take place in one of the server paths specified in the build workspace. If you don't want a check-in (that's in a server path specified in the build workspace) to trigger automatic builds, specify ***NO_CI*** in the Comment field when checking in the changeset. A changeset containing ***NO_CI*** in the Comment field doesn't trigger a CI build. You can obtain this special string from the NoCICheckInComment property of the IBuildServer interface (discussed later in section 2.1.11).

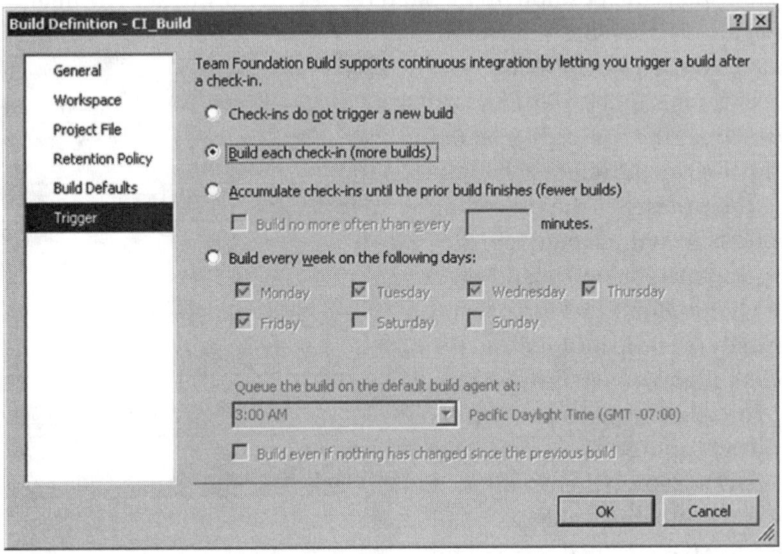

Figure 2.13   Use the Trigger tab to generate CI, rolling, or scheduled builds.

2.1.5 *Launching and queuing builds*

Team Build queues build requests if another build belonging to the same team project is in progress. In such an event, the build requests are put in a queue and executed one at a time. This is a major difference between the build engines of TFS 2005 and TFS 2008. TFS 2005 displayed an error message if you tried to concurrently execute a build type belonging to the same team project in the same build machine.

Keep in mind that similar to TFS 2005, TFS 2008 can still execute only a single build definition per team project using a given build agent. As discussed, the difference is that if you try to concurrently execute another build definition that belongs to the same team project (using the same build agent), TFS 2008 will queue the build request instead of producing an error message. Of course, using multiple build agents, you can always run build definitions from the same team project in parallel. (Also, as discussed, typically a single build agent runs on a single build machine, although it's possible to configure multiple build agents to run on a single build machine.)

Support for queued builds in TFS 2008 allows you to send build requests to build agents without worrying about the current status of the build machine. Build queues are also helpful for CI builds, since Team Build can queue up multiple build requests when a build is in progress (instead of rejecting pending requests).

To launch a new build, right-click a build definition and click Queue New Build from the context menu. In the Queue Build dialog box (see figure 2.14), you can specify a build agent for executing the build. You can also indicate the priority of the build request. Based upon a build request's priority relative to other build requests in the queue, the build agent displays the position of the build request in the queue. The queue position gives you an idea of when the build might get executed. You may not be able to predict the exact time, since you may not know how long the preceding build requests in the queue might take; furthermore, the priority of the preceding build requests could change or they could be postponed or cancelled.

In the Queue Build dialog box, you can also specify the drop location and the command-line parameters to pass to MSBuild. The ability to pass parameters to MSBuild at runtime is an enhancement over TFS 2005, where you had to edit the TFSBuild.rsp file to send parameters to MSBuild (you can still do this in TFS 2008). Modify the TFS-Build.rsp file for durable parameters and use the Queue Build dialog box for ad hoc choices.

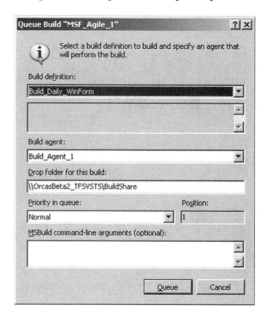

Figure 2.14 The Queue Build dialog box provides various runtime options for build execution.

2.1.6 Build definitions and security

After you create a build definition, you might want to limit who can execute it and generate builds. If you've created multiple build definitions—for example, for development, SQA, and release builds (possibly based on different source control folders as well as other settings)—you'd probably want to restrict the groups of people who can run each build definition.

Unfortunately, in TFS 2008, you can't apply security on build definitions. Any user who has access to a team project can execute all the build definitions contained in it. This deficiency is expected to be corrected in a future version of TFS.

For now, the best you can do is prevent people from editing the build definitions. To prevent a group of users from editing a build definition, select the folder in TFVC that contains the corresponding TFSBuild.proj file and deny Read permission to the group. If a user from the prohibited group tries to edit the build definition, TFS 2008 will display an error message (see figure 2.15).

Figure 2.15 TFS 2008 displays an error message if a user attempts to edit a build definition but doesn't have Read access to the folder containing the corresponding TFSBuild.proj file.

2.1.7 Running parallel builds

Running builds in parallel can speed up the build process for large projects. MSBuild 3.5 introduces support for launching parallel builds on multi-processor or multi-core machines. Team Build uses the MSBuild engine to generate builds. To generate parallel builds using MSBuild, you need to do two things:

- Set the `BuildInParallel` task parameter to `true`.
- Specify a value (greater than 1) for the `/maxcpucount` (or `/m` for short) command-line parameter.

You should set up project-to-project references in your solutions so that MSBuild can resolve the dependencies and create parallel builds in the correct order. For more information regarding how MSBuild creates parallel builds, visit http://msdn2. microsoft.com/en-us/library/bb383805(VS.90).aspx and http://msdn2.microsoft. com/en-us/library/bb651793(VS.90).aspx.

Since Team Build invokes MSBuild behind the scenes to create builds, Team Build needs to pass the correct parameter values to MSBuild in order to launch parallel builds. This is achieved as follows.

Team Build attempts to build each configuration and each solution in parallel, if possible. In the Microsoft.TeamFoundation.Build.targets file (located in the %ProgramFiles%\MSBuild\Microsoft\VisualStudio\TeamBuild directory), the MSBuild task is called with the `BuildInParallel` task parameter set to the values of the `BuildConfigurations-InParallel` or `BuildSolutionsInParallel` variables (see listings 2.1 and 2.2). The values of `BuildConfigurationsInParallel` and `BuildSolutionsInParallel` are initialized to `true` in the Microsoft.TeamFoundation. Build.targets file.

Team Build offers a key named `MaxProcesses` in the TfsBuildService.exe.config file, where you can specify the number of worker processes that MSBuild should generate (the default is 1). The value you specify should depend upon the number of processors or cores in your machine. The value specified in the `MaxProcesses` key is passed to MSBuild at runtime.

Listing 2.1   The `CoreCompile` target invokes the MSBuild task

```
<!-- Main compile target -->
 <Target Name="CoreCompile"
        DependsOnTargets="$(_CoreCompileDependsOn)"
        Outputs="@(CompilationOutputs)">

   <MakeDir Directories="$(BinariesRoot)"
        Condition="!Exists('$(BinariesRoot)')" />

   <MSBuild BuildInParallel="$(BuildConfigurationsInParallel)"
        Projects="@(ConfigurationList)"
        Targets="CompileConfiguration"
        StopOnFirstFailure="$(StopOnFirstFailure)">
    <Output TaskParameter="TargetOutputs" ItemName="CompilationOutputs"
    />
   </MSBuild>

 </Target>
```

Listing 2.2   The `CoreCompileConfiguration` target invokes the MSBuild task

```
<!-- Compile an individual configuration -->
<Target Name="CoreCompileConfiguration"
  DependsOnTargets="$(CoreCompileConfigurationDependsOn)">

  <MSBuild BuildInParallel="$(BuildSolutionsInParallel)"
        Projects="@(SolutionList)"
        Targets="CompileSolution"
        StopOnFirstFailure="$(StopOnFirstFailure)">
   <Output TaskParameter="TargetOutputs" ItemName="CompilationOutputs"
   />
  </MSBuild>

  <!-- Add Platform and Configuration metadata to CompilationOutputs. -->
  <ItemGroup>
   <CompilationOutputs>
    <Platform>$(Platform)</Platform>
    <Configuration>$(Configuration)</Configuration>
   </CompilationOutputs>
  </ItemGroup>

 </Target>
```

2.1.8   Using the Build Explorer

The Build Explorer acts as the build management dashboard, providing access to queued as well as completed builds. To view the Build Explorer, right-click the Builds node in Team Explorer and select View Builds from the context menu (or double-click the All Build Definitions element located under the Builds node). There are two tabs in Build Explorer—Queued and Completed. The Queued tab (see figure 2.16) shows build requests that are currently in the execution queue. The Completed tab (see figure 2.17) shows builds that have been generated already. Note that the columns available in these two tabs are different. The options available in the build toolbar also change depending on which tab is currently selected.

The Queued tab in Build Explorer displays builds that are in progress as well as ones waiting in the queue. Using the build toolbar or the context menu associated with a build entry, you can stop in-progress builds and postpone or cancel queued builds. You can also change the priority of a queued build.

Note the Requested By column is available in both tabs in Build Explorer. This is a new piece of metadata associated with a build that wasn't captured in TFS 2005. Knowing who initiated a build is useful in many organizations, since it helps the audit process. For CI builds, the Requested By column displays the name of the developer whose check-in triggered the build. If there are multiple accumulated check-ins, the

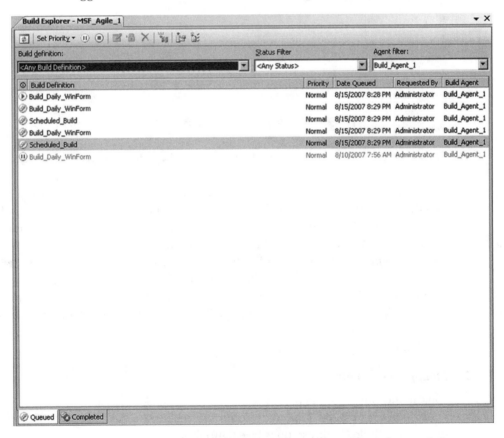

Figure 2.16 **The Queued tab in Build Explorer displays builds that are waiting to be executed.**

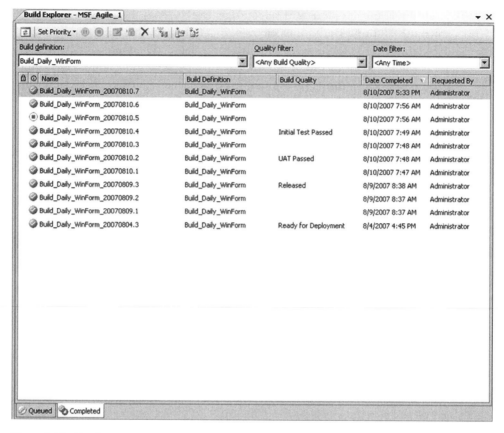

Figure 2.17   The Completed tab in Build Explorer displays builds that have been generated.

Requested By column shows the name of the user associated with the last (highest numbered) check-in. For scheduled builds, Team Build displays "Team Build System Account" in the Requested By column. For builds launched manually, the name of the TFS user who launched the build is displayed in the Requested By column.

The Completed tab in Build Explorer is similar to the one available in TFS 2005, but contains additional options. You can filter builds using build definition, build quality, and build date. When you right-click a build, the context menu offers options to delete the build, indicate the build quality, retain the build indefinitely, navigate to the drop location, and so on. As in TFS 2005, you can double-click an entry to view the detailed build report.

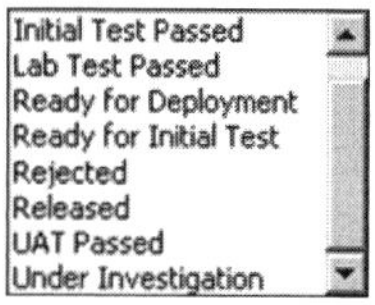

2.1.9   *Managing build qualities*

You can indicate the build quality using the Build Quality drop-down in Build Explorer. Note that TFS 2008 offers more Build Quality settings (see figure 2.18) than were available in TFS 2005. You can also customize the available build quality settings. On the Build menu,

Initial Test Passed
Lab Test Passed
Ready for Deployment
Ready for Initial Test
Rejected
Released
UAT Passed
Under Investigation

Figure 2.18   Use the Build Quality drop-down to indicate the testing and release status of a build.

click Manage Build Qualities to launch the Edit Build Qualities dialog box (see figure 2.19). Changing the build quality settings in Build Explorer triggers TFS events. You can monitor the build quality change events and take appropriate actions (such as copying files from the drop location to a testing, staging, or production server).

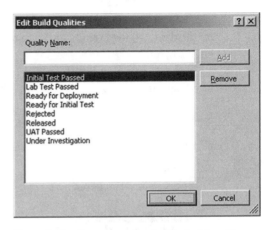

Figure 2.19 You can customize the build quality options to suit your development process.

2.1.10 *Generating incremental builds*

TFS 2008 introduces two properties (specified in the TFSBuild.proj file) that facilitate downloading only the changed source files as well as generating only the affected binaries. They are

- `IncrementalGet`—Set this property to `true` if you want Team Build to download only the modified source files (the files that have been changed since the last build). By default, Team Build downloads every source file located in the server paths specified in the build workspace.
- `IncrementalBuild`—Set this property to `true` if you want to download only the modified source files and generate only the corresponding binaries. By default, Team Build downloads all source files associated with the workspace and regenerates all binaries. For more information regarding how `IncrementalBuild` works, visit http://msdn2.microsoft.com/en-us/library/aa833876(vs.90).aspx.

Incremental builds are especially useful when creating CI builds for large projects. Downloading the full source code and doing a full build every time could create a potential bottleneck in the build process (depending on project size, check-in frequency, build schedule, hardware setup, connectivity speed, and so forth).

2.1.11 *Exploring the Team Build object model*

TFS 2008 introduces a new object model for Team Build. Conceptually, the object model acts as the access point to the build system. Behind the scenes, the object model communicates with the Team Build service to perform requested actions and return corresponding results.

The top-level interface in the new Team Build object model (in TFS 2008) is called `Microsoft.TeamFoundation.Build.Client.IBuildServer`. In TFS 2005, the top-level class was called `Microsoft.TeamFoundation.Build.Proxy.BuildStore` and it was a thin wrapper around the build web services. The build object model in TFS 2008 is a lot richer.

`IBuildServer` is implemented by an internal sealed class named `Microsoft.Team-Foundation.Build.Client.BuildServer`, located in the `Microsoft.TeamFoundation.Build.Client` assembly. Since the `BuildServer` class is internal, you can't instantiate it directly. When you call the GetService method of the Microsoft.TeamFoundation. Client.TeamFoundationServer class and pass IBuildServer as the service type, the method internally creates an instance of the BuildServer class and returns the reference to you.

As you can see in figure 2.20, IBuildServer exposes methods to create and delete build agents and build definitions, queue builds, stop in-progress builds, and run

Figure 2.20　The IBuildServer interface offers methods to interact with the build system.

queries (in order to get information about builds, build agents, build definitions, build qualities, and so on).

Other important interfaces include `IBuildAgent` (represents a build agent), `IBuildDefinition` (represents a build definition), and `IBuildDetail` (represents an individual build). See Figure 2.21 to learn about their properties and methods.

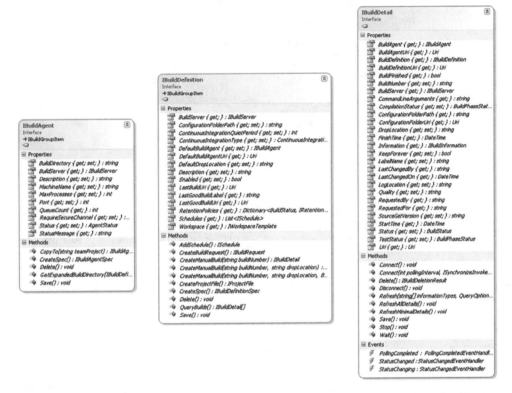

Figure 2.21 `IBuildAgent`, `IBuildDefinition`, **and** `IBuildDetail` **provide information about build machines, build definitions, and specific builds, respectively.**

Now that we have an overview of the Team Build object model, let's look at two examples of how this knowledge can be applied to solve real-life problems.

2.1.12 *A sample program for queuing builds*

In this section, we look at a sample program that finds the build agent that's least busy and queues a build in it (see listing 2.3). The steps are as follow:

1. Get a reference to the build server and get a list of build agents. The build server offers a method named `QueryBuildAgents` for retrieving the collection of build agents.

2. Iterate the collection of build agents and select the build agent that has the lowest number of build requests queued. The `IBuildAgent` interface contains a property named `QueueCount` to report the number of requests currently queued in the build agent.

3 Retrieve the build definition from the build server (using the `GetBuildDefini-tion` method) and create a build request from it. The `IBuildDefinition` interface contains a method named `CreateBuildRequest` for creating build requests. After creating a build request, we can customize its properties. In particular, we set the `BuildAgent` property to the build agent selected in the previous step.

4 Finally, queue the build in the selected build agent, using the `QueueBuild` method of the build server.

Listing 2.3   Queuing a build in the build agent with the lightest load

```
using System;
using System.Diagnostics;
using System.Collections.Generic;

using Microsoft.TeamFoundation.Client;
using Microsoft.TeamFoundation.Build.Client;

namespace OrcasBuildTests
{
    class TeamBuildHelper
    {
        string _tfsUrl = TFS_NAME;                              Change these
        string _teamProject = TEAM_PROJECT_NAME;                values for
        string _buildDefinition = BUILD_DEFINITION_NAME;        your project

        public void QueueBuildDefinition()
        {
            try
            {                                                   Get reference
                                                                to TFS
                TeamFoundationServer tfs =
                  new TeamFoundationServer(_tfsUrl);                    Get
                                                                       reference
                IBuildServer buildServer =                             to build
                  (IBuildServer)tfs.GetService(typeof(IBuildServer));  server

                IBuildAgent[] buildAgents =                     Get list of agents that
                  buildServer.QueryBuildAgents(_teamProject);   belong to project

                //find the build agent with the lowest queue count
                IBuildAgent selectedBuildAgent = null;
                int lowestQueueCount = 0;

                foreach (IBuildAgent buildAgent in buildAgents)
                {
                    if (selectedBuildAgent == null)
                    {                                           Initialize
                        selectedBuildAgent = buildAgent;        currently
                        lowestQueueCount = buildAgent.QueueCount; selected
                        continue;                               agent if
                    }                                           empty

                    if (buildAgent.QueueCount < lowestQueueCount)
                    {                                           Select
                        selectedBuildAgent = buildAgent;        agent if
                        lowestQueueCount = buildAgent.QueueCount; queue
                    }                                           count is
                }                                               lower
```

```
                  //now queue the build definition to the
                  //selected build agent

                  //retrieve the build definition and create a new build
                  //request using the selected build agent
                  IBuildDefinition buildDefinition =
                     buildServer.GetBuildDefinition(
                     _teamProject, _buildDefinition);

                  IBuildRequest buildRequest =
                     buildDefinition.CreateBuildRequest();

                  buildRequest.BuildAgent = selectedBuildAgent;

                  buildServer.QueueBuild(buildRequest);        ◁──┐ Queue build
               }                                                  │ request in
               catch (Exception ex)                              │ selected agent
               {
                  Debug.WriteLine(ex);
                  throw;
               }
            }
         }
      }
}
```

2.1.13 *Determining which build contains a particular fix*

Continuing our discussion of the new Team Build object model, let's look at another real-life problem. A common request from SQA groups involves knowing which build contains a particular work item. In order to retrieve this information, you could launch the Build Explorer, go through each build, and view the Associated Work Items section of each build report (see figure 2.22) to identify the build that contains

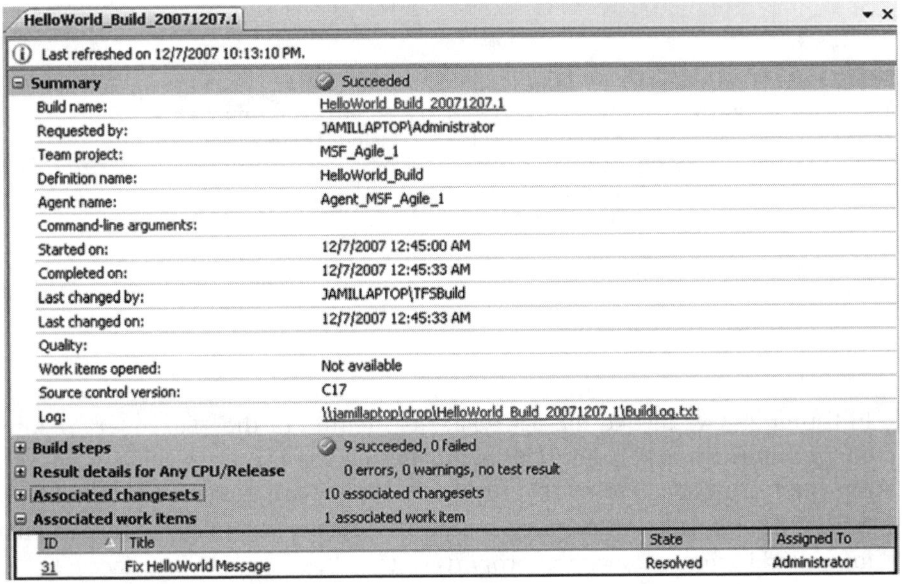

Figure 2.22 The build report includes information regarding associated work items.

the work item. Although this manual method would work, it would be time consuming. An easier approach would be to determine this information using a custom program, leveraging the object model. Listing 2.4 shows the code needed to obtain the corresponding build number, given a work item number.

Listing 2.4　Finding which build contains a specific work item

```
public void FindBuild()
{
    string found_in_build = null;

    try
    {
        TeamFoundationServer tfs =                              Get reference
          new TeamFoundationServer(_tfsUrl);                    to TFS

        IBuildServer buildServer =                                  Get reference
          (IBuildServer)tfs.GetService(typeof(IBuildServer));       to build server

        IBuildDetail[] buildDetails =
          buildServer.QueryBuilds(_teamProject);

        foreach (IBuildDetail buildDetail in buildDetails)
        {
          List<IWorkItemSummary> workitems =
          InformationNodeConverters.GetAssociatedWorkItems(buildDetail);

          foreach (IWorkItemSummary workitem in workitems)
          {
           if (_workitem_number == workitem.WorkItemId)
           {
            found_in_build = buildDetail.BuildNumber;
            break;
           }
          }
        }

        if (found_in_build != null)
          Debug.WriteLine("Work Item Id:" + _workitem_number +
                  " found in build:" + found_in_build);
        else
          Debug.WriteLine("Work Item Id:" + _workitem_number +
                  " not found");
    }
    catch (Exception ex)
    {
      Debug.WriteLine(ex);
      throw;
    }
}
```

In listing 2.4, we invoke the QueryBuilds method of the IBuildServer interface to obtain information related to all builds for a given team project. The information is returned as a collection of IBuildDetail objects. We iterate over the collection and extract the information exposed by the IBuildDetail interface. In particular, we're interested in the Information property of the IBuildDetail interface.

The `Information` property is of type `IBuildInformation` and contains a `Nodes` collection (see figure 2.23). Each member of the `Nodes` collection is of type `IBuildInformationNode`. The members of the `Nodes` collection represent build steps, associated changesets, associated work items, and so forth. Instead of parsing the information contained in `IBuildInformationNode`, we take a simpler approach and use the `InformationNodeConverters` class.

The `InformationNodeConverters` class is a utility class that offers various static methods for adding and retrieving build steps, associated changesets, associated work items, and so on (see figure 2.24). We use the `GetAssociatedWorkItems` method of the `InformationNodeConverters` class to obtain the list of work items associated with a particular build. This method returns a collection of `IWorkItemSummary` objects. The `WorkItemId` property belonging to the `IWorkItemSummary` interface contains the

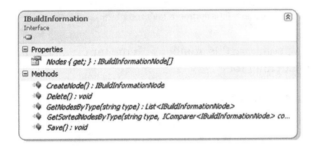

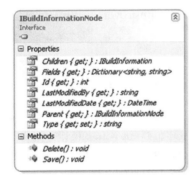

Figure 2.23
`IBuildInformation`, `IBuildInformationNode`, and `IWorkItemSummary` interfaces enable you to obtain detailed information about a specific build.

Figure 2.24 The `InformationNodeConverters` class offers useful methods to configure build execution as well as to retrieve information about completed builds.

actual work item number. We compare this number with the input work item number to identify the build we're searching for.

2.2   *Team Foundation version control*

Compared to Team Build, the changes in TFVC are incremental. But there are significant performance-related improvements that may not be immediately obvious, unless you're working on large projects. In this section, we discuss the features of TFVC that have undergone improvements in TFS 2008.

2.2.1   *Get the latest on check-out*

TFS 2005 didn't provide a way to automatically download the latest version when checking out a file. When you checked out a file, TFS 2005 simply made the current version of the file (the version that the server believed to be in your workspace) editable. If there was a later version of the file in the server, it wasn't download to the local workspace.

This behavior was not a bug but a feature. The idea was rooted in the fact that since files are often modified in a group (a feature or a change request could affect multiple files), downloading the latest version of a single file while leaving others unchanged could make the software in the local workspace inconsistent. Hence, the preferred way of downloading changes from the server was to deliberately fetch the appropriate version of all related files. This can be done (both in TFS 2005 and TFS 2008) at the file or folder level using the context menu. Right-click a file or folder and select Get Latest Version or Get Specific Version from the context menu (see figure 2.25). If you perform this

Figure 2.25 You can download a specific version of a file from TFVC using the context menu associated with files and folders.

operation at the folder level, the changes in that folder as well as in mapped subfolders will be downloaded recursively.

The default check-out behavior remains unchanged in TFS 2008. But TFS 2008 provides an option (turned off by default) to automatically download the latest version when checking out a file or folder. Many users have voiced this need when attempting to ensure that developers are always working on the latest version of a file; people often forget to consciously download the latest version. In the Tools menu, click Options. In the Options dialog box, expand the Source Control node in the tree and click the Visual Studio Team Foundation Server element; make your selection using the Get Latest Version of Item on Check Out check box (see figure 2.26).

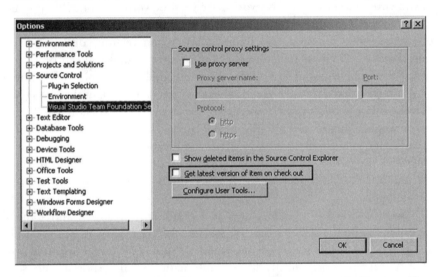

Figure 2.26 The Options dialog box enables you to configure whether checking out a file will automatically download the latest version.

If this check box is selected, TFS 2008 will automatically download the latest version of a file or folder when you click Check Out for Edit from the context menu. If the check box is cleared, TFS 2008 will simply make the current version of the file or folder editable (by pending an edit). However, when you double click the file to open it (or select View from the right-click context menu), TFS 2008 will inform you that there's a mismatch between the server and local versions and ask which version you want to open (see figure 2.27). Furthermore, you can find out which files in your workspace are outdated by looking at the Latest column in the Source Control Explorer (see figure 2.28).

In the Select Item dialog box (see figure 2.27), you have the option of working with either the server version or the local version of

Figure 2.27 TFVC displays the Select Item dialog box when there's a mismatch between the server and workspace versions of a file.

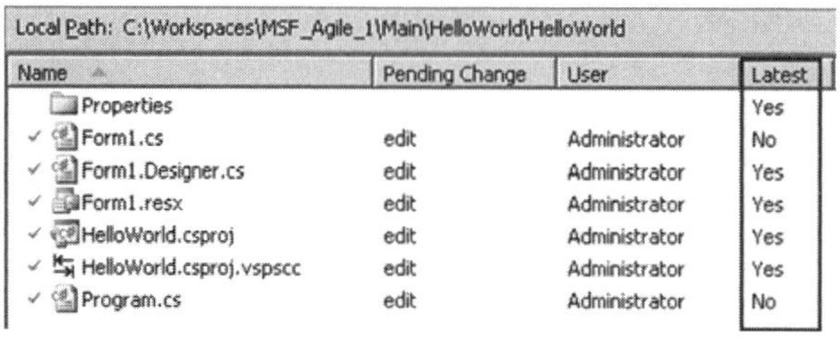

Name ▲	Pending Change	User	Latest
📁 Properties			Yes
✓ Form1.cs	edit	Administrator	No
✓ Form1.Designer.cs	edit	Administrator	Yes
✓ Form1.resx	edit	Administrator	Yes
✓ HelloWorld.csproj	edit	Administrator	Yes
✓ HelloWorld.csproj.vspscc	edit	Administrator	Yes
✓ Program.cs	edit	Administrator	No

Local Path: C:\Workspaces\MSF_Agile_1\Main\HelloWorld\HelloWorld

Figure 2.28   The Latest column in Source Control Explorer displays the status of files in the workspace relative to the server.

a file. Recall that this dialog box is displayed for any file that has a mismatch between its workspace and server versions.

If you choose to work with the workspace version, you'll encounter a conflict when checking in the changes (since the server version is different), and you'll be asked to resolve the version conflicts (see figure 2.29). When version conflicts are detected during check-in, TFS 2008 halts the check-in process so that you can resolve the conflicts and verify the changes (otherwise, untested code will be uploaded to the server). After you're satisfied that the changes are valid, you can check in the changes.

On the other hand, if you choose to work with the server version, you'll encounter an error when trying to save the file (since the workspace version is different and is still read-only); you can choose to overwrite the local file or save the file using a different filename. Regardless of whether you work with the server version or the workspace version, ultimately you'll need to synchronize the two versions when you try to check in the changes.

If you've checked out a file (there is a pending edit on it), and someone else changes the file on the server (while it's still checked out to you), TFS 2008 will display a merge window if you try to get the latest version. The merge window provides a mechanism for you to selectively (or automatically) incorporate the server-side changes with the version in your workspace.

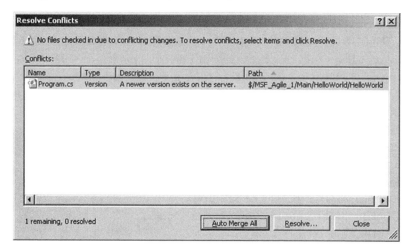

Figure 2.29   The Resolve Conflicts dialog box enables you to resolve conflicts between the workspace and server versions.

If you haven't checked out the file (there is no pending edit on it), and someone else modifies the file on the server, you won't get a merge window when you try to get the latest version; TFS 2008 will simply overwrite the workspace version with the server version. Consequently, be careful when trying this if you don't have pending edits—the operation will unconditionally overwrite your workspace files with files downloaded from the server. You can get into this situation if you go offline (see section 2.2.2), make changes, and then set the read-only attribute. If you wish to merge server-side changes with the version in your workspace, check out the file (pend an edit) and then get the latest version.

2.2.2 Working offline

TFS 2005 didn't provide an option in the interface to work offline. If you needed to work offline in TFS 2005, you had to remove the read-only attributes of the source files, make necessary changes, and then use the `tfpt` power tool (with the `online` option) to pend the changes (once the server was back online). In TFS 2008,

Figure 2.30   Visual Studio 2008 can switch to offline mode if TFVC is unavailable.

Figure 2.31   Click the Go Online icon to synchronize local changes with TFVC.

although the general approach remains unchanged from TFS 2005, offline support is integrated into the Visual Studio IDE and you don't need to use a command-line tool.

When opening a project or solution, the IDE checks whether TFS is available and switches to offline mode if it isn't (figure 2.30 shows the message box that's displayed). When in offline mode, the Solution Explorer window also displays an extra icon (named Go Online) in the toolbar (see figure 2.31). When connectivity to TFS is restored, click the Go Online icon to pend appropriate changes to the files in your workspace. You can also select the Go Online option from the right-click context menu associated with the solution or file in Solution Explorer. TFS 2008 supports edit, add, and delete operations in offline mode, but not rename operations.

In offline mode, you can't check out a file from the server, since the server isn't available. You can only work on the files in your local workspace. Since the files in your workspace are read-only (unless you've performed a check-out), when you try to save your changes, you'll encounter a warning screen saying that the file can't be saved (see figure 2.30). Click Overwrite to remove the read-only attribute and save your changes.

When you click Go Online (after server connectivity is restored), Visual Studio will scan your local workspace and display a dialog box indicating appropriate changes (see

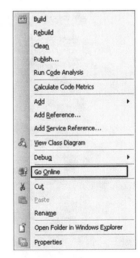

Figure 2.32   The Go Online option is also available from the context menu associated with a solution or file in Solution Explorer.

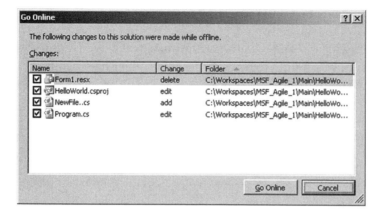

Figure 2.33
When synchronizing local changes with the server, TFVC marks each locally modified file with the appropriate type of change.

figure 2.33). Keep in mind that the logic responsible for determining edit and add operations checks the file attributes in the workspace. For edits and adds, the read-only attribute on the impacted files shouldn't be set. If you set the read-only attribute to `true`, the file won't be displayed in the Go Online dialog box (and won't have edits or adds pended for check-in).

2.2.3   *Folder comparison*

In TFS 2005, you couldn't compare folders (server or local) from the Visual Studio IDE. This commonly requested feature has been implemented in TFS 2008. Right-click a folder in the Source Control Explorer and select Compare from the context menu. In the Compare dialog box, specify the source and target folders (see figure 2.34).

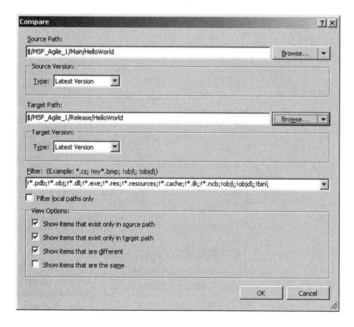

Figure 2.34   The Compare dialog box enables you to compare server or workspace folders and specify various options.

Use the Browse buttons to navigate to the chosen folders—you can specify server or local folders. You can also specify the source and target version types, based on labels, changesets, dates, latest versions, and so on.

Furthermore, you can filter the files that appear in the output list by typing excluded file names, file extensions, or folder names in the Filter box. For example, if you want to exclude all .config files, type !*.config in the Filter box. If you want to exclude a folder named "settings", type !settings\ in the Filter box. Separate the entries using a semicolon (;). The output of the Compare operation is displayed in figure 2.35.

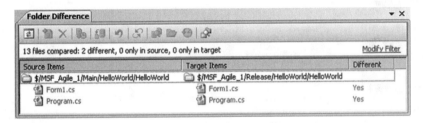

Figure 2.35   The Folder Difference window displays the files which differ between the specified folders.

2.2.4   *Annotate*

In TFS 2008, the annotate feature of the tfpt power tool has been integrated into the user interface. To invoke the annotate feature, right-click a file and select Annotate from the context menu.

The annotate functionality enables you to see the changes made to a file by various users, along with corresponding changeset information (see figure 2.36). You can view additional information about a changeset by clicking the changeset number. The annotation information serves as an audit trail regarding the changes to a file and enables you to see who did what, and when. In case of pending edits, the changes that have occurred in the workspace but haven't yet been checked in are marked Local.

```
BasicMath.cs;C16 (Annotated)   Source Control Explorer   Start Page          ▼ ✕

14  John   10/29/2007   using System;
                        using System.Collections.Generic;
                        using System.Linq;
                        using System.Text;

                        namespace MyMath
                        {
                            public class BasicMath                I
                            {
16  Lori   10/29/2007         /// <summary>
                              /// Adds two decimals together
                              /// </summary>
                              /// <param name="a">First number</param>
                              /// <param name="b">Second number</param>
                              /// <returns>The value of a + b</returns>
15  Steve  10/29/2007         public decimal Add(decimal a, decimal b)
14  John   10/29/2007         {
                                  return a + b;
                              }

15  Steve  10/29/2007
16  Lori   10/29/2007         /// <summary>
                              /// Subtracts two decimals
                              /// </summary>
                              /// <param name="a">First Number</param>
                              /// <param name="b">Second Number</param>
                              /// <returns>The value of a - b</returns>
15  Steve  10/29/2007         public decimal Subtract(decimal a, decimal b)
                              {
                                  return a - b;
                              }

16  Lori   10/29/2007         /// <summary>
                              /// Multiplies two values together
                              /// </summary>
                              /// <param name="a">First Number</param>
                              /// <param name="b">Second Number</param>
                              /// <returns>The value of a * b</returns>
                              public decimal Multiply(decimal a, decimal b)
                              {
                                  return a * b;
◄                                                                          ►
```

Figure 2.36   The annotated file displays granular audit information regarding its change history.

You can gather additional information about a change by hovering the mouse pointer over an annotation entry. You can also right-click an annotation entry and select the options available in the context menu (see figure 2.37; the context menu options are different for entries marked Local). For example, click Annotate This Version to open the version indicated by the changeset number and display annotation information for that version. Select Compare with Previous Version to compare the current version of the file with the version indicated by the changeset number.

View Changeset Details...

View History

Compare With Previous Version...

Annotate This Version

Get This Version

Stop Annotation

Figure 2.37   The context menu associated with annotation entries contains options to obtain additional information about the change.

2.3 *Summary*

As we saw in this chapter, TFS 2008 contains a number of significant improvements that make the product more stable, efficient, and usable. We looked at new features in Team Build such as support for various kinds of builds, a new object model, better security, and so on. We also reviewed new features of TFVC, such as offline support, folder comparison, better annotation support, and more.

The next version of TFS (codenamed *Rosario*) promises even more significant enhancements. Upcoming features in Rosario include support for managing multiple TFS instances and multiple projects, creating hierarchical work items, improved test management, relating tests and test results back to requirements, better traceability and ability to conduct impact analysis, and so on.

In the next chapter, we look at another major component of VSTS 2008 that's now available as an integrated product—Visual Studio Team System 2008 Database Edition. VSTS 2008 Database Edition brings database professionals into the mainstream development process by providing support for schema extraction, versioning, comparison, and deployment.

Introducing VSTS 2008 Database Edition

This chapter covers

- Database change management
- Database testing
- Integrating with Team Build

Few applications work without interacting with a database. Databases typically contain configuration settings, lookup values, user and transaction information, application metadata, persisted state information, business rules, auditing information, historical records, and a host of other crucial data. However, despite their obvious importance and relevance, database development and management have traditionally been outside the scope of the mainstream application development process. Application developers have typically used the latest development methodologies, the greatest software configuration management (SCM) systems and the slickest IDEs, whereas database developers have languished in obsolete environments that don't support many basic modern features (such as IntelliSense). Their activities remain opaque, noncommunicable, unauditable, and sometimes, unmaintainable. Without integrating the activities of database developers into the mainstream development process, the full potential of the development team remains unrealized, and application development becomes difficult.

Visual Studio Team System 2008 Database Edition (DB Pro) helps you unlock the knowledge contained in your SQL Server databases. DB Pro can extract the schema from existing databases. Once decoupled, the stand-alone schema becomes available for versioning, distribution, and replication. For instance, to share the schema of a production database between distributed development teams—a common requirement—you don't need to schedule the database administrator's (DBA's) time to create an accurate and complete script (or an empty database backup). You can use DB Pro to easily import the schema from an existing database, with full fidelity and high granularity, facilitating fine-grained change management by distributed teams. You can also create sample data, run database unit tests, and compare the data as well as the schema of one database with another.

While many of these functions can be performed today using custom programming or isolated solutions, DB Pro provides an integrated toolset that operates in unison with other VSTS products as well as TFS. For example, the unit-testing framework works with Team Test, the schema is versioned using Team Foundation version control (or other third-party systems), database changes are associated with work items using work item tracking, and public database builds are created using Team Build. Using an integrated product simplifies learning, increases reach, reduces friction, and helps you take a holistic approach toward software lifecycle management.

This chapter takes a practitioner's view of DB Pro. We dive into the concepts, steps, and issues involved in typical database maintenance activities. We explore the product's main features and extensibility points. As such, the material in this chapter is introductory in nature.

The primary goal of the chapter is to demonstrate how database maintenance activities can be integrated into the mainstream software process. I show how DB Pro makes it possible to construct, evolve, version, build, and deploy database code similar to how developers typically create and maintain application code.

In this chapter, you'll learn about the following:

- *How to create an offline view of a database and make schema changes in a controlled manner*—Changing the schema of an existing production database is usually a high-risk activity due to various dependencies, which aren't easily discoverable. DB Pro offers the capability to modify a schema in a *sandbox*. You can make changes across various dependencies, compare one schema with another, and deploy the changes safely. Another benefit of "shredding" the database schema into a set of data definition language (DDL) fragments is the ability to version the schema at a granular level and share it across the development team. Once the schema is stored in the version control repository, you can use a common label to tie the application code and the corresponding database schema together, creating a complete package.

- *How to generate test data*—Creating a test dataset manually is often a painful task, especially when you have to satisfy complex referential integrity constraints, ensure certain statistical distributions, or maintain proportionality between related tables. DB Pro allows you to generate test data using built-in as well as custom data generators.

- *How to create database unit tests*—Application developers have recognized the value of unit tests for several years now, as evidenced by the popularity of agile development methodologies such as test-driven development (TDD), extreme programming (XP), and so on. But database professionals have had no straightforward way to create unit tests for database logic (stored procedures, functions, and triggers). DB Pro provides this missing functionality and offers an extensible model where, in addition to using predefined conditions for validating test results, you can create custom conditions.

- *How to integrate DB Pro with Team Build*—Team Build enables you to create public builds from the source control repository. Certain development methodologies emphasize continuous integration, where a new build is generated as soon as a source file is checked in. Other practices include daily or weekly builds for development, staging, and production environments. DB Pro integrates with Team Build and can participate in the build process, along with the application code. You can customize the Team Build project file to automatically deploy the database build script to a target database.

3.1   *A quick tour of DB Pro*

The best way to get an overview of the features available in DB Pro is to walk through a common scenario (see figure 3.1). Our scenario involves modifying an existing production database. Since it's dangerous to make any but the most trivial changes directly on a production server, a better strategy is to extract the schema, make changes in isolation, test the modified database separately, and then apply the changes to the production server (assuming the tests pass). As a by-product of this process, you get a standalone schema and database project that can be stored in Team Foundation version control (TFVC), shared with team members, and used to make public builds.

When working with a real-life production database, practical considerations come into play. For instance, developers usually don't have direct access to production databases. Consequently, a production DBA gets involved and the steps are typically as follows (see figure 3.2).

Figure 3.1   A representative database maintenance process

1 A DBA extracts the schema from the production database using DB Pro and checks it in to TFVC.

2 Developers download the schema into their local workspaces and make modifications locally. Since the developers don't have access to the production database, it becomes difficult to compare their local schema changes with the schema of the production server. Also, if developers can't access the production server then when they build the database project, DB Pro will generate a Create script (to create the database from scratch), not an Update script (to incrementally update the structure). To resolve this problem, you can create a structural mirror of the production database in a development machine. The mirror database may contain representative data from the production database—mirrored data should be scrubbed to remove sensitive information. The mirror enables developers to compare their changes with the reference database, and to generate the appropriate change scripts for updating the production database.

3 The DBA obtains the database change script from TFVC or from a public build created using Team Build. He can also create the database change script himself by downloading the appropriate version of the database project from TFVC and building the project using DB Pro. Using DB Pro, he can also compare the schema changes with the current structure of the production database. After verifying that the changes are valid, he applies the changes to the production database.

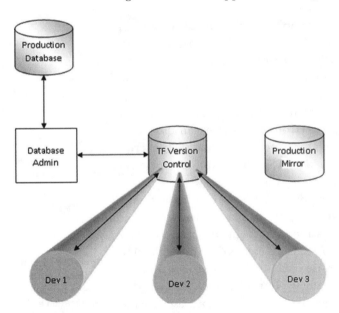

Figure 3.2 In a typical scenario, the DBA extracts the schema from a production database and makes it available to developers via TFVC. The DBA also applies the schema changes back to the production database.

3.1.1 Creating a database project

Launch Visual Studio and bring up the New Project dialog box. Note that DB Pro has installed four project templates for creating database projects (see figure 3.3). Select the

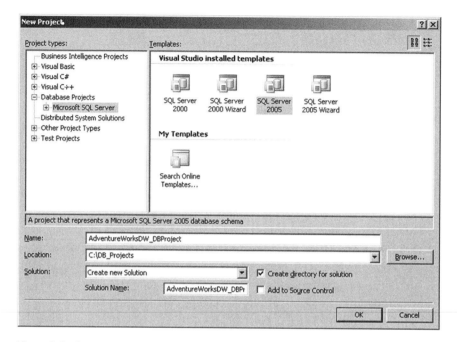

Figure 3.3   Create a database project for working with the schema of a database.

SQL Server 2005 project template. This template creates an empty database project. To extract a schema from an existing database, right-click the project name in Solution Explorer and select Import Database Schema from the context menu (see figure 3.4).

A schema can be created in other ways as well. You can always create a new schema from scratch. You can also create schemas by reverse engineering an existing T-SQL script (right-click the project name in Solution Explorer and select Import Script from the context menu).

The Import Database Schema menu option is available for new projects only (projects that don't have database objects). This option is removed from the context menu after a database is imported. This means that you can't reimport the schema of a source database if the structure of the source database has changed. To update the database project with schema changes from the source database, use the Schema Compare feature (discussed later in the chapter).

Figure 3.4   Import a database schema to create fine-grained DDL fragments for modification and versioning.

Clicking Import Database Schema launches the Import Database Wizard. Create a new connection to the production database (or reuse an existing connection) and follow the instructions in the wizard. When you click Finish, DB Pro imports the schema information to the database project (see figure 3.5).

Note that the Schema Objects node in Solution Explorer contains the bulk of the structural information. The schema information is imported in a collection of .sql files. The .sql files contain T-SQL code and can be executed in the Query Editor (available in DB Pro IDE as well as in Microsoft SQL Server 2005 Management Studio). The schema information is imported in a fine-grained manner as DDL fragments that are as small as possible. For example, instead of lumping all table-related information in a single .sql file, separate files are created for each table, key, constraint, trigger, and index. In DB Pro v1, you can only import schema information from relational databases; analytical databases aren't supported at this time.

Note also in figure 3.5 that DB Pro presents two views named Solution Explorer and Schema View. The Solution Explorer view displays the contents of the filesystem as they are. The Schema View creates an object-oriented representation, similar to the Object Explorer in Microsoft SQL Server 2005 Management Studio. For example, in Schema View, the columns, indexes, keys, and triggers associated with a table are displayed under the node for that table.

Internally, DB Pro creates an empty design database to validate the schema

Figure 3.5 The imported schema is decomposed into a set of T-SQL files.

information (see figure 3.6). The name of the design database is in the format *<your_database_project_name>*_DB_*<number>*. You can specify a local SQL Server instance name where the design database will be created—if you don't specify anything, the design database will be created in the default instance. To select an instance name, in the Tools menu, click Options. Then, in the Options dialog box, expand the Database Tools node, click Design-time Validation Database, and type the instance name in the Connection Options/SQL Server Instance Name text box.

The design database mimics the structure of the imported database, but doesn't contain any data. DB Pro keeps the structure of the design database and the contents of the local .sql files in sync. If you edit a .sql file, the changes are automatically

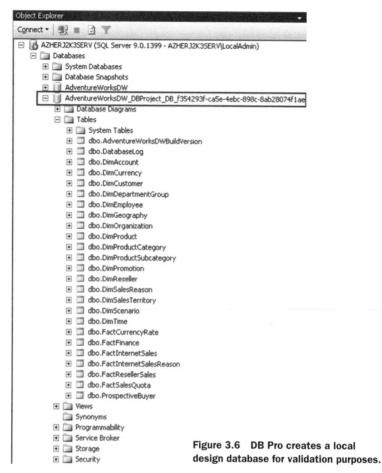

Figure 3.6   DB Pro creates a local design database for validation purposes.

reflected in the design database. If for some reason the two get out of sync, you can click the synchronize icon in Schema View to bring the design database and the file system back in sync.

3.1.2   *Making changes offline*

Once a database project is created, you can work on the schema files without worrying about impacting the source database. As previously discussed, the schema is deserialized into a collection of granular .sql files in your local file system. Changes made in those files have no effect on the original database from which the schema was derived. (DB Pro automatically synchronizes these changes with the local design database.)

You can check the files in to TFVC for versioning as well as sharing among team members. The schema files are treated like any other source files in TFVC. You can apply the usual source control practices, such as branching, labeling, associating changes with work items, enforcing check-in policies, and so on. Like other Visual Studio projects, you can add the schema files to TFVC during project creation, or subsequently by right-clicking the solution in Solution Explorer and selecting Add Project to Source Control from the context menu.

DB Pro supports rename refactoring. If you rename an item or an element, DB Pro displays all the places that will be impacted by the change. You can then apply the changes once you're satisfied that they're safe. To perform rename refactoring, right-click an item or an element in Schema View,

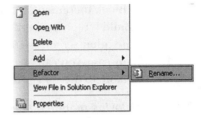

Figure 3.7 Rename refactoring allows you to make changes safely.

point to Refactor in the context menu, and select Rename (see figure 3.7). You can also select Refactor from the Data menu. DB Pro allows you to preview the changes (see figure 3.8) and apply them globally. This feature is a great time saver and enables you to make schema changes safely. Support for other kinds of refactoring is expected in future versions.

When doing rename refactoring, watch out for potential data loss. For example, when you rename a column, DB Pro creates a temporary table with the new column name, copies data from the old table to the temporary table (except for the data residing in the renamed column), drops the old table, and finally renames the temporary table to reflect the name of the old table. During this process, the data for the renamed column isn't copied from the old table to the temporary table, resulting in loss of data. If you tell DB Pro to prevent data loss in the target database—by selecting

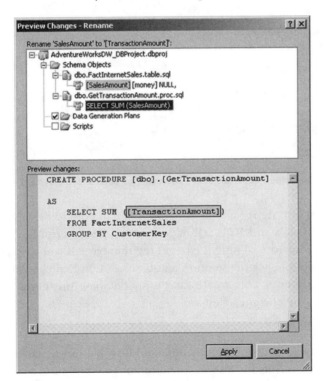

Figure 3.8 The Preview Changes screen displays the lines that are affected by rename refactoring.

the Block Incremental Deployment if Data Loss Might Occur option in the Properties or Build screen or the Block Schema Updates if Data Loss Might Occur option in one of the other screens—DB Pro won't update the target database if it contains any rows. In any case, you can always manually edit the update script and migrate data from the old table to the refactored table.

3.1.3 Deploying modified schema to a test database

DB Pro allows you to create a deployment script for modifying the schema of a target database. To specify the name of the target test database, as well as select various build options, right-click the solution name in Solution Explorer and select Properties from the context menu. Select the Build tab and specify your choices (see figure 3.9).

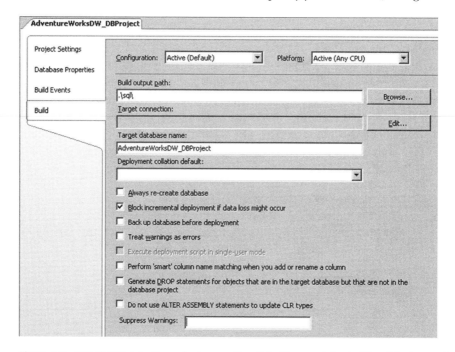

Figure 3.9   The Build tab in the project properties dialog box contains build and deployment options.

To create a deployment script, right-click the solution name in Solution Explorer and select Build from the context menu. This action generates a T-SQL script file that you can give to a DBA for creating or updating the target test database. If you have permissions to create databases, right-click the solution name in Solution Explorer and select Deploy from the context menu. This creates an empty database on the target SQL Server instance, based on the current schema.

3.1.4 Generating test data

Once you create a test database, you need to populate it with representative values. You could create your own scripts for test data generation or use DB Pro's automatic data generation capability. To use DB Pro's data generation feature, in Solutions

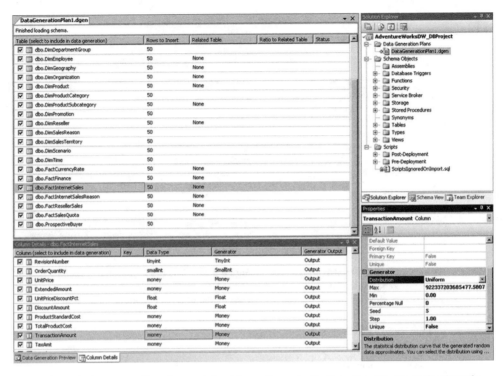

Figure 3.10   A data generation plan contains information regarding how the data for each column in each table will be generated.

Explorer, right-click the Data Generation Plans node, point to Add, and then click Data Generation Plan. This creates a new data generation plan (see figure 3.10).

In the top pane, select a table to work with. In the bottom pane, click the Column Details tab. For each column in the table, using the drop-down in the Generator column, specify the type of data generator you want to use. Customize the data generation options using the Properties pane. You can specify options such as the statistical distribution type, whether the generated values should be unique, what percent of generated values should be null, and so on. Select the Data Generation Preview tab to preview the output of the data generator before populating the target database with test data.

The list of available data generators depends on the corresponding column type. In addition to the type-specific data generators (String, Integer, Float, and so forth) there are two generators that merit special attention:

- *Regular Expression generator*—Available for string data types, this generator creates strings based on syntactical rules. For example, if you're generating test data for a phone number field using a String generator, you get gibberish values, as shown in figure 3.11. This isn't very meaningful and may not yield useful test results. Instead, use a Regular Expression generator and specify an expression to construct phone numbers (see figure 3.12). The result is displayed in figure 3.13.

Figure 3.11   The default String generator generates a random sequence of characters.

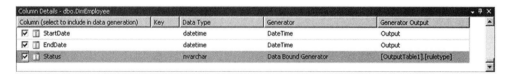

Figure 3.12   Use the Expression property of the Regular Expression generator to specify the pattern of generated strings.

Figure 3.13   A Regular Expression generator creates meaningful strings.

- *Data Bound generator*—Use this generator to look up data values from a lookup table and generate valid values for a column (see figure 3.14). In the Properties pane, specify the connection information and the SELECT query to fetch values from the lookup table (see figure 3.15). In the Column Details window, select one of the columns returned by the SELECT query as the value for the Generator Output column. Figure 3.16 shows the final result. Note that the Data

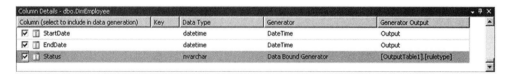

Figure 3.14   A Data Bound generator creates values based upon a lookup table.

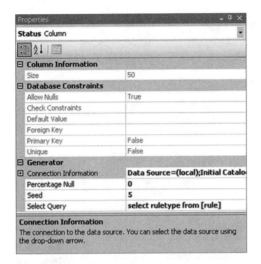

Figure 3.15   Specify a SELECT query to be used by the Data Bound generator.

Figure 3.16   A Data Bound generator populates the column with the values fetched from another table.

Bound generator isn't suited for populating a table with static data from a lookup table when you need to maintain the original sequence and content. The Data Bound generator copies a random set of values from the lookup table. If you need to clone a table, do it in the post-deployment script.

The generators are smart enough to recognize primary key/foreign key constraints and produce data in the correct sequence, so that the referential integrity constraints aren't violated. You can also specify the ratio of rows inserted in a particular table to rows in a related table. If none of the built-in generators meet your needs, you can create custom data generators (more on this in later sections).

3.1.5   Creating unit tests

Once the target database is populated with test data, the next task is to create unit tests to check the validity of the schema and the data. DB Pro offers the capability to test stored procedures, functions, and triggers using T-SQL code (although under the hood, it generates C# or VB.NET code). This feature saves time by allowing you to call the database code directly, without writing wrapper functions for unit testing. Database professionals finally get a unit-testing framework similar to what application developers have been utilizing for years.

Unlike unit tests for application code, code coverage information isn't captured when running unit tests for databases in VSTS 2005 or VSTS 2008. Support for this is planned for a future version.

On the Test menu, click New Test. In the Add New Test dialog box, select Database Unit Test and choose a C#, VB.NET, or C++ test project type (see figure 3.17). In the Project Configuration dialog box (see figure 3.18), specify the target database connection, whether the database project schema should be deployed, and whether the

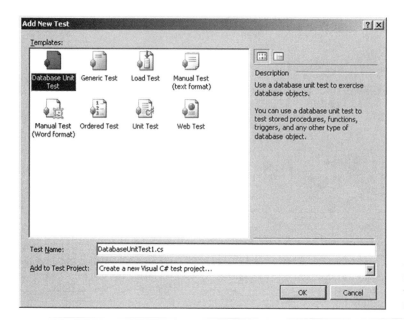

**Figure 3.17
Create a Database
Unit Test project
for constructing
database unit tests.**

database should be prepopulated using a specified data generation plan prior to executing unit tests.

In the unit test designer, write the appropriate T-SQL code to invoke database stored procedures, functions, and triggers (see figure 3.19). Use the Test Conditions drop-down to select a mechanism to test the validity of the unit test. Use the Properties pane

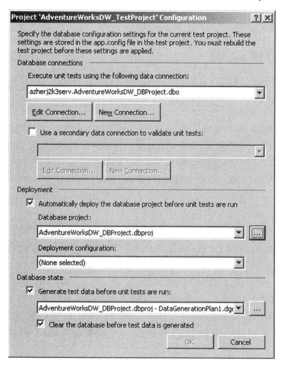

**Figure 3.18   The Project Configuration
dialog box contains options for connecting
to and preconfiguring the target database.**

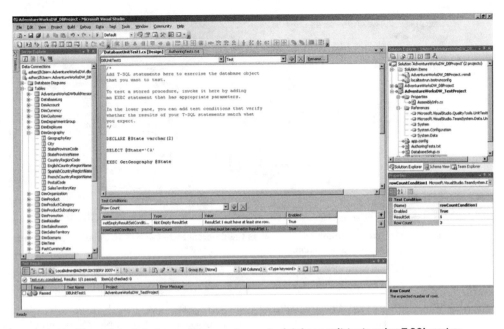

Figure 3.19   The unit test designer allows you to create database unit tests using T-SQL syntax.

to specify various parameters associated with the test conditions. The default test condition specified by DB Pro is Inconclusive. Just like the `Assert.Inconclusive` method in application unit tests, the Inconclusive test condition essentially means that no validations have taken place.

The built-in test conditions are somewhat coarse-grained. They include whether an empty or populated resultset was returned, how many rows were returned, what values were returned, whether execution time exceeded a defined limit, and so on. You can create custom test conditions by inheriting from the `Microsoft.VisualStudio.TeamSystem.Data.UnitTesting.Conditions.TestCondition` abstract class (see figure 3.20). For more information on how to create custom test conditions, refer to http://msdn2.microsoft.com/en-us/library/aa833409(VS.80).aspx.

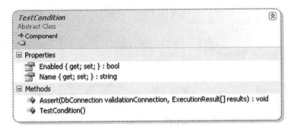

Figure 3.20   Create a custom test condition by inheriting from the `TestCondition` class.

3.1.6   *Deploying the modified schema to production database*

Once you're satisfied that your changes are valid, the next step is to deploy the changes to the production database. Prior to undertaking this, you might want to visually compare the modified schema in the database project with the current schema of the

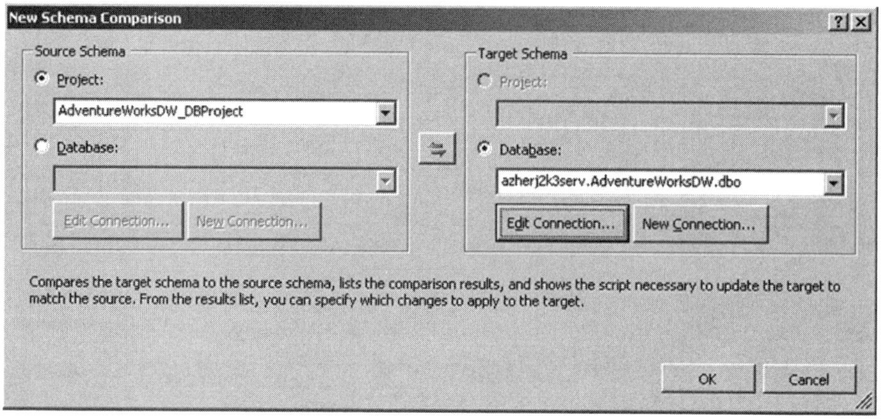

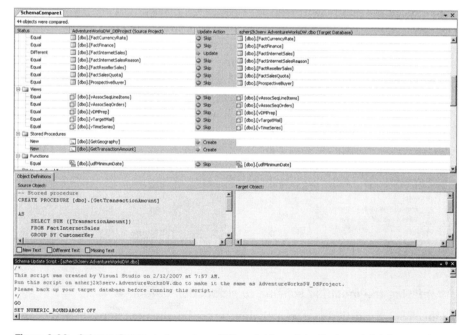

Figure 3.21   **Schema Compare determines the differences between two databases or between a database project and a database.**

production database, to ensure that your changes are still valid. Somebody else could have modified the production database since you last imported the schema.

On the Data menu, point to Schema Compare, and click New Schema Comparison. In the New Schema Comparison dialog box, specify the locations of the source and target schemas (see figure 3.21). DB Pro displays the differences between the two schemas. At the bottom of the schema comparison screen, DB Pro displays a script for updating the target schema to make it identical to the source schema (see figure 3.22). Click

Figure 3.22   **Schema Compare generates a SQL script to update the target database and synchronize it with the source database or project.**

Export to Editor to open the update script in Query Editor. The update script is database-agnostic. You can hand off the update script to a DBA for applying the changes to the target database, or if you have the necessary rights, you can apply the changes yourself by clicking Write Updates.

Exercise caution if you're updating a target database that contains important data, since changing the schema might cause loss of data. To prevent data loss, on the Tools menu, click Options. In the Options dialog box, expand the Database Tools node, click Schema Compare, and select Block Schema Updates if Data Loss Might Occur (see figure 3.23). This option is turned on by default. If you're updating a test database where data loss isn't an issue, turn off this option if DB Pro is preventing you from updating the target schema. For more information regarding the options available in this screen, refer to http://msdn2.microsoft.com/EN-US/library/aa833438(VS.80).aspx.

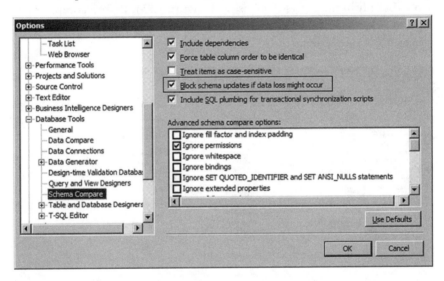

Figure 3.23 In the Options window, you can customize how Schema Compare updates the target database.

You can filter the visible objects in Schema Compare based on the type of update action. On the Schema Compare toolbar, click the Filter icon and specify the filter condition (see figure 3.24).

When you compare against a database project, the schema comparison feature actually compares against the underlying design database that corresponds to the project. Consequently, if an object in your project has errors, it isn't included in schema comparison, since the faulty object doesn't get created in the design database.

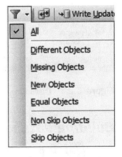

Figure 3.24 Click the Filter icon to filter which objects are visible in the schema comparison screen.

In DB Pro v1, when running Schema Compare, you can't delete objects if the target happens to be a project. In the comparison dialog box, if the target project doesn't contain an object that the source contains, the update action is displayed as *Skip*, instead of *Delete*.

Also in DB Pro v1, you can't compare the schema of a database project with the schema of another database project. This feature would've been useful in order to determine what schema changes have been made between two versions of a database project, for example.

On a related note, it's worth knowing that DB Pro also offers the capability to compare the data stored in two databases. On the Data menu, point to Data Compare and select New Data Comparison. The data comparison screen has tabs that display which rows are identical, which are different, which exist only in the source database, and which exist only in the target database (see figure 3.25). Before comparing two tables using Data Compare, make sure that they have identical schemas and the same primary key or unique index.

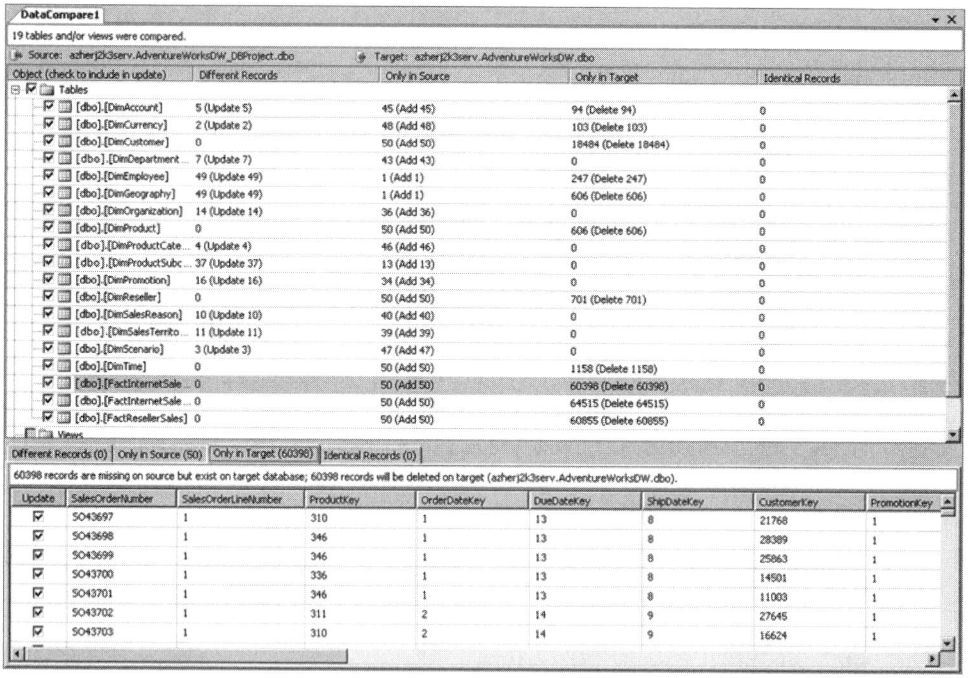

Figure 3.25   Data Compare compares the contents of two databases.

3.2   *Building database projects*

A *build* in the context of a database project means the creation of a .sql file that can synchronize the structure of a target database (specified in the Build tab of the project's properties) with a database project. If the Always Re-create Database option is selected (see figure 3.9 displayed previously) or the target database doesn't exist, the output .sql file contains the necessary T-SQL commands (such as CREATE commands) to generate the target database from scratch. If this option isn't selected and the target database is accessible, the output .sql file contains only the necessary commands (such as ALTER commands) to modify the schema of the target database.

You can create builds from the Visual Studio IDE, from the command line using MSBuild, or from Team Build projects. DB Pro introduces a new targets file to support building database projects. This file is named Microsoft.VisualStudio.TeamSystem.Data. Tasks.targets. It's located in the %ProgramFiles%\MSBuild\Microsoft\VisualStudio\ v8.0\TeamData folder for TFS 2005 and in the %ProgramFiles%\MSBuild\Microsoft\ VisualStudio\v9.0\TeamData folder for TFS 2008. The `SqlBuildTask` task (used in the targets file) creates the .sql script. The `SqlDeployTask` task updates the target database. But `SqlDeployTask` doesn't regenerate the .sql file; it expects to find an existing .sql file. Listing 3.1 shows the contents of the targets file in TFS 2005; listing 3.2 shows the contents of the targets file in TFS 2008. The targets file is imported into the database project file.

Although listings 3.1 and 3.2 are quite long, we decided to include the full content of the targets files, so that you can build a comprehensive knowledge of their inner workings while reading the book.

Note in listing 3.1 that in TFS 2005, the `BuildScriptName` and `TargetDatabase` properties are defined unconditionally. This means that if these property values are defined in your database project file (the .dbproj file) prior to the line that imports the targets file, the values defined in the database project file will be overridden by the values specified in the targets file. This problem doesn't show up when building from the Visual Studio IDE or when building using MSBuild, but manifests itself when building from Team Build (more on this in later sections). This is a bug in DB Pro/TFS 2005 and has been fixed in DB Pro/TFS 2008.

Listing 3.1 Targets file for building database projects in TFS 2005

```
<?xml version="1.0" encoding="Windows-1252"?>
<Project InitialTargets="CheckRequiredProperties"
    xmlns="http://schemas.microsoft.com
    /developer/msbuild/2003">

    <!--Some properties must be set in the main project file,
        before using this .TARGETS file-->
    <Target Name="CheckRequiredProperties">
    </Target>

    <UsingTask TaskName="SqlBuildTask"
        AssemblyName=
        "Microsoft.VisualStudio.TeamSystem.Data.Tasks,
        Version=2.0.0.0, Culture=neutral,
        PublicKeyToken=b03f5f7f11d50a3a"/>
    <UsingTask TaskName="SqlDeployTask"
        AssemblyName=
        "Microsoft.VisualStudio.TeamSystem.Data.Tasks,
        Version=2.0.0.0, Culture=neutral,
        PublicKeyToken=b03f5f7f11d50a3a"/>
```

```xml
<UsingTask TaskName="SqlBuildScriptNameTask"
   AssemblyName=
   "Microsoft.VisualStudio.TeamSystem.Data.Tasks,
   Version=2.0.0.0, Culture=neutral,
   PublicKeyToken=b03f5f7f11d50a3a"/>
   <UsingTask TaskName="DataGeneratorTask"
   AssemblyName=
   "Microsoft.VisualStudio.TeamSystem.Data.Tasks,
   Version=2.0.0.0, Culture=neutral,
   PublicKeyToken=b03f5f7f11d50a3a"/>

<!--This makes the project files a dependency of all
   targets so that things rebuild if they change-->
<PropertyGroup>
   <MSBuildAllProjects>
      Microsoft.VisualStudio.TeamSystem.Data.Tasks.targets
   </MSBuildAllProjects>
</PropertyGroup>

<!--Output and path properties-->
<PropertyGroup>
   <!--The ScriptName autogenerated by the
      SqlBuildScriptName target if not specified as
      a build argument-->
   <BuildScriptName></BuildScriptName>

   <!--
      We default to the name of the project file
      for the name of TargetDatabase if the property
      is not specified
   -->
   <TargetDatabase>$(MSBuildProjectName)</TargetDatabase>

</PropertyGroup>

<Target Name="SqlBuildScriptName"
   Condition="$(BuildScriptName)==''">
   <SqlBuildScriptNameTask
      TargetConnectionString="$(TargetConnectionString)"
      TargetDatabase="$(TargetDatabase)"
      ProjectName="$(ProjectName)">
         <Output TaskParameter="BuildScriptName"
            PropertyName="BuildScriptName"/>
   </SqlBuildScriptNameTask>
</Target>

<!--Build-->
<PropertyGroup>
   <SqlBuildDependsOn>SqlBuildScriptName</SqlBuildDependsOn>
</PropertyGroup>

<Target
   Name="SqlBuild"
   DependsOnTargets="$(SqlBuildDependsOn)">

   <SqlBuildTask
      SourceItems="@(Build)"
      PostDeployItems="@(PostDeploy)"
      PreDeployItems="@(PreDeploy)"
```

```
            TargetConnectionString="$(TargetConnectionString)"
            TargetDatabase="$(TargetDatabase)"
            OutputPath="$(OutDir)"
            BuildScriptName="$(BuildScriptName)"
            ProjectName="$(MSBuildProjectName)"
            DBProduct="$(DBProduct)"
            EnableClrIntegration="$(EnableCLRIntegration)"
            AutoClose="$(AutoClose)"
            AutoCreateStatistics="$(AutoCreateStatistics)"
            AutoShrink="$(AutoShrink)"
            AutoUpdateStatistics="$(AutoUpdateStatistics)"
            AutoUpdateStatisticsAsynchronously
               ="$(AutoUpdateStatisticsAsynchronously)"
            CloseCursorOnCommitEnabled
               ="$(CloseCursorOnCommitEnabled)"
            DefaultCursor="$(DefaultCursor)"
            ArithmeticAbort="$(ArithAbort)"
            NumericRoundAbort="$(NumericRoundAbort)"
            ConcatNullYieldsNull="$(ConcatNullYieldsNull)"
            AnsiNulls="$(AnsiNulls)"
            AnsiPadding="$(AnsiPadding)"
            AnsiWarnings="$(AnsiWarnings)"
            QuotedIdentifier="$(QuotedIdentifier)"
            AnsiNullDefault="$(AnsiNullDefault)"
            DatabaseChaining="$(DatabaseChaining)"
            EnableServiceBroker="$(EnableServiceBroker)"
            RecursiveTriggersEnabled="$(RecursiveTriggersEnabled)"
            Trustworthy="$(Trustworthy)"
            DatabaseState="$(DatabaseState)"
            DatabaseAccess="$(DatabaseAccess)"
            UpdateOptions="$(UpdateOptions)"
            Parameterization="$(Parameterization)"
            Recovery="$(Recovery)"
            PageVerify="$(PageVerify)"
            TornPageDetection="$(TornPageDetection)"
            AllowSnapshotIsolation="$(AllowSnapshotIsolation)"
            ReadCommittedSnapshot="$(ReadCommittedSnapshot)"
            EnableFullTextSearch="$(EnableFullTextSearch)"
            DeploymentCollationPreference
               ="$(DeploymentCollationPreference)"
            DefaultCollation="$(DefaultCollation)"
            AlwaysCreateNewDatabase="$(AlwaysCreateNewDatabase)"
            GenerateDropsIfNotInProject
               ="$(GenerateDropsIfNotInProject)"
            SingleUserMode="$(SingleUserMode)"
            BlockIncrementalDeploymentIfDataLoss
               ="$(BlockIncrementalDeploymentIfDataLoss)"
            UseFuzzyMatchForColumns="$(UseFuzzyMatchForColumns)"
            TreatWarningsAsErrors="$(TreatWarningsAsErrors)"
            PerformDatabaseBackup="$(PerformDatabaseBackup)"
            NoAlterAssemblyStatements="$
               (DoNotUseAlterAssemblyStatementsToUpdateCLRTypes)"
            SuppressWarnings="$(SuppressWarnings)"
        />

    </Target>
```

```xml
<!-- Deploy -->
<PropertyGroup>
   <SqlDeployDependsOn>
      SqlBuildScriptName
   </SqlDeployDependsOn>
</PropertyGroup>
<Target Name="SqlDeploy"
   DependsOnTargets="$(SqlDeployDependsOn)">

   <SqlDeployTask
      BuildScriptPath="$(OutDir)$(BuildScriptName)"
      DBProduct="$(DBProduct)"
      TargetConnectionString="$(TargetConnectionString)"
      TargetDatabase="$(TargetDatabase)"
      SetVariablesXml="$(SetVariables)"/>
</Target>

<Import Project="$(MSBuildBinPath)\Microsoft.Common.targets" />

<PropertyGroup>
   <AllDependsOn>Build;Deploy</AllDependsOn>
</PropertyGroup>
<Target Name="All" DependsOnTargets="$(AllDependsOn)" />

   <PropertyGroup>
      <BuildDependsOn>
         PreBuildEvent;SqlBuild;PostBuildEvent
      </BuildDependsOn>
   </PropertyGroup>
<Target Name="Build"
   DependsOnTargets="$(BuildDependsOn)">
   <OnError ExecuteTargets="PostBuildEvent"
      Condition="'$(RunPostBuildEvent)'=='Always'"/>
   <OnError ExecuteTargets="_CleanRecordFileWrites"/>
</Target>

<PropertyGroup>
   <DeployDependsOn>SqlDeploy</DeployDependsOn>
</PropertyGroup>

<Target Name="Deploy" DependsOnTargets="$(DeployDependsOn)" />

<PropertyGroup>
   <CleanDependsOn>SqlBuildScriptName</CleanDependsOn>
</PropertyGroup>
<Target Name="Clean" DependsOnTargets="$(CleanDependsOn)">
   <Delete Files="$(OutDir)$(BuildScriptName)"/>
</Target>

<!-- CreateManifestResourceNames target: empty target -->
<PropertyGroup>
   <CreateManifestResourceNamesDependsOn>
   </CreateManifestResourceNamesDependsOn>
</PropertyGroup>

<Target Name="CreateManifestResourceNames"
   DependsOnTargets
   = "$(CreateManifestResourceNamesDependsOn)"/>

</Project>
```

Listing 3.2 shows the contents of the Microsoft.VisualStudio.TeamSystem.Data.Tasks. targets file in TFS 2008.

Listing 3.2 Targets file for building database projects in TFS 2008

```xml
<?xml version="1.0" encoding="Windows-1252"?>
<Project InitialTargets="CheckRequiredProperties" xmlns="http://
  schemas.microsoft.com/developer/msbuild/2003">

 <!--Some properties must be set in the main project file, before using
  this .TARGETS file-->
 <Target Name="CheckRequiredProperties">
 </Target>

 <UsingTask TaskName="SqlBuildTask"
  AssemblyName="Microsoft.VisualStudio.TeamSystem.Data.Tasks,
Version=9.0.0.0, Culture=neutral,
PublicKeyToken=b03f5f7f11d50a3a"/>
 <UsingTask TaskName="SqlDeployTask"
  AssemblyName="Microsoft.VisualStudio.TeamSystem.Data.Tasks,
Version=9.0.0.0, Culture=neutral,
PublicKeyToken=b03f5f7f11d50a3a"/>
 <UsingTask TaskName="DataGeneratorTask"
  AssemblyName="Microsoft.VisualStudio.TeamSystem.Data.Tasks,
Version=9.0.0.0, Culture=neutral,
PublicKeyToken=b03f5f7f11d50a3a"/>

 <!--This makes the project files a dependency of all targets so that
  things rebuild if they change-->
 <PropertyGroup>
  <MSBuildAllProjects>
   $(MSBuildAllProjects);
   $(MSBuildExtensionsPath)\Microsoft\VisualStudio\v9.0\TeamData\
   Microsoft.VisualStudio.TeamSystem.Data.Tasks.targets
  </MSBuildAllProjects>
 </PropertyGroup>

 <!--Output and path properties-->
 <PropertyGroup>
  <TargetExt>.dbmeta</TargetExt>
  <!--Ensure DefaultDataPath has a trailing slash, so it can be
   concatenated -->
  <DefaultDataPath Condition="'$(DefaultDataPath)' != '' and
   !HasTrailingSlash('$(DefaultDataPath)')">$(DefaultDataPath)\
  </DefaultDataPath>
  <!--TargetName property is defined here for the unit tests to pass -->
  <TargetName Condition=" '$(TargetName)' == '' ">$(MSBuildProjectName)
  </TargetName>
  <BuildScriptName Condition="'
   $(BuildScriptName)' == ''">$(MSBuildProjectName).sql
  </BuildScriptName>
  <ReferenceAssemblyName Condition="'
   $(ReferenceAssemblyName)' == ''">$(TargetName)$(TargetExt)
  </ReferenceAssemblyName>

  <IntermediateOutputPath>$(OutputPath)</IntermediateOutputPath>
```

```xml
<!--
We default to the name of the project file for the name of the
TargetDatabase if the property is not specified
-->
<TargetDatabase Condition="'
 $(TargetDatabase)' == ''">$(MSBuildProjectName)
</TargetDatabase>

</PropertyGroup>

<Target Name="_SetupSqlBuildInputs"
      Outputs="@(SqlBuildInputItems)">
 <CreateItem Include="$(MSBuildAllProjects)">
  <Output TaskParameter="Include" ItemName="__SqlBuildInputItems"/>
 </CreateItem>
 <CreateItem  Include="@(Build)">
  <Output TaskParameter="Include" ItemName="__SqlBuildInputItems"/>
 </CreateItem>
 <CreateItem  Include="@(NotInBuild)">
  <Output TaskParameter="Include" ItemName="__SqlBuildInputItems"/>
 </CreateItem>
 <CreateItem  Include="@(PostDeploy)">
  <Output TaskParameter="Include" ItemName="__SqlBuildInputItems"/>
 </CreateItem>
 <CreateItem  Include="@(PreDeploy)">
  <Output TaskParameter="Include" ItemName="__SqlBuildInputItems"/>
 </CreateItem>
 <CreateItem  Include="@(ReferencePath)">
  <Output TaskParameter="Include" ItemName="__SqlBuildInputItems"/>
 </CreateItem>
 <CreateItem  Include="$(MSBuildProjectFullPath)">
  <Output TaskParameter="Include" ItemName="__SqlBuildInputItems"/>
 </CreateItem>

 <CreateItem Condition="Exists('$(MSBuildProjectFullPath).user')"
   Include="$(MSBuildProjectFullPath).user">
  <Output TaskParameter="Include" ItemName="__SqlBuildInputItems"/>
 </CreateItem>

 <CreateItem  Include="@(__SqlBuildInputItems->'%(FullPath)')">
  <Output TaskParameter="Include" ItemName="SqlBuildInputItems"/>
 </CreateItem>
</Target>

<Target Name="_SetupSqlDeployReferences"
      Outputs="@(SqlDeployReferences)">
 <CreateItem Include="@(Reference)">
  <Output TaskParameter="Include" ItemName="SqlDeployReferences"/>
 </CreateItem>
 <CreateItem Include="@(ProjectReference)">
  <Output TaskParameter="Include" ItemName="SqlDeployReferences"/>
 </CreateItem>
</Target>

<Target Name="_SetupSqlBuildOutputs"
      Outputs="@(SqlBuildOutputItems)">
 <CreateItem Include="$(OutDir)$(ReferenceAssemblyName)">
```

```
   <Output TaskParameter="Include" ItemName="__SqlBuildOutputItems"/>
  </CreateItem>
  <CreateItem  Include="$(OutDir)$(BuildScriptName)">
    <Output TaskParameter="Include" ItemName="__SqlBuildOutputItems"/>
  </CreateItem>
  <CreateItem  Include="@(__SqlBuildOutputItems->'%(FullPath)')">
    <Output TaskParameter="Include" ItemName="SqlBuildOutputItems"/>
  </CreateItem>
</Target>

<!--Build-->
<PropertyGroup>
<SqlBuildDependsOn>ResolveReferences;_SetupSqlBuildInputs;
  _SetupSqlBuildOutputs;
  </SqlBuildDependsOn>
</PropertyGroup>
<Target Name="SqlBuild"
       DependsOnTargets="$(SqlBuildDependsOn)"
       Inputs="@(SqlBuildInputItems)"
       Outputs="@(SqlBuildOutputItems)"
       >

  <SqlBuildTask
    SourceItems="@(Build)"
    PostDeployItems="@(PostDeploy)"
    PreDeployItems="@(PreDeploy)"
    TargetConnectionString="$(TargetConnectionString)"
    TargetDatabase="$(TargetDatabase)"
    OutputPath="$(OutDir)"
    BuildScriptName="$(BuildScriptName)"
    ReferenceAssemblyName="$(ReferenceAssemblyName)"
    ProjectPath="$(MSBuildProjectFullPath)"
    References="@(ReferencePath)"

    DBProduct="$(DBProduct)"
    EnableClrIntegration="$(EnableCLRIntegration)"
    AutoClose="$(AutoClose)"
    AutoCreateStatistics="$(AutoCreateStatistics)"
    AutoShrink="$(AutoShrink)"
    AutoUpdateStatistics="$(AutoUpdateStatistics)"
    AutoUpdateStatisticsAsynchronously=
    "$(AutoUpdateStatisticsAsynchronously)"
    CloseCursorOnCommitEnabled="$(CloseCursorOnCommitEnabled)"
    DefaultCursor="$(DefaultCursor)"

    ArithmeticAbort="$(ArithAbort)"
    NumericRoundAbort="$(NumericRoundAbort)"
    ConcatNullYieldsNull="$(ConcatNullYieldsNull)"
    AnsiNulls="$(AnsiNulls)"
    AnsiPadding="$(AnsiPadding)"
    AnsiWarnings="$(AnsiWarnings)"
    QuotedIdentifier="$(QuotedIdentifier)"
    AnsiNullDefault="$(AnsiNullDefault)"

    DatabaseChaining="$(DatabaseChaining)"
    EnableServiceBroker="$(EnableServiceBroker)"
    RecursiveTriggersEnabled="$(RecursiveTriggersEnabled)"
```

```
        Trustworthy="$(Trustworthy)"
        DatabaseState="$(DatabaseState)"
        DatabaseAccess="$(DatabaseAccess)"
        UpdateOptions="$(UpdateOptions)"
        Parameterization="$(Parameterization)"
        Recovery="$(Recovery)"
        PageVerify="$(PageVerify)"
        TornPageDetection="$(TornPageDetection)"
        AllowSnapshotIsolation="$(AllowSnapshotIsolation)"
        ReadCommittedSnapshot="$(ReadCommittedSnapshot)"
        EnableFullTextSearch="$(EnableFullTextSearch)"
        DeploymentCollationPreference="$(DeploymentCollationPreference)"
        DefaultCollation="$(DefaultCollation)"
        AlwaysCreateNewDatabase="$(AlwaysCreateNewDatabase)"
        GenerateDropsIfNotInProject="$(GenerateDropsIfNotInProject)"
        SingleUserMode="$(SingleUserMode)"
        BlockIncrementalDeploymentIfDataLoss=
        "$(BlockIncrementalDeploymentIfDataLoss)"
        UseFuzzyMatchForColumns="$(UseFuzzyMatchForColumns)"
        TreatWarningsAsErrors="$(TreatWarningsAsErrors)"
        PerformDatabaseBackup="$(PerformDatabaseBackup)"
        NoAlterAssemblyStatements=
        "$(DoNotUseAlterAssemblyStatementsToUpdateCLRTypes)"
        SuppressWarnings="$(SuppressWarnings)"
        FileGroups="$(FileGroups)"
        SetVariablesXml="$(SetVariables)"
        FileGroupSetVariablesXml="$(FilegroupSetVariables)"
        CompatLevel ="$(CompatLevel)"
        />

    </Target>

    <!-- Deploy -->
    <PropertyGroup>
      <SqlDeployDependsOn>_SetupSqlDeployReferences;</SqlDeployDependsOn>
    </PropertyGroup>
    <Target Name="SqlDeploy"
            DependsOnTargets="$(SqlDeployDependsOn)">

      <SqlDeployTask
        BuildScriptPath="$(OutDir)$(BuildScriptName)"
        DBProduct="$(DBProduct)"
        TargetConnectionString="$(TargetConnectionString)"
        TargetDatabase="$(TargetDatabase)"
        SetVariablesXml="$(SetVariables)"
        FileGroupSetVariablesXml="$(FilegroupSetVariables)"
        References="@(SqlDeployReferences)"
        />

    </Target>

    <Import Project="$(MSBuildBinPath)\Microsoft.Common.targets" />
    <PropertyGroup>
      <AllDependsOn>Build;Deploy</AllDependsOn>
    </PropertyGroup>
    <Target Name="All" DependsOnTargets="$(AllDependsOn)" />

    <!-- Build -->
```

```xml
<PropertyGroup>
  <BuildDependsOn>BeforeBuild;PrepareForBuild;PreBuildEvent;SqlBuild;
    PostBuildEvent;AfterBuild
  </BuildDependsOn>
</PropertyGroup>

<Target Name="Build"
      DependsOnTargets="$(BuildDependsOn)"
      Outputs="@(SqlBuildOutputItems)">

  <OnError ExecuteTargets="PostBuildEvent"
  Condition="'$(RunPostBuildEvent)'=='Always'"/>
  <OnError ExecuteTargets="_CleanRecordFileWrites"/>
</Target>

<!-- Deploy -->
<Target
  Name="PreDeployEvent"
  Condition="'$(PreDeployEvent)'!='' And Exists($(OutDir))">
  <Exec WorkingDirectory="$(OutDir)" Command="$(PreDeployEvent)" />
</Target>

<Target
Name="PostDeployEvent"
Condition="'$(PostDeployEvent)'!='' And Exists($(OutDir))">
  <Exec WorkingDirectory="$(OutDir)" Command="$(PostDeployEvent)" />
</Target>

<PropertyGroup>
  <DeployDependsOn>PreDeployEvent;SqlDeploy;PostDeployEvent</
  DeployDependsOn>
</PropertyGroup>
<Target Name="Deploy" DependsOnTargets="$(DeployDependsOn)">

  <OnError ExecuteTargets="PostDeployEvent"
  Condition="'$(RunPostDeployEvent)'=='Always'"/>
</Target>

<!-- Clean -->
<PropertyGroup>
  <CleanDependsOn>_SetupSqlBuildOutputs</CleanDependsOn>
</PropertyGroup>
<Target Name="Clean" DependsOnTargets="$(CleanDependsOn)">
  <Delete Files="@(SqlBuildOutputItems)"/>
</Target>

<!-- CreateManifestResourceNames target: empty target -->
<PropertyGroup>
  <CreateManifestResourceNamesDependsOn>
  </CreateManifestResourceNamesDependsOn>
</PropertyGroup>

<Target Name="CreateManifestResourceNames"
  DependsOnTargets="$(CreateManifestResourceNamesDependsOn)"/>

<!--
============================================================
Overriding BuiltProjectOutputGroup
============================================================
-->
```

```xml
<Target
    Name="BuiltProjectOutputGroup"
    Outputs="@(BuiltProjectOutputGroupOutput)"
    DependsOnTargets="$(BuiltProjectOutputGroupDependsOn)">

 <CreateItem Include="$(OutDir)$(ReferenceAssemblyName)"
    AdditionalMetadata="IsKeyOutput=true;
    TargetPath=$(ReferenceAssemblyName)">
   <Output TaskParameter="Include"
        ItemName="_BuiltProjectOutputGroupOutputIntermediate"/>
 </CreateItem>

 <CreateItem Include="$(OutDir)$(BuildScriptName)"
   AdditionalMetadata="TargetPath=$(BuildScriptName)">
   <Output TaskParameter="Include"
   ItemName="_BuiltProjectOutputGroupOutputIntermediate"/>
 </CreateItem>

 <!-- Convert intermediate items into final items; this way we
   can get the full path for each item -->
 <CreateItem Include=
"@(_BuiltProjectOutputGroupOutputIntermediate->'%(FullPath)')">
   <Output TaskParameter="Include"
     ItemName="BuiltProjectOutputGroupOutput"/>
 </CreateItem>
</Target>

<!--
  ============================================================
  Overriding SourceFilesProjectOutputGroup
  ============================================================
  -->
 <Target
    Name="SourceFilesProjectOutputGroup"
    Outputs="@(SourceFilesProjectOutputGroupOutput)"
    DependsOnTargets="$(SourceFilesProjectOutputGroupDependsOn)">

 <AssignTargetPath Files="@(Build)"
   RootFolder="$(MSBuildProjectDirectory)">
   <Output TaskParameter="AssignedFiles"
   ItemName="_BuildWithTargetPath" />
 </AssignTargetPath>

 <AssignTargetPath Files="@(PreDeploy)"
   RootFolder="$(MSBuildProjectDirectory)">
   <Output TaskParameter="AssignedFiles"
   ItemName="_PreDeployWithTargetPath" />
 </AssignTargetPath>

 <AssignTargetPath Files="@(PostDeploy)"
   RootFolder="$(MSBuildProjectDirectory)">
   <Output TaskParameter="AssignedFiles"
   ItemName="_PostDeployWithTargetPath" />
 </AssignTargetPath>

 <AssignTargetPath Files="@(NotInBuild)"
   RootFolder="$(MSBuildProjectDirectory)">
   <Output TaskParameter="AssignedFiles"
```

```
            ItemName="_NotInBuildWithTargetPath" />
        </AssignTargetPath>

        <!-- First we deal with Compile, EmbeddedResource and AppConfig -->
        <CreateItem Include="@(_BuildWithTargetPath->
    '%(FullPath)');@(_PreDeployWithTargetPath->
    '%(FullPath)');@(_PostDeployWithTargetPath->
    '%(FullPath)');@(_NotInBuildWithTargetPath->
    '%(FullPath)');@(_EmbeddedResourceWithTargetPath->
    '%(FullPath)');@(AppConfigWithTargetPath->
    '%(FullPath)')">
            <Output TaskParameter="Include"
            ItemName="SourceFilesProjectOutputGroupOutput"/>
        </CreateItem>

        <!-- Include the project file -->
        <CreateItem Include="$(MSBuildProjectFullPath)"
          AdditionalMetadata="TargetPath=$(ProjectFileName)">
            <Output TaskParameter="Include"
            ItemName="SourceFilesProjectOutputGroupOutput"/>
        </CreateItem>
    </Target>
</Project>
```

Looking at listings 3.1 and 3.2, you can see how the target file for database projects has evolved from TFS 2005 to TFS 2008. As stated before, these listings are quite long, but we included them so that you have access to the full content of the targets files while reading the book. We feel that by looking at their inner workings, you'll be able to learn a lot about how the database build system really works.

3.2.1 Using MSBuild to build database projects

The MSBuild utility enables you to create builds and deploy changes from the command prompt. To build a database project and generate the output .sql script, type the following at the Visual Studio command line:

```
MSBuild <database_project_filename>
```

This command executes `SqlBuildTask` and generates the output .sql file, using the property values specified in the database project file (the .dbproj file) and the project user file (the .user file). The settings in the .user file override the ones in the .dbproj file. The predeployment and postdeployment scripts are also added to the output .sql file.

To deploy the modified schema to the local server, type the following at the command prompt:

```
MSBuild <database_project_filename> /t:Deploy
```

This command executes `SqlDeployTask` and applies the schema modifications to the target database. As discussed, you need to have an existing .sql file to deploy, since the `SqlDeployTask` task doesn't regenerate the file.

To deploy to a remote server, use the `TargetConnectionString` and `TargetDatabase` properties as follows:

```
MSBuild <database_project_filename> /t:Deploy
/p:TargetConnectionString = <target_DBConnection_string>
/p:TargetDatabase = <target_database_name>
```

The TargetConnectionString property makes sense in the context of the Deploy target only. You don't need to specify the TargetConnectionString property if you're deploying to a local database instance.

The ability to specify the target connection string and database name is also useful if you need to deploy the same script to multiple servers. Using the Visual Studio IDE, you can deploy to a single target server only. When using the MSBuild command to deploy to multiple servers, you don't need to create a different .sql file for each target database. Create a single .sql file and run the deployment target multiple times, specifying a new target database name each time.

If you wish to rename the .sql file (to better reflect its purpose, for example), use the BuildScriptName property with the MSBuild command (with or without the /t:Deploy switch).

> **TIP** When performing a build using MSBuild from the command line, you can use the database solution filename (the name of the .sln file) instead of the database project filename (the name of the .dbproj file). If you use the solution filename, all projects inside the solution will be built. But you can't use the database solution filename when using the /t:Deploy switch with MSBuild, since Deploy isn't a standard target for Visual Studio solutions. You must use the database project filename when using the /t:Deploy switch with MSBuild.

3.2.2   *Using Team Build to build database projects*

Team Build enables you to create public builds on a dedicated build machine. Team Build fetches the latest source files from TFVC and generates the SQL build script. The build machine needs to have a local instance of SQL Server installed so that DB Pro can create a local design database. The build machine also needs to have DB Pro installed.

As is the case when building C# or VB.NET projects, Team Build uses MSBuild to build database projects. But as discussed, for database projects, the output is a .sql script, not an executable file. By default, Team Build doesn't deploy the schema changes to the target database (although you can customize the Team Build script to do so).

CHOOSING A CONFIGURATION

When creating a build type for a database project, you need to be aware of configuration issues. When you create a database project, you get a configuration named Default (see figure 3.26). But when you create a new Team Build project, your configuration options are Debug and Release (see figure 3.27). As a result of this mismatch, when you try to build the Team Build project, it fails.

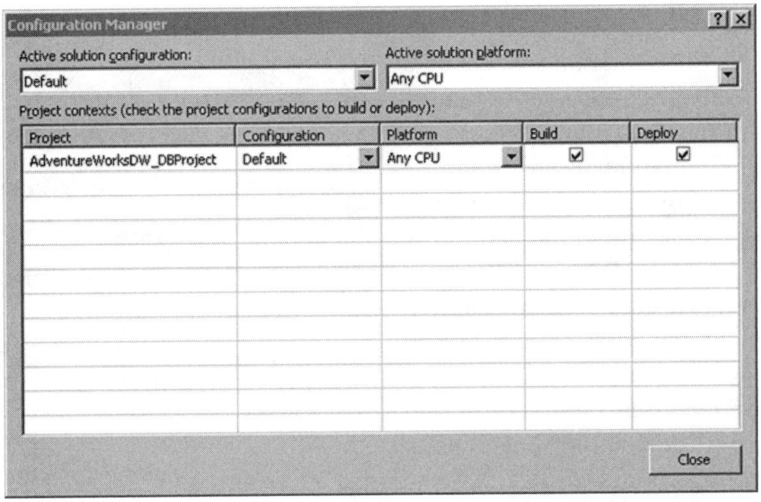

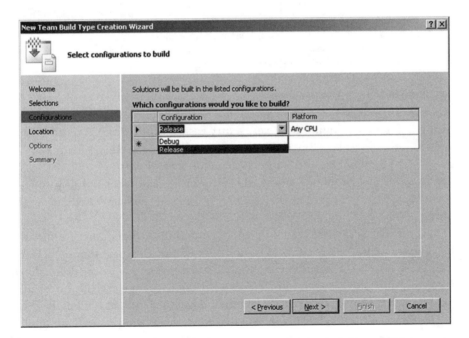

Figure 3.26 Use the Configuration Manager to create configurations containing different set of options.

Figure 3.27 Team Build allows you to specify two configurations—Debug and Release.

You can solve the configuration mismatch problem in two ways:

- *Option 1*—Using the Configuration Manager in Visual Studio, create a new Debug or Release configuration in the database project. Select Configuration Manager from the Solution Configurations drop-down in the Visual Studio toolbar. In the Configuration Manager dialog box, select New from the Active Solution Configuration drop-down to launch the New Solution Configuration dialog box (see figure 3.28). You can copy the options from an existing configuration.

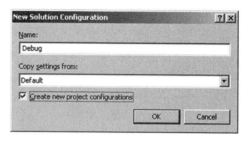

Figure 3.28 When creating a new configuration, you can inherit the settings from an existing configuration.

- *Option 2*—Modify the configuration section of the build script to use the Default configuration, as shown in listing 3.3. You can also simply type "Default" in the configuration dialog box in Team Build.

Listing 3.3 The build script modified to use the default configuration

```
<ConfigurationToBuild Include="Default|Any CPU">
  <FlavorToBuild>Default</FlavorToBuild>
  <PlatformToBuild>Any CPU</PlatformToBuild>
</ConfigurationToBuild>
```

SPECIFYING A TARGET DATABASE

When you specify a target database name in the Build tab of the project properties dialog box (refer to figure 3.9), your entry is stored in the database project user file (the .dbproj.user file). But the .dbproj.user file isn't used by Team Build. Consequently, the generated build script may contain invalid entries.

To solve this problem, modify the .dbproj file and specify valid values for the TargetDatabase, TargetConnectionString, and DefaultDataPath properties (see listing 3.4).

If you're using TFS 2005, move the property definition block after the line containing the Import statement for the Microsoft.VisualStudio.TeamSystem.Data.Tasks.targets file. As previously discussed, the TargetDatabase property is unconditionally overwritten in the Microsoft.VisualStudio.TeamSystem.Data.Tasks.targets file. Check in the database project file to TFVC and make sure that developers don't accidentally overwrite it.

If you're using TFS 2008, you don't need to move the property definition block. Moreover, you can specify the values for TargetDatabase, TargetConnectionString, and DefaultDataPath in the Queue Build dialog box or in the TFSBuild.rsp file in Team Build.

Listing 3.4 Specifying valid values in the database project file

```
<PropertyGroup Condition=" '$(Configuration)' == 'Default' ">
    <DefaultDataPath>
        <Valid_Path_in_Target_Machine>
    </DefaultDataPath>
    <TargetDatabase>
        <Your_Target_Database_Name>
    </TargetDatabase>
    <TargetConnectionString>Data
        Source=<Your_DBServer_Name>;Integrated
        Security=True;Pooling=False
    </TargetConnectionString>
</PropertyGroup>
```

DEPLOYING SCHEMA CHANGES

As discussed, by default, Team Build doesn't deploy the schema changes to one or more target databases. But you can easily achieve this goal by overriding the `AfterDropBuild` target and launching the `MSBuild` task with the `Deploy` target, as shown in listing 3.5. The account under which the Team Build service is running should have the necessary permissions to create and update the design database as well the target database.

Listing 3.5 Deploying the schema changes and overriding the target

```
<Target Name="AfterDropBuild">
    <MSBuild
        Projects="$(SolutionRoot)\SolutionName\
        DatabaseProjectName\DatabaseProjectName.dbproj"
        Properties="Configuration=Default;OutDir=
        $(SolutionRoot)\..\binaries\Default\"
        Targets="Deploy" />
</Target>
```

In this section, we've seen how to set up Team Build to build database projects. In the next section, we switch gears and look at another topic that frequently comes up when populating a test database as part of a build process—how to create custom data generators to produce meaningful data.

3.3 *Technical review: creating a custom data generator*

In this section, we create a custom data generator that outputs prime numbers, subject to a user-specified limit. You'll be able to use the same technique to create custom data generators that meet your own requirements.

Custom generators are created by extending the `Microsoft.VisualStudio.TeamSystem.Data.DataGenerator.Generator` class (see figure 3.29). The abstract `Generator` class is located in an assembly named Microsoft.VisualStudio.TeamSystem.Data.dll. The basic technique is simple; here are the steps:

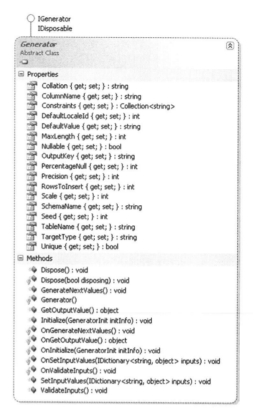

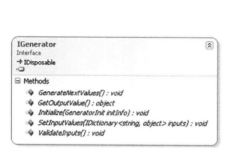

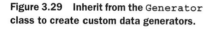

Figure 3.29   Inherit from the `Generator` class to create custom data generators.

- Create a Class Library Project. Add reference to the Microsoft.VisualStudio. TeamSystem.Data.dll assembly.

- Create a property to specify the prime number limit. Decorate the property with the `Input` attribute. This attribute marks the property as an input property; users can enter its value from the Properties pane in the Visual Studio IDE. You can have one or more input properties.

- Create a property to return the computed prime number to the Visual Studio IDE. Decorate the property with the `Output` attribute. This attribute marks the property as an output property. The value returned in this property is inserted in the target database and represents the result of all the work that's done in the custom generator. You can have one or more output properties.

- Override the `OnInitialize` method to perform necessary initializations. We use this method to insert the first prime number in the prime numbers array.

- The `OnGenerateNextValues` method is called each time a new value is needed—once for each row in the target table. Override this method, perform necessary computations, and store the results in one or more output properties. Visual Studio will pick up the results from the output properties.

- Sign the assembly and compile. Custom data generators are required to be strong-named assemblies.

- Register the assembly with Visual Studio by following steps described in http://msdn2.microsoft.com/en-us/library/aa833163(VS.80).aspx. The basic approach is to create a custom .Extensions.xml file in the %ProgramFiles%\Microsoft Visual Studio 9.0\DBPro folder and copy the custom assembly to the %ProgramFiles%\Microsoft Visual Studio 9.0\Common7\IDE\PrivateAssemblies folder.

The source code for the custom prime number generator is shown in listing 3.6.

Listing 3.6 Source code for custom prime number generator

```
using System;
using System.Collections.Generic;
using System.Text;

using Microsoft.VisualStudio.TeamSystem.Data.DataGenerator;
using System.Collections;

namespace CustomDataGenerator
{
    public class PrimeNumberGenerator : Generator
    {

        private int _result;
        private int _limit;
        private int _lastprime;
        private bool _isFirstAccess;
        private const int _FIRST_PRIME = 2;
        private ArrayList _primes = new ArrayList();

        [Input]
        public int Limit
        {
            get { return _limit; }
            set { _limit = value; }
        }

        [Output]
        public int Result
        {
            get { return _result; }
            set { _result = value; }
        }

        /// <summary>
        /// this method is called when the generator
        /// is initialized
        /// </summary>
        protected override void OnInitialize(
            GeneratorInit initInfo)
        {
            _primes.Add(_FIRST_PRIME);          Initialize
            _lastprime = _FIRST_PRIME;           variables
            _isFirstAccess = true;
```

```csharp
/// <summary>
/// this method is called every time a new
/// value is required
/// </summary>
protected override void OnGenerateNextValues()
{
    //generate a prime number every time this
    //method is called; If limit reached,
    //return last biggest prime number

    if (_isFirstAccess)
    {
        this.Result = _lastprime;
        _isFirstAccess = false;
    }
    else if (_lastprime == Limit)
    {
        this.Result = _lastprime;
    }
    else
    {//calculate the next prime number

        bool isPrimeFound = false;
        for (int i = _lastprime + 1; i <= Limit; i++)
        {
            bool isDivisible = false;

            foreach (int prime in _primes)
            {
                if (i % prime == 0)
                {
                    isDivisible = true;
                    break;
                }
            }                                      // Divide number
                                                   // by existing
            if (!isDivisible)                      // primes
            {
                // prime found!
                _primes.Add(i);
                _lastprime = i;
                this.Result = i;
                isPrimeFound = true;
                break;
            }
        }

        if (!isPrimeFound)                         // Return last prime
            this.Result = _lastprime;              // if no more found
    }
}
```

3.4 Summary

The modern software development process—no matter which methodology you follow—is largely about maximizing productivity through effective team collaboration. More and more, success and failure are measured at the team level, not at the individual level. In the twenty-first century, enterprise software development is no longer a solo act. Technology has become too broad and too deep for one person to know it all. The more you can integrate and synchronize the activities of a diverse group of specialists, the more successful you'll be. The essential purpose of TFS is just that. DB Pro extends the platform to include database support.

In this chapter, we saw how DB Pro enables database professionals to become part of the mainstream application development process. We learned that DB Pro offers an integrated toolset to manage the database lifecycle in a holistic way. By facilitating schema extraction, database refactoring, schema and data comparison, test data generation, unit testing, and safe deployment, DB Pro has changed the way databases will be managed in the days to come.

In the next part of the book, we switch gears and dive deep into solving real-life application development problems using TFS. The material is more in-depth than what we've covered so far. But you'll gain an actionable understanding regarding how to use and extend TFS to meet the needs of your own organization.

Part 2

Diving deep into version control and Team Build

In part 2 of the book, we dive down into selected areas to better understand the inner workings of TFS. The material is technically deeper than the discussions in part 1, which provided a broad context of how TFS works and prepared us for in-depth exploration.

In part 2 we investigate how to use Team Foundation version control and Team Build to solve selected real-life problems. In any software development effort, effective management of source code assets and creation of high-quality builds are essential for mitigating execution risks.

We take a practitioner's point of view and walk through some common issues that come up during a typical day in a development shop. Version control and Team Build are crucial features to master regardless of your development process. After all, without source code and output assemblies, you have no software!

Understanding
branching in
version control

This chapter covers

- Branching concepts
- How branches differ from labels and folders
- Using branches for sharing code
- Building from branches

Version control systems, officially called *software configuration management (SCM)* systems, help you manage the evolution of your codebase. Depending on the level of sophistication, version control systems store source code in shared repositories using efficient algorithms (forward, reverse, or interleaved deltas), provide secure access to distributed team members, enable multiple developers to work together efficiently, associate code changes with work items, maintain audit trails, facilitate parallel development, and recover previous file versions. They also provide atomic check-in for consistency, support private workspaces, revert local workspaces to previous points in time, maintain coding standards, and work with various IDEs. SCM systems support build creation, offline activities, disaster recovery, and high availability. They also provide notification of key events such as check-ins. Additionally, SCM systems perform scores of other functions to safeguard your software assets in a consistent, accessible, and reliable manner. Without a good version control system, you'll find it virtually impossible to hold your team together and manage the evolution of your software.

As you work with version control systems, one of the most important decisions you'll need to make is how to set up the branch structure. *Branching* allows you to perform parallel development in isolation as well as define different policies for your codebase. *Merging* is the process of transferring the accumulated changes from one branch to another. As you work with multiple feature teams, multiple geographies, multiple versions of the software under simultaneous development, and multiple software releases, service packs, and emergency patches, you'll discover that without an effective branching and merging strategy, you can't maintain order and consistency. Failing to choose a judicious branching configuration and maintain it vigilantly will cause various problems. These include increased incidences of overwriting each other's changes, regressed bugs, duplication of efforts, incorrect builds with wrong files, inordinate amounts of time spent resolving collisions, the wrong version being shipped to the clients, and so on.

Team Foundation version control (TFVC) provides a low-overhead branching model that can help streamline your development process. TFVC lets you branch easily and intuitively. When it comes to merging back the changes, TFVC takes into account the branch and merge histories of the associated files, making the process quite intelligent. For advanced operations, you can go beyond the user interface and use the command-line utility, the Team Foundation Server Power Tools (TFS Power Tools), or the programming APIs to meet your needs. In this chapter, we explore various functionalities of TFVC related to creating and sustaining an effective branching structure.

This chapter focuses on how to effectively use the branching and merging features of TFVC. We talk about how to resolve specific branching and merging-related issues. This chapter isn't a general introduction to TFVC.

We start with a product-agnostic discussion regarding various branching concepts and the implications of adopting each approach. We then explore how branches differ from labels and folders in TFVC, and how you should organize each element for flexibility and maintainability. Finally, we discuss how to limit the scope of Team Build to files, changesets, and work items associated with a specific branch.

In this chapter, you'll learn about the following:

- *Branching strategies*—The various branching models, and how to select a branching pattern depending on team size, code policy, and release planning considerations.
- *Differences between branches and labels*—When you should create a new branch and when you can simply create a label.
- *Differences between branches and folders*—The relationship between branches and folders and how to organize them for scalability and maintainability.

- *How to share code between team projects*—If you have common code located in a separate team project, learn how to consume the code from other team projects.

- *How to build from a branch*—By default, when you run a Team Build script, the full source code from the entire team project is downloaded in the build machine, and the entire codebase (contained in the team project) is labeled. This causes Team Build to relate the build with work items associated with check-ins in all branches. We discuss how to avoid this problem using branch-specific builds.

- *How to use the Team Foundation Sidekicks*—TFS Sidekicks are third-party tools that enable you to visually manage branches, learn about merge candidates, and so on. Learn how to use these tools to improve your productivity.

4.1 Benefits of using a version control system

If you've been writing software for a while, you've probably faced the need to store files in a shared repository as well as keep multiple versions of files. If you only use a shared folder for file storage, you'll face the following issues over time:

- If your fellow developers maintain private folder structures, how would you know that a particular file has been changed and needs to be integrated? If team members don't know about concurrent changes to the same file, then whoever copies the file last to the shared folder overwrites everyone else's changes. Even if people somehow find out about concurrent changes, how would you manage the merge operations? How do you decide who merges first, who merges next, and so on? You'll probably need to get the parties together and work out a conflict resolution strategy. As the number of people or the number of files increases, you'll run into major problems if you follow an ad hoc strategy for managing code.

- There's no audit trail. When suspicious changes are found in the shared location, you don't know who made the changes, when they were made, or why. Fixes that were made earlier mysteriously disappear and new problems get introduced—and the worst part is, you don't know who's responsible. This problem alone is enough to create grave misunderstandings between team members and cause chaos at critical times.

- It can be extremely difficult to reverse incorrect changes or restore the system to a previous state. If you've been keeping frequent backups of the shared folder then you might be able to revert to a previous state. But unless you're backing up the shared folder before every change (a potentially cumbersome process), you're at risk of losing the file that was just overwritten. In real life, you may run into desperate situations, usually at the worst possible times, when you can't undo incorrect changes in critical files.

A modern version control system watches over your software assets and improves team productivity. Let's look at selected issues that'll help you to better manage your source code.

4.2   Company types and branching issues

Regardless of your company's size, you'll probably benefit from using branching and merging. Otherwise, you may run into difficulties with concurrent change conflicts. In modern development organizations, where you have multiple versions under simultaneous development by globally distributed teams working in different time zones, as well as development, quality assurance, and release teams working in unison but under different environments and change control policies, it's difficult to manage the development process without using effective branching and merging strategies.

4.2.1   Small companies

If you work for a small company, consider adopting branching patterns that don't require too much maintenance, but still facilitate parallel development and long-term product support. Since you may not have dedicated people to manage the version control system, you don't want to create too many branches unnecessarily and end up spending a lot of time merging changes back and forth. Look at the code promotion model, the codeline-per-release model, and the branch-by-release model (discussed later in section 4.3), and decide whether one of these patterns meet your requirements.

4.2.2   Large companies

Branching patterns that are relevant for small companies also apply to large companies. Many of the challenges associated with software development issues are universal—supporting parallel development, preparing code for a release, testing release candidates exhaustively, releasing binaries to customers, and servicing the release. The code promotion model, the codeline-per-release model, and the branch-by-release model represent different strategies for dealing with software configuration management.

However, in large companies that implement large projects, there are additional considerations that stem from the sheer number of components that are developed in parallel. Conceptually, each component in a large project can be thought of as a small project by itself, each with its own lifecycle. Subdividing the management of a large project in this manner enables you to reduce complexity and facilitate independent evolution. Of course, at regular intervals, you need to create integrated builds to validate cross-component dependencies and assumptions. You also need to establish quality gates before merging code from lower levels to more stable branches. Experience from the field suggests that this approach is an effective strategy for managing large teams—divide the problem and conquer it in pieces.

4.2.3   Large companies with distributed TFS

For a company that has multiple TFS servers in geographically distributed locations, the obvious challenge is coordinating the work. TFS doesn't have built-in synchronization and replication capability. Therefore, the multiple TFS servers in your enterprise operate in an autonomous fashion. Consequently, you need to figure out a strategy to propagate as well as integrate changes and resolve conflicts. No matter what approach you select, some of the key considerations are as follow:

- In a distributed scenario, the remote team may have its own TFS server to work with. The remote TFS server is used to support the activities of the remote team—associating check-ins with work items, storing shelvesets, enforcing check-in policies, performing unit tests, creating builds, and so on. Without a remote TFS server, these software engineering activities would be supported by the main TFS server—a proposition that could be impractical due to bandwidth, security, and organizational reasons. When the remote development reaches a stable point, the code is uploaded to the main TFS server.

- The remote team needs to download the latest sources from the main TFS server as well as upload their changes to it. TFS 2005 Service Pack 1 introduces support for basic and digest authentication, enabling remote clients to connect over Internet without requiring a VPN connection (for more information, visit http://msdn.microsoft.com/en-us/library/aa833874.aspx). The remote team can speed up the file downloads from the main TFS Server by installing TFS Proxy at their location. TFS Proxy caches files locally after first time access. However, the proxy server needs a VPN connection to the main TFS server (even if you're using TFS 2005 Service Pack 1). To configure the proxy server, on the Tools menu, click Options; in the Options dialog box, expand the Source Control node and click Visual Studio Team Foundation Server (see figure 4.1). For more information on setting up the proxy server, visit http://msdn2. microsoft.com/en-us/library/ms252490(VS.80).aspx.

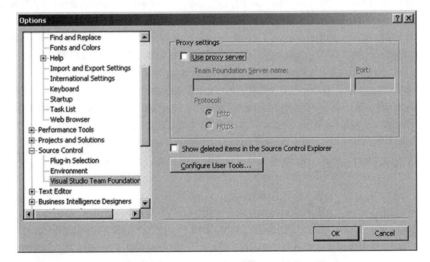

Figure 4.1   You can use the proxy server to cache files downloaded from TFVC.

- You need to figure out a way to download not only the source files but also the work items from the main TFS server to the remote server. Otherwise, the remote team will have difficulty managing their team activities and associating changesets with work items. But since you're using two different TFS servers, the work item numbers (which are system generated) may not match when you transfer the work items between servers. The solution is to have a reference number field—which stores, for example, the work item number generated by the primary TFS server—for correlating the work items between the two systems.

- The remote team can check in their changes to the main TFVC server using Team Explorer or an automated process. They don't need to necessarily check in every new changeset that was added to their local TFVC (it depends on the team workflow model). Once the remote team has a stable and tested codebase, they can check in the files only from the tip of the remote branch. In this case, when checking in code to the main TFS server, they need to associate all the work items that are resolved by the cumulative check-in. You may be better off creating an automated process for the cumulative check-in. Otherwise, the remote team will have to manually determine which work items have been resolved on the remote TFS server since the last cumulative check-in to the main TFS server. Recall that the remote team doesn't check in every single changeset that exists in the remote TFS server—they perform a cumulative check-in from the tip of the branch, after the code passes certain quality criteria.

4.3   Branching models

There are many branching patterns that you can adopt to support the lifecycle of your applications (see the references section at the end of the chapter for further reading on this subject). When selecting a branching model, consider your team's size and geographic locations; the product's development, release and maintenance plans; and other relevant factors.

I want to point out two general issues as you think about setting up a branching structure in TFVC. Although you can branch at any level in TFVC—from a team project down to a file—it's usually a best practice to branch at a solution level. A solution file references the project files using relative server paths. That's why it's easiest to manage the source files if you branch at the level of the solution (or higher, of course). Going beyond a single solution, try to branch everything needed for a build—as you branch, try to include the related solutions that go into a build.

Another issue to keep in mind is that you can't branch to a target folder that's a child of the source folder. For example, don't check in files directly under the root of the team project—you can't branch the root folder because all folders under the root are, by definition, children of the root (although you can branch individual files located in the root folder). Furthermore, keep in mind that when using the Source Control UI, you can only merge between branches that have a parent-child relationship.

Let's now review some commonly used branching models.

4.3.1   The code promotion model

The *code promotion model* is a simple branching strategy widely used in development organizations. The idea is to "promote" a file from one level to another as it becomes more stable. In some version control systems, the promotion model is implemented in a single codeline, with a file attribute indicating whether the file belongs to the development, testing, or production level. We feel that this approach can become cumbersome under various circumstances (depending on the version control tool being used), such as when a file is promoted and then demoted, when a new revision of the file has been promoted but you need to re-create a previous configuration, and so on. In TFVC, we can implement the code promotion pattern using branches (see figure 4.2). TFVC doesn't have a file attribute indicating the file's promotion level.

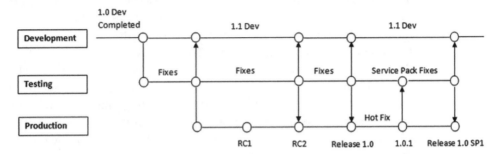

Figure 4.2 The code promotion branching model

The code promotion branching model works as follows:

- Developers make their routine changes in the development branch. Bug fixes and feature implementations take place in this branch. The development branch serves as the main codeline (see the Mainline pattern in Berczuk and Appleton's *Software Configuration Management Patterns*) and always contains the latest version of the code. Builds are made from the tip of this branch at regular intervals—or as soon as a changeset is checked in, depending upon your development methodology (the continuous integration pattern advocates creating a build immediately after a changeset is checked in). Build verification tests are executed to test the stability of the code. Although there are usually some minimum quality criteria for the code to be checked in to the development branch (the code should at least build and pass a minimum set of build verification tests), there's usually no guarantee that the latest code is stable from a usage perspective. (Depending on your needs, you can create a separate branch to host the stable codebase; that way, the team members will always have a branch from where they can get the latest stable code.) You should label well-tested stable points in the development codeline so that team members can resynchronize their workspaces to known-good points if the tip of the codeline becomes unstable.

- Once the code in the development branch is ready for a release, a label is applied to the set of files in the development branch; for example, the label could read "Version 1.0 Ready for Testing." A testing branch is created based on the label. The code under test is subjected to a full suite of regression tests in anticipation of the release. The releases for which branching takes place could be internal or external. The releases can be based on milestones in the project plan or represent stable points that aggregate a set of features or fixes. The idea is that the codebase under test is now isolated from the main development line and the development branch can continue to evolve as usual, without having to be "frozen" for the particular release. As bugs are discovered and fixed in the testing branch (recall that the development branch is being used for the next version), they are *reverse integrated* back to the main development branch as appropriate. If critical bug fixes or important feature implementations take place in the main branch while testing is underway, selected changes can be *forward integrated* from the development branch to the testing branch. In the interest of stability, only a limited group of people are allowed to make changes in the testing branch. Once the SQA group certifies the code to be fit for release, the code in the testing branch is labeled—for example, "Version 1.0 Ready for Production"—and the code is branched into a production branch. As the release candidates are deployed and tested in various environments, the bugs discovered from this process are fixed in the testing branch. Furthermore, bugs discovered after the final release are also fixed in this branch, and appropriate service packs are produced for distribution. After validation by the SQA team, the bug fixes are merged with the development and production branches.

- The production branch contains the code that's deemed fit to be a release candidate. The production code is isolated in its own branch because this gives greater flexibility for providing hot fixes. After a release, emergency bug fixes can take place in the production branch, but changes made in the production branch need to be reverse integrated in the testing branch as well as the main branch. If you're patching an old release, you may sometimes find that the development branch has evolved to a point where reverse integrating changes from the production branch doesn't make any sense and could introduce errors (the code structure may have changed significantly in the meantime). In such cases, you need to manually edit the appropriate files in the development branch and apply only the relevant fixes.

4.3.2   The codeline-per-release model

As you think about the code promotion model, you might wonder about the need to create a separate production branch from the testing branch. Why not just create a single branch for the release-preparation work, as in figure 4.3? In this new strategy, a single release branch is created where testing, bug fixes, and releases take place. If you need to provide emergency hot fixes, you can create a new branch from the release branch.

The difference between the code promotion model (as shown in figure 4.2) and the codeline-per-release model (as shown in figure 4.3) is that in the codeline-per-release

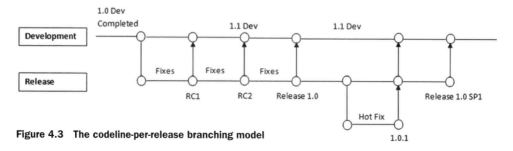

Figure 4.3   The codeline-per-release branching model

model, you essentially work with two branches and create the third branch (the hot fix branch) only on demand. If a hot fix isn't needed, the third branch isn't created. In the code promotion model, you always have three branches.

Moreover, in the codeline-per-release model, you can reverse and forward integrate directly between the release branch and the main branch—TFVC allows you to directly merge files only between a parent branch and its children. In the code promotion model, you can't reverse or forward integrate changes between the production branch and the main branch directly—you have to go through the testing branch. Although this is usually a good thing—you typically want to update the testing branch—there are cases where testing (especially for emergency fixes) is done using the binaries created from the release branch, and merging with the testing branch is redundant. For example, if the SQA group has no plans to test the code again from the testing branch because they've already tested the fix from the hot fix release branch, it's better to merge the code directly from the production branch to the main branch.

In the code promotion model, you can perform a *baseless merge* (discussed later in section 6.7) between the main branch and the production branch. But this operation tends to be complicated and isn't supported from the user interface in TFVC. In the codeline-per-release model, you can merge directly between the release branch and the main branch, because they have a parent-child relationship. Of course, once you create a hot fix branch (see figure 4.3) you need to reverse integrate with the principal release branch and then merge the principal release branch with the main branch. You can't directly merge between the hot fix branch and the main branch, since they don't have a parent-child relationship. You could of course do a baseless merge from the command prompt.

Despite the difficulties associated with merging files between noncontiguous branches, one of the advantages of maintaining separate testing and production branches is ease of administration. Since SQA and release management functions are performed by separate teams in many organizations, separate branches provide more fine-grained access control capability. Evaluate your organizational and project needs and come up with a branching strategy that's effective in your scenario.

A potential issue with both the code promotion model and the codeline-per-release model is propagating changes from old releases to new releases. Imagine finding and fixing a bug in an old release. Since the release branches don't have parent-child relationships with one another, you need to first reverse integrate the changes from the old release to the mainline. Once the fixes are in the mainline, you need to forward integrate them to each of the release branches.

There are numerous problems with this approach. First of all, when you try to reverse integrate the changes from the old release branch to the mainline, you may find that the code in the mainline has evolved to a point where a successful merge from an old release is counterproductive or even impossible. When merging, you can only merge with the latest files in the mainline—it's not possible to merge with files which aren't at the tip of a branch. Additionally, once the fixes are somehow applied to the mainline, you'll need to forward integrate the changes from the mainline to each release branch (assuming the fixes are relevant in the subsequent releases that have already taken place). Since the mainline contains many current changes, you'll need to carefully "cherry pick" the changesets and select only the ones containing the appropriate fixes. Given the potential friction associated with the whole approach, you may end up manually applying the changes in each release branch, instead of trying to propagate a fix from an earlier release.

4.3.3   The branch-by-release model

Another approach traditionally used in version control systems is the branch-by-release model (also called the *staircase model*). In this model, as soon as development for a particular release is completed, a new branch is created (see figure 4.4). All development activities unrelated to the current release are performed in the new branch. The old branch goes through code chill, code freeze, testing, and release phases.

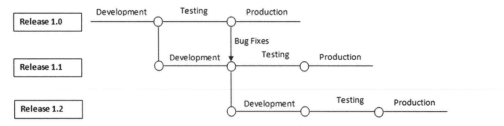

Figure 4.4   The branch-by-release branching model

Although the branch-by-release model is widely used and seems like a natural way to maintain multiple versions, you need to be aware of the following limitations associated with this approach:

- Before a new branch is created, if a developer wants to work on longer-term tasks that won't be included in the current release, she's likely to run into source code management problems. A fundamental feature of various version control systems (including TFVC) is that you need to check in code in the same branch from which you originally checked it out. You can't check out files from one branch and check them in to another branch without going through a lot of circuitous steps, such as manually copying and pasting files between folders in the local workspace. Even if you shelve your code in TFVC, when you unshelve the code and try to check it in, the code will be checked in to the branch from which the shelveset was created. Again, you could use workarounds to accomplish this, but this introduces unnecessary hassles. You could wait for the code freeze period to be over (and the code released) before checking in your changes, but by that time, the branch becomes a maintenance branch for the released code and your longer-term changes should probably go in the new branch, not the old one. As discussed, you can't propagate your changes to the new branch in a straightforward way. As a side note, in TFVC, to find out whether users have pending changes that they haven't uploaded to the server, type the following at the command prompt:

```
tf status /user:*
```

- Every time a new branch is created, developers need to adjust their workspaces to point to the new branch. Although this isn't a major problem, developers don't find it exciting to have to change their workspace mappings every time a new version is released.

4.3.4 *A branching model for large projects*

For large projects, figure 4.5 shows a representative branching solution. The core ideas are as follow:

- The main branch is reserved for tested, stable code. Nobody checks in code directly to this branch. Designated team members reverse integrate approved code changes from the integration branch to the main branch (once the changes pass appropriate quality criteria). After the main branch is updated, the changes are forward integrated to the feature branches.

- Release branches are created from the main branch when the code is mature. The management of the release branch is similar to the codeline-per-release model, discussed previously. By creating separate release branches (such as alpha, beta, or release candidate branches), you avoid the need to freeze the main branch for a release. After a release branch is created, the main branch moves forward and accumulates the changes for the next version.

- As its name implies, the integration branch serves as the central receiving line where stable features are brought together and the application is tested holistically. The code in this branch is tested exhaustively at various levels (such as component, system, and business levels) to determine conformance with the requirements, both functional and nonfunctional. Once the codebase is deemed to be stable and accurate, the changes are promoted to the main branch.

- Each feature team works on a separate branch, created from the integration branch. In large projects, you'll want to create two feature branches—one for active development and another for hosting stable code. If you're working on large complicated components, you might want to have a third branch devoted to testing; only tested code is promoted to the stable feature branch (similar to the code promotion model discussed earlier). In the development branch, feature team members check in code at a rapid pace. The development branch contains the "bleeding-edge" code. At designated points, the code from the feature development branch is tested and merged with the code in the stable feature branch. After extensive regression testing, the stable code is promoted to the integration branch.

- If a subgroup within a feature team wants to undertake a significantly different development effort—such as for R&D purposes—the team can create additional "bridge" or "private" branches under the feature development branch. The code in the R&D branch can be merged with the feature development branch if the outcome is successful, or discarded otherwise.

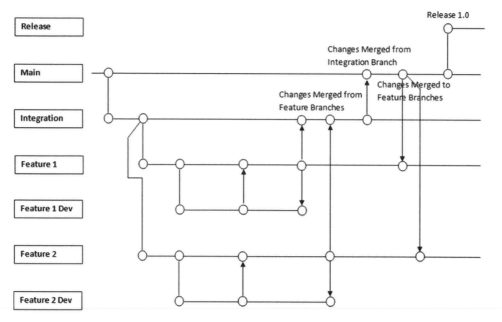

Figure 4.5   Development branch structure for a large project

Note that in the proposed branching model, the main, integration, release, and feature branches (at least the stable feature branches) contain *all* code for the application. This is because as a best practice, as discussed earlier, it's recommended that you keep all code that goes into a particular build in the same branch. In addition to the source files, you should store the build script and other build-related artifacts. This approach simplifies source code management and provides explicit traceability—allowing you to reproduce builds easily. In large projects, you'll find this simple approach especially useful when chasing down elusive bugs reported from customer sites or when patching releases.

Furthermore, having the full application source code in each feature branch allows the feature team members to debug problems across components. Frequently, when your component interacts with other external components, you'll need to debug mysterious problems by delving into the source code of the external components in order to understand the failure. Having access to the full source code provides significant value to the process of troubleshooting.

In TFVC, the folder structure is independent of the branching structure. You can select any folder structure you want to organize the codebase. Figure 4.6 shows a representative folder structure.

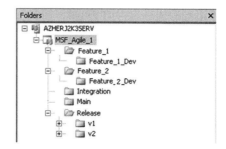

Figure 4.6   Create a folder hierarchy to organize the codebase; the folder hierarchy is independent of the branch hierarchy.

4.3.5 A remote branch model for distributed teams

You can set up a separate branch in the main repository to receive the changes made by remote teams. The remote branch can be derived from either the mainline or the local branch, depending on your workflow model (see figures 4.7 and 4.8). Keep in mind that in TFVC, normal merges can be done between a parent and its children only. You can of course do baseless merges between other kinds of branches, but they're more difficult.

The goal of having a separate remote branch is that the on-site team can work with stable versions of the remote deliveries. Coordination between distributed teams in different time zones is inherently difficult, no matter how efficient an organization or a vendor happens to be. Given the realities of the software development process, you'll inevitably have change conflicts. Discussions will need to take place between the local and remote teams to determine who's right and who's wrong. Consequently, it makes sense to keep the stable remote changes in a separate branch and "pull" the changes to the local branches when you're ready to undertake the integration process.

Broadly speaking, you can merge local as well as remote changes to the main integration branch (as shown in figure 4.7), or you can merge changes directly to the local

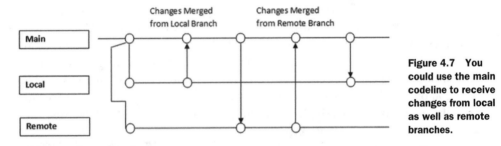

Figure 4.7 You could use the main codeline to receive changes from local as well as remote branches.

active development line (as shown in figure 4.8). You can create many variations of the basic idea, as appropriate. For example, you could use a separate integration branch (instead of the main codeline) to provide greater isolation and ensure stability of the mainline. If you're working on a large project, you could create a separate remote development branch associated with each component. The goal is to minimize unexpected friction and handle conflicts when you're ready. Set up a schedule, such as weekly, so that the conflict detection and resolution process don't suffer undue delay.

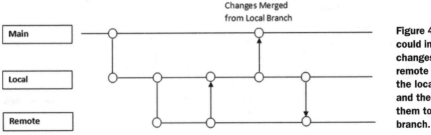

Figure 4.8 You could integrate changes from the remote branch to the local branch, and then promote them to the main branch.

Now that we have a conceptual understanding of the pros and cons associated with various branching models, let's think about when we need to actually create branches and when can use some of the other features offered by source control systems.

4.4 *Branches versus labels*

When working with TFVC, you'll sometimes wonder whether to create a label or a branch. The simple philosophy that I recommend is to think about isolation and policy requirements. If you expect to work on a codebase in parallel with the current codeline (such as patching a release), you should create a separate branch. Also, if you need to apply a different policy (for example, for access control) to your codebase, you should create a new branch as well.

TFVC supports *path space* branching. To the user, this kind of branching appears similar to copying a folder in Windows Explorer. But internally, a file isn't copied until it's changed in the new or the old branch. This approach saves space. Consequently, don't hesitate to create branches if you feel you need isolation or policy variation—the overhead isn't significant from a technical point of view. But from a process point of view, keep in mind that the code you branch may need to be merged back with the main codeline sooner or later (unless that branch will wither and die, such as when making a unique change for a single client). The later you merge, the greater the pain. Therefore, it doesn't make sense to unnecessarily fork the main codeline and deal with the subsequent difficulties of merging divergent codebases unless there's good reason.

A lot of times, you'll be able to meet your needs by creating a simple label instead of branching the codeline. Labels in TFVC are powerful. A label represents a collection of files. Labels in TFVC can span team projects—you can include files from multiple team projects in a single label. But labels aren't versioned. TFVC doesn't maintain a history of changes that take place in a label; it only knows about the current contents of a label.

Contrary to popular conception, a label in TFVC doesn't represent a "point in time" subset of the repository. A label can include files from different points in time. When adding a file to a label, you can specify the version of the file you want (see figure 4.9). You may choose to add the latest version or a previous version—use the Version dropdown shown in figure 4.9 to find the correct file version.

Before creating labels to group files that aren't from the same point in time—such as, "three files from

Figure 4.9   You can select the file version when creating a label.

changeset 101, two files from changeset 105, and five files from changeset 109"—think long and hard about whether you really need to do this, since this approach increases logical complexity. Sometimes the reasons may be valid. For example, you may have created a label to mark the source files for release, and now need to change a few files to fix some last-minute bugs. Instead of creating a new label, you might want to update the previous one, since only a few files may have changed (and you don't want the tip of the codeline to go into the release). Another way you could end up with files from different periods in a label is if the label was created based upon your workspace, and the workspace contained files from different points in time.

Once a label is created, you can specify who can change it. Right-click a folder in Source Control Explorer, click Properties from the context menu, click the Security tab, and specify permissions for Administer Labels entries. See figure 4.10; the Label entry allows you to specify who can create labels.

When branching, you can choose to branch from a label (see figure 4.11). Recall that a label may contain files from different points in time. After branching, to determine where a file came from, right-click the file, click Properties from the context menu, and click the Branches tab. You'll be able to view which version of the source file happens to be the parent of the selected file (see figure 4.12).

You might want to branch from a label for a variety of reasons. One reason might be clarity. If you create a label containing files with appropriate version numbers, explicitly

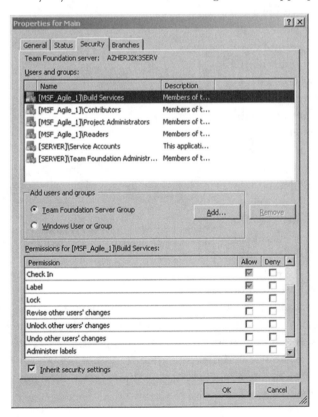

Figure 4.10 You can specify the access permissions for labels in the Security tab.

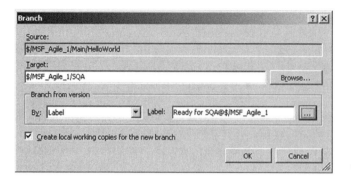

Figure 4.11   TFVC allows you to create a branch from a label.

name the label for the intended purpose, and then branch from the label, you'll have a logical reference to the files that are branched. You can also use the Comment field in the label to indicate the purpose of branching. Although you can't tell by looking at the files in the target branch whether they were branched from a label, you'll still have a logical reference persisted in the source branch encapsulating the files that were branched (assuming you haven't updated the contents of the label after the branch was created).

Another reason for branching from a label might be the need to do maintenance work on the labeled files. After you modify one or more of the labeled files, where will you check them in? You could check the modified files in to the tip of the codeline. But depending on the changes that have occurred in the codeline since the label was created, this action could be massively disruptive. A better option is to create a branch from the label to host the modified files.

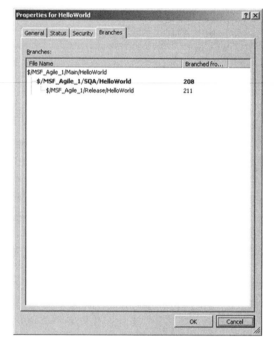

Figure 4.12   The Branches tab displays the branching hierarchy.

A third reason for branching from a label might be the need to create a partial branch. In TFVC, you can't select multiple files in a folder and branch them. TFVC allows you to branch specific files or folders (and their children) only. If you want to create a branch containing the selected files in a folder (and not branch the files that remain unselected), you can create a label containing the selected files and then create a branch from the label.

4.4.1 *Identifying changes after creating a label*

After you apply a label to an active branch, you may later want to find out what changes have taken place in the branch since the label was applied. It takes a bit of effort to answer the question.

The first approach to try would be to use the tf history command. Type the following at the command prompt; this command shows you what happened between the time when the label was created and now:

```
tf history <branch_path> /recursive
/format:detailed /version:L<your_label_name>~T /noprompt
```

When you execute this command, you may be surprised to see that changesets belonging to various items within the label appear in the output. Your goal was to see only those changesets that were added *after* the label was created. This behavior takes place because version ranges in TFVC (specified with the /version: option) are inclusive—the output includes the contents of the starting range as well as the ending range. To identify the changesets that were added to the branch after the label was created, you need to identify the highest changeset number in the label. When analyzing the output of tf history, only consider the changesets that have a higher number than the highest changeset number found in the label. You can identify the changesets included in a label by typing the following at the command prompt:

```
tf labels <your_label_name> /owner:* /format:detailed
```

You could create a script to parse the output of the tf labels command, determine the highest changeset number, and then parse the output of tf history and filter the changesets that are higher in number. Alternatively, you could create a simple program using the TFVC API to determine the changes which have taken place after a label is created (see listing 4.1).

TIP If you're interested in seeing the changes that took place between two labels, type the following at the command prompt:

```
tf history <branch_path> /recursive /format:detailed
/version:L<label_name_1>~L<label_name_2> /noprompt
```

Listing 4.1 Identifying changes in a branch after applying a label

```
/// using statements omitted for brevity ..

namespace LabelTests
{
  class Program
  {
    static void Main(string[] args)
    {
      string labelName;
      string labelScope;
      string branchPath;

      pGetParams(args, out labelName,
        out labelScope, out branchPath, out _vcServer);
```

```
        int highestChangesetInLabel = 0;
        try
        {
          VersionControlLabel[] labels =
            _vcServer.QueryLabels(labelName,
            labelScope, null, true);

          foreach (VersionControlLabel label in labels)
          {
            foreach (Item item in label.Items)
            {
              if (item.ChangesetId >
                highestChangesetInLabel)
                highestChangesetInLabel =
                  item.ChangesetId;
            }
          }

          IEnumerable changesets =
            _vcServer.QueryHistory(branchPath,
            VersionSpec.Latest, 0, RecursionType.Full,
            null, new LabelVersionSpec(labelName),
            VersionSpec.ParseSingleSpec(
            "T", null), int.MaxValue, true, false);

          foreach (Changeset changeset in changesets)
          {
            if (changeset.ChangesetId >
              highestChangesetInLabel)
              Console.WriteLine(
                changeset.ChangesetId);
          }

          Console.WriteLine("Completed");
        }
        catch (Exception ex)
        {
          Console.Error.WriteLine("Error: " + ex.Message);
          Environment.Exit(1);
        }

      }

      /// <summary>
      /// Retrieves and validates the Command-line arguments.
      /// </summary>
      /// <param name="args"></param>
      /// <param name="labelName"></param>
      /// <param name="scope"></param>
      /// <param name="branchPath"></param>
      /// <param name="vcServer"></param>
      private static void pGetParams(string[] args,
        out string labelName, out string scope,
        out string branchPath,
        out VersionControlServer vcServer)
      {
        // If no arguments provided or the number of
        // arguments is less than four then
```

Determine highest changeset number

Select only changesets with higher numbers

```
        // one or more required arguments are missing.
        // If so, display error and exit the program.
        if (args.Length < 4)
        {
            Console.Error.WriteLine(
                @"Error: Please input server name,
                label name, label scope and branch name");
            Console.Error.WriteLine(
                @"Pattern: LabelTests <server_name>
                <label_name> <label_scope> <branch_name>");
            Console.Error.WriteLine(
                @"Example: LabelTests TFSServer
                LabelName LabelScope BranchPath ");
            Environment.Exit(1);
        }

        TeamFoundationServer tfServer = null;
        try
        {
            tfServer = new TeamFoundationServer(args[0],
                new UICredentialsProvider());
            tfServer.EnsureAuthenticated();
        }
        catch (Exception ex)
        {
            // If exception is thrown then the
            //user may not be authenticated or the TFS
            //server may not exist. Exit the application.
            Console.Error.WriteLine(ex.Message);
            Environment.Exit(1);
        }
        vcServer = (VersionControlServer)
            tfServer.GetService(typeof(VersionControlServer));

        scope = args[2];
        if (!vcServer.ServerItemExists(scope, ItemType.Any))
        {
            Console.Error.WriteLine(
            "Error: Server path for label scope not valid");
            Environment.Exit(1);
        }

        branchPath = args[3];

        if (!vcServer.ServerItemExists(
            branchPath, ItemType.Any))
        {
            Console.Error.WriteLine(
                "Error: Server path for branch is not valid");
            Environment.Exit(1);
        }

        labelName = args[1];
    }
  }
}
```

Obtain reference to TFS and authenticate

Get reference to version control server

Validate server path for label scope

Validate server path for branch

Note that the change detection technique described for labels will only work accurately if the labels are "snapshots" in time. This is because the technique depends on finding the highest changeset number in a label and determining the subsequent changesets whose numbers are greater. If a label contains files from different points in time (see the earlier discussion regarding labels in TFVC), this technique doesn't work, and computing changes becomes more complicated. But it's still possible to determine what changes have taken place. The `GenCheckinNotesUpdateWorkItems` task invoked by Team Build implements the fully accurate logic required to determine changes between labels, regardless of the temporal location of the files in a label.

4.5   *Branches versus folders*

Branches and folders are independent entities in TFVC. Failure to grasp this idea causes a lot of confusion. In TFVC, you can create a new folder by right-clicking on the right pane and selecting New Folder from the context menu (see figure 4.13).

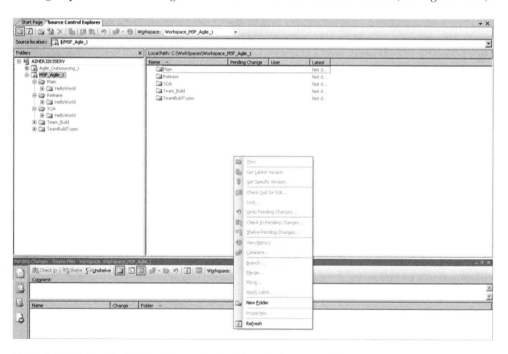

Figure 4.13   Folders in TFVC enable you to visually organize your codebase.

To create a branch, right-click a folder and select Branch from the context menu (see figure 4.14), or select a folder, click the File menu, point to Source Control, and click Branch.

Folders are typically created to visually organize the code for the sake of clarity and maintainability. Create a branch when you need to define different administrative policies on the codeline, or when you're developing in parallel and want to merge changes later. It isn't possible to tell by looking at the folder structure whether the files in various folders are related or not (by *related*, we mean having a common ancestor branch). For example, look at figure 4.15. The HelloWorld folders located under Main, SQA, and Release all appear as peers. But if you look at the branching hierarchy, you'll see that SQA is a child of Main, and Release is a child of SQA (see figure 4.16). To avoid confusion, try to keep the folder names and branch names similar, but bear in mind that the folder and branching hierarchies are independent.

In the next section, we apply our knowledge of branching to solve the problem of sharing code between team projects. This exercise will hopefully give you some insights regarding how to solve code management problems in your own organization.

Figure 4.14   Create a branch for isolation or policy variation.

Figure 4.15   The folder structure doesn't provide any information about branch relationships.

Figure 4.16   The branching hierarchy may be different from the folder hierarchy.

4.6   *Sharing code between team projects*

In large projects, you may face situations where common framework code resides in a separate team project. The reasons for this could be administrative, organizational, or procedural. The shared component might be developed by a separate project team with different stakeholders or development methodology, or in a different geographical location. For a variety of reasons, you may have to depend on components that aren't located in the same team project as your code. In such cases, you could subscribe to a component at the binary level and treat the internal implementation of the component as a black box. In many cases, this approach will work fine, but in my experience, for complicated cross-component interactions (especially when the external component itself is evolving), there's tremendous value in working with a component at the source-code level. In my experience, many hours of frustration can be avoided if you have access to the full source code of the shared component and can debug all the way through. Many unforeseen side effects can be understood and controlled, mysterious crashes can be resolved, and input parameters adjusted accordingly.

TFVC allows you to branch codelines across team projects. You can create a team project containing the common codebase and branch the codeline in team projects where the shared component needs to be reused. Let's walk thorough a concrete example.

Start by creating a team project named Common_Framework. This project contains the common framework code that will be used in other team projects. Add a test solution named CommonFrameworkCode.sln and a class file named Common-Code.cs (see figure 4.17).

Figure 4.17   Create a team project for housing the common framework code.

Create a new team project named MSF_Agile_1 that will host your main application. Create a folder named Common_Framework (see figure 4.18). This folder will store a copy of the shared code. Map this folder to your workspace.

At this point, you're now ready to branch the shared code from the Common_Framework team project to the MSF_Agile_1 team project, where it will be referenced and used. Switch to

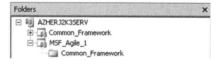

Figure 4.18   Create a new folder to store the shared framework code.

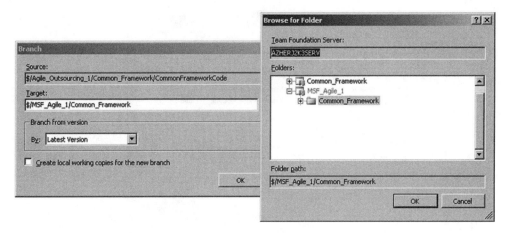

Figure 4.19 Codelines can be branched across team projects.

the workspace where MSF_Agile_1 is mapped, right-click the solution folder in the Common_Framework team project, and click Branch from the context menu. In the Branch dialog box, click Browse and select the Common_Framework folder in the MSF_Agile_1 team project (see figure 4.19). Notice that you aren't limited to folders within the same team project; the target folder can belong to a different team project. Click OK in the Browse for Folder dialog box; then click OK in the Branch dialog box. TFVC will populate the target folder with the shared framework code files from the source folder (see figure 4.20).

To verify the branch hierarchy, right-click the solution folder in the MSF_Agile_1 project and click Properties from the context menu. Then click the Branches tab. You'll see that the solution folder in the MSF_Agile_1 team project is a child of the corresponding folder in the Common_Framework team project (see figure 4.21).

At this point, a copy of the shared code is available in the application team project (MSF_Agile_1). Recall from previous discussion that a code file isn't actually copied until it's changed in the parent or in the child branch. This is an internal implementation detail that you can't see from the user interface. The point is that unlike some other version control systems, the shared component files in the application team project are completely decoupled from those located in the common framework team project.

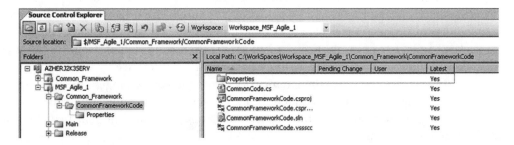

Figure 4.20 After branching, the code files are replicated in the target team project.

Figure 4.21   Branching hierarchies can span multiple team projects.

In a typical usage scenario, the common files will be updated in the common framework team project by the framework team. The framework team will then forward integrate the changes to the application team projects. To test this scenario, modify the CommonCode.cs file in the Common_Framework team project. Switch to the workspace where MSF_Agile_1 is mapped, right-click the solution directory in the Common_Framework team project, and select Merge from the context menu. In the Source Control Merge Wizard dialog box, make sure that the target branch corresponds to the common framework branch in MSF_Agile_1 (see figure 4.22). The changes will be merged from the solution directory in the Common_Framework team project to the corresponding folder in the MSF_Agile_1 team project. Make sure that you have the target folder mapped in the current workspace before initiating the merge operation.

Once the changes are applied to the Common_Framework folder in MSF_Agile_1, the feature teams can pick up the shared code changes from the local branch. The developers working on the main application will find the whole process seamless—they'll simply get the updates locally, although the original code is located in a different team project. For isolation purposes, the developers working in the MSF_Agile_1 team project might want to create a child branch from the local common framework branch and use this branch as reference. The updated shared code—remember that the framework team makes changes to the common code—may be forward integrated to the reference branch only after running extensive regression tests, once the application developers are confident that the shared code is compatible.

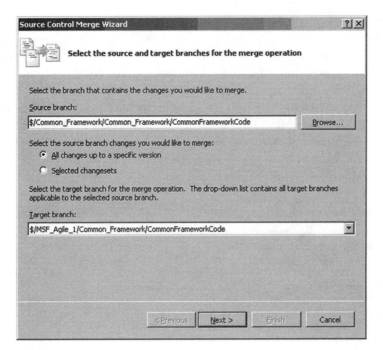

Figure 4.22 Merge
operations can span
team projects.

4.7   Branches and builds

Builds created using Team Build are independent of
branches. Team Build doesn't have built-in awareness of branches. You can create a build type that contains solutions from one or more branches, but in
most cases, you'll probably want to create a separate
build type for each branch. In TFS 2005, the Team-
BuildTypes folder under the root of your team project contains all the build types (see figure 4.23). In
TFS 2005, you can't put the Team Build types under
the corresponding source branches (this limitation

Figure 4.23 The TeamBuildTypes
folder contains the build-related files.

doesn't exist in TFS 2008). In TFS 2005, although you could manually check in a copy
of the build artifacts under the corresponding code branches, when you execute a build
from Team Explorer, TFVC looks for the corresponding build files under the Team-
BuildTypes directory. In TFS 2008, you can put the MSBuild file for the build definition
(TFSBuild.proj) in any folder.

   To create a build type for a specific branch, when creating a new build definition,
select only the specific solutions that belong to the source branch. Don't include solutions from other branches. Even if you select solutions from a single branch, when you
execute the build, Team Build will download all files in the team project, not just the
files in the source branch. This could potentially waste time and resources, especially
if your project is large.

To fix this problem, in TFS 2005, edit the corresponding WorkspaceMapping.xml file. Change the server mappings to point to the source branch only (see listing 4.2). Note the change in the `InternalMapping` element; the `ServerItem` attribute points to the branch where the solution is located. The `LocalItem` attribute is left unchanged; Team Build doesn't use this attribute. Depending on how the server mapping has been set up, you may also need to edit the solution path in the `SolutionToBuild` element in the build script, so that Team Build can find the solution file during build execution.

In TFS 2008, the WorkspaceMapping.xml file is no longer used. Use the Workspace tab in the Build Definition wizard to remove the unneeded server paths and eliminate unnecessary file downloads during build execution.

Listing 4.2 Modified WorkspaceMapping.xml

```
<?xml version="1.0" encoding="utf-8"?>
<SerializedWorkspace xmlns:xsi="http://www.w3.org/2001/XMLSchema-
    instance" xmlns:xsd="http://www.w3.org/2001/XMLSchema">
    <Mappings>
        <!-- comment out and change the following mapping --!>
        <!--
        <InternalMapping ServerItem="$/MSF_Agile_1"
            LocalItem="C:\WorkSpaces\Workspace_MSF_Agile_1"
            Type="Map" />
        --!>
        <!— modified ServerItem mapping points to the source
            branch --!>
        <InternalMapping ServerItem="$/MSF_Agile_1/Main"
            LocalItem="C:\WorkSpaces\Workspace_MSF_Agile_1"
            Type="Map" />
    </Mappings>
</SerializedWorkspace>
```

Another problem is that if you make changes or associate work items with changesets in any branch, the changesets and work item associations will show up in the build report, even if you're building solutions in a different branch. In figure 4.24, the changesets and associated work items belong to check-ins on a *different* branch.

The core problem is that the automatic label created by Team Build includes all files in all branches of the team project. The `GenCheckinNotesUpdateWorkItems` task

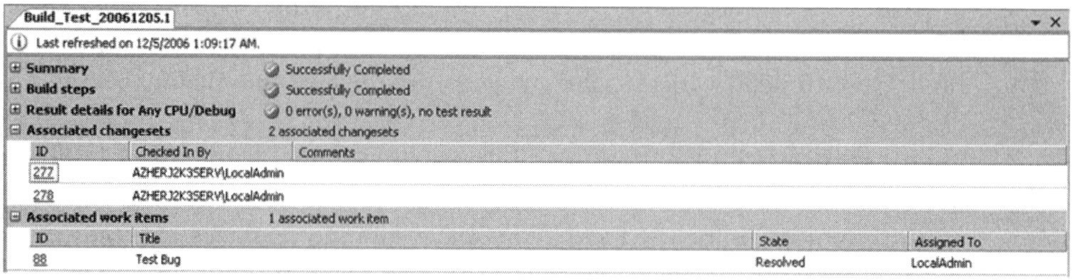

Figure 4.24 The build report shows all changesets and work items associated with check-ins since the last build.

in Team Build accepts two labels—the label for the last successful build and the label for the current build. Depending on the files included in the labels, the `GenCheckin-NotesUpdateWorkItems` task determines the changesets and work item associations that have occurred since the last successful build.

To resolve this problem, override the `CoreLabel` target so that the labels created by Team Build include only files that are located in your designated branch. The instructions for modifying the build script can be found at http://msdn2.microsoft.com/en-us/library/ms181737(VS.80).aspx. The modified build script is shown in listing 4.3.

Alternatively, you can modify the workspace mapping information, as discussed previously. If you limit the workspace mapping to point to a specific server path, only the files resident in that path (and below) will be included in the label. Consequently, you'll get the expected behavior—only the changesets and work item associations related to the files in the server path will be included in the build report.

Listing 4.3   Team Build script modified to label only branch-specific files

```xml
<?xml version="1.0" encoding="utf-8"?>
<Project DefaultTargets="DesktopBuild"
   xmlns="http://schemas.microsoft.com/developer/msbuild/2003">

   <!-- Do not edit this -->
   <Import
      Project="$(MSBuildExtensionsPath)\Microsoft\
      VisualStudio\v8.0\TeamBuild\
      Microsoft.TeamFoundation.Build.targets" />
      <ProjectExtensions>
      <!-- DESCRIPTION
      The description is associated with a
      build type. Edit the value for making changes.
      -->
      <Description>
      </Description>
      <BuildMachine>azherj2k3serv</BuildMachine>
      </ProjectExtensions>
      <PropertyGroup>
         <!-- TEAM PROJECT
         The team project which will be built using
         this build type.
         -->
         <TeamProject>MSF_Agile_1</TeamProject>
         <BuildDirectoryPath>c:\build</BuildDirectoryPath>
         <DropLocation>\\azherj2k3serv\drop</DropLocation>
         <RunTest>false</RunTest>
         <WorkItemFieldValues>Symptom=build break;Steps To
         Reproduce=Start the build using Team Build
         </WorkItemFieldValues>
         <RunCodeAnalysis>Never</RunCodeAnalysis>
         <UpdateAssociatedWorkItems>
            True
         </UpdateAssociatedWorkItems>
         <!-- Title for the work item created
```

```
      on build failure -->
      <WorkItemTitle>
         Build failure in build:
      </WorkItemTitle>
      <!-- Description for the work item
         created on build failure -->
      <DescriptionText>This work item was created
         by Team Build on a build failure.
      </DescriptionText>
      <!-- Text pointing to log file location
         on build failure -->
      <BuildlogText>
         The build log file is at:
      </BuildlogText>
      <!-- Text pointing to error/warnings file
         location on build failure -->
      <ErrorWarningLogText>
         The errors/warnings log file is at:
      </ErrorWarningLogText>
   </PropertyGroup>
<ItemGroup>
   <SolutionToBuild
      Include="$(SolutionRoot)\Test\HelloWorld\
         HelloWorld.sln" />
</ItemGroup>
<ItemGroup>
   <ConfigurationToBuild Include="Debug|Any CPU">
      <FlavorToBuild>Debug</FlavorToBuild>
      <PlatformToBuild>Any CPU</PlatformToBuild>
   </ConfigurationToBuild>
</ItemGroup>
<ItemGroup>

   <MetaDataFile Include=" ">
      <TestList> </TestList>
   </MetaDataFile>
</ItemGroup>
<ItemGroup>
</ItemGroup>

<!-- Add the following lines for modified Label creation -->
<PropertyGroup>
   <BranchPath>
      Main/HelloWorld
   </BranchPath>
</PropertyGroup>
<Target Name="CoreLabel"
   Condition=" '$(IsDesktopBuild)'!='true' "
   DependsOnTargets="$(CoreLabelDependsOn)" >
   <!-- Label all the latest non deleted files in workspace -->
   <Label
      Condition=" '$(SkipLabel)'!='true' "
      Workspace="$(WorkspaceName)"
      Name="$(BuildNumber)@$/$(TeamProject)
      /$(BranchPath)"
      Version="W$(WorkspaceName)"
```

```
        Files="$/$(TeamProject)/$(BranchPath)"
        Recursive="true" />
    </Target>
</Project>
```

At this point, we've learned how to constrain Team Build to work with branch-specific files and changes. In the next section, we look at a third-party utility that makes working with TFVC easier.

4.8   *Using Team Foundation Sidekicks*

Team Foundation Sidekicks is a freely downloadable product suite (get it from the Attrice Corportation web site at http://www.attrice.info/cm/tfs/index.htm) designed to improve productivity when working with TFVC. There is another companion product that works with MSBuild. The utilities provide a graphical interface to various functionalities that are only available through the command-line interface in TFVC. I believe that power users will find these tools to be an intuitive and time-saving solution. In this section, we look at a few utilities that can make working with TFVC easier.

The History Sidekick offers various helpful features when working with branches and merge operations. As you navigate the folder hierarchy in the left pane, information about branch structure, merge history, and merge candidates is available from the tabs in the right pane (see figure 4.25).

You can use the Status Sidekick to determine which users have pending check-ins and what kind of lock they're holding (see figure 4.26). As discussed earlier, this information is useful when you're about to freeze a particular branch and would like all

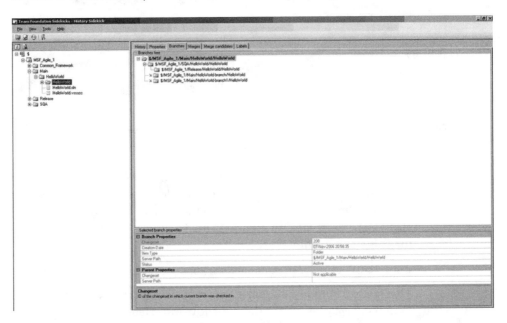

Figure 4.25   The History Sidekick offers an easy-to-use graphical interface for various advanced TFVC command-line functions.

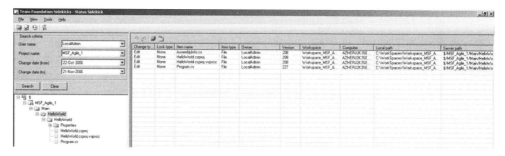

Figure 4.26   The Status Sidekick provides information regarding uncommitted check-outs and lock types.

developers to check in their changes. Knowing which users have checked out files from the branch helps you to alert them regarding an impending code freeze. If you need to forcibly remove a lock held by a developer, you have the following options:

- *Delete the workspace for the user holding the lock*—This option is useful if the developer has left the organization or his machine has crashed. Use the Workspace Sidekick to delete the workspace (see figure 4.27) or type the following at the command prompt (assuming you have Administer workspaces permission):

```
tf workspace /delete <workspace>;<username>
```

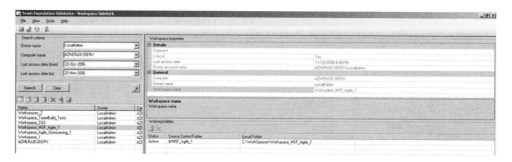

Figure 4.27   The Workspace Sidekick allows you to copy and delete workspaces.

- *Unlock the file*—The person performing the operations needs to have Unlock Other Users' Changes permission for the file. To access the permissions screen, right-click the folder or the file, select Properties from the context menu, and click the Security tab (see figure 4.28). To unlock the file, type the following at the command prompt:

```
tf lock <file> /lock:none /workspace:<workspace>;<username>
```

The *<file>* parameter should contain the fully qualified server filename; for example, $/MSF_Agile_1/Main/HelloWorld/HelloWorld/Program.cs.

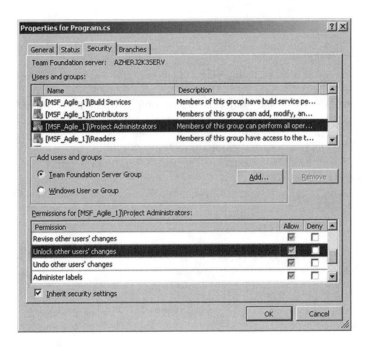

Figure 4.28 Permissions associated with being able to unlock other people's changes can be specified in the Security tab of the Properties dialog box.

4.9 Summary

TFVC provides powerful features for supporting your organization's source control requirements. You can create branches at any level in the source control tree, even across team projects. Good tool support is essential for correctly propagating changes from one branch to another, especially when you're performing large-scale branch and merge operations.

Unlike some other version control systems, TFVC doesn't support branching with built-in awareness of inheritance hierarchies, referred to as *stream-based branching*. Instead, TFVC copies files within the path structure of the source code repository, referred to as *path-space branching*. (As discussed, to conserve space, a copy isn't made until a file in the parent or child branch is actually modified.) Although there are pros and cons associated with each approach, I believe that you'll find your version control requirements to be adequately supported by TFVC, either out of the box, or using the command-line tools, third-party utilities, or programming APIs.

In this chapter, we learned about branches, labels, and folders. We applied our branching knowledge to solve the problem of sharing code among team projects. We also saw how to create builds based on a specific branch.

In the next chapter, we review how to associate policies with branches. Since one of the main reasons for creating branches is to associate different access control and check-in policies with branched codebases, it's important to learn how to create, deploy, and manage branch policies effectively.

4.10 *References*

Bellagio, David, and Tom Milligan. *Software Configuration Management Strategies and IBM Rational ClearCase.* IBM Press, 2005. ISBN: 0-321-20019-5.

Berczuk, Stephen, and Brad Appleton. *Software Configuration Management Patterns.* Addison Wesley, 2003. ISBN: 0-201-74117-2.

Birmele, Chris. "Branching and Merging Primer." Microsoft Corporation, August 2006. http://msdn2.microsoft.com/en-us/library/aa730834(vs.80,d=printer).aspx.

"Streamed Lines: Branching Patterns for Parallel Software Development." CM Crosroads. http://www.cmcrossroads.com/bradapp/acme/branching/branch-structs.html.

"Microsoft Team Foundation Server Branching Guidance." Microsoft Corporation. http://www.codeplex.com/BranchingGuidance.

Walrad, Chuck, and Darrel Strom. "The Importance of Branching Models in SCM." *IEEE Computer,* September 2002 (pp. 31–38).

Understanding
branch policies

5

This chapter covers

- Access-control policies
- Check-in policies
- Customizing check-in policies

Branch policies determine what kinds of changes can be made in a branch and who can make them. This topic is important because typically you don't want team members to be able to make unrestricted changes in every branch. Depending on whether a particular branch contains code for development, integration, quality control, or production purposes, you'll want to limit access to branches and only allow certain kinds of check-ins. For example, you may want to prevent direct check-ins in a quality control branch and only allow updates to that branch via merge operations from the development branch.

In this chapter, you'll learn about access control policies and check-in policies. Access control policies determine who can access a branch and what kinds of actions they can perform. Check-in policies specify the preconditions that must be satisfied before code can be committed in a branch. Most of this chapter is devoted to check-in policies, since there's a lot to learn about how they're created and enforced.

In this chapter, you'll learn about the following:

- *Determining effective access control policies*—Since security settings in TFVC can be inherited from higher levels, it's often not obvious who has what kind of access permissions in a given branch. We create a simple custom utility to obtain branch-specific security permissions.
- *Customizing check-in policies*—Out-of-the-box, check-in policies can be defined at the team project level, not at the branch level. However, you can use TFS Power Tools to apply custom policies at the branch level. In this chapter, we also create a custom policy to better organize branch-specific policies.

5.1   *Policies and branches*

As discussed, one of the primary reasons for branching is because you want to associate different policies with a codeline. (The other main reason is for parallel development.) You should create a branch when you need to apply a different policy to a codebase. Policies come in two general flavors—access control policies and check-in policies.

5.1.1   *Access control policies*

Access control policies control security permissions. TFVC allows you to specify access control policies at any level—on a team project, folder, subfolder, or individual files. You can also specify whether policies at a particular level inherit policies defined at higher levels. (Do this by selecting the Inherit Security Settings check box in the Security tab of the Properties dialog box.) The other point to remember is that `Deny` settings have priority over `Allow` settings, regardless of whether those settings are specified at the current level or inherited from higher levels. If a permission is denied at a higher level, you can't change that setting at a lower level (assuming Inherit Security Settings is selected at the lower-level folder).

To specify the security settings for a branch, right-click a folder in Source Control Explorer and select Properties from the context menu; then click the Security tab in the Properties dialog box. You can specify the permissions for the branch at the Windows or TFS group level (this is recommended), or even at the individual Windows user level. You can also specify security settings from the command prompt using the `tf permission` command. For more information regarding TFS and TFVC security, visit the Microsoft web site at http://msdn2.microsoft.com/en-us/library/ms252587(VS.80).aspx.

TIP   Keep in mind that `Deny` permission settings take precedence over `Allow` permission settings.

5.1.2   *Check-in policies*

Check-in policies help enforce your organization's development methodology and ensure that the code being checked in passes the necessary quality requirements. In addition to using the predefined check-in policies, you can create custom ones. Check-in policies are specified at the team project level. (If you download TFS Power Tools, you can use the Custom Path policy to associate policies with branches.)

Depending on the branch where the code is being checked in, you may want to specify different preconditions. For example, when checking in code in the main development branch, you may require that the code pass unit testing and static analysis, whereas code being checked into a private branch may be subjected to less scrutiny.

5.2 *Determining access control policies*

To determine your effective permissions for an item (a folder or a file), you can invoke the VersionControlServer.GetEffectivePermissions method (see listing 5.1). You can also use the VersionControlServer.GetEffectiveGlobalPermissions method to display the global permissions associated with a user. Both methods accept a username parameter (the GetEffectivePermissions method also accepts another parameter indicating the name of the target item). But you can only specify the name of the current user running the program.

Listing 5.1 Source code to display access control permissions

```
using System;
using System.Collections.Generic;
using System.Text;

using Microsoft.TeamFoundation.Client;
using Microsoft.TeamFoundation.VersionControl.Client;
using System.Net;

namespace GetPermissions
{
    class Program
    {
        static void Main(string[] args)
        {
            string tfsServer = "VSTS";           These should
            string item =                        point to your
                "$/MSF_Agile_1/Main/HelloWorld/HelloWorld";   server

            try
            {
                TeamFoundationServer tfs =
                    new TeamFoundationServer(
                    tfsServer, new UICredentialsProvider());
                tfs.EnsureAuthenticated();

                VersionControlServer vcServer
                    = tfs.GetService(typeof(       Get reference
                    VersionControlServer))         to TFVC
                    as VersionControlServer;

                string[] globalPermssions =
                    vcServer.GetEffectiveGlobalPermissions(
                    tfs.AuthenticatedUserName);

                string[] itemPermssions =
                    vcServer.GetEffectivePermissions(
                    tfs.AuthenticatedUserName, item);
```

```
        Console.WriteLine("Global permissions for "
          + tfs.AuthenticatedUserName);

        foreach (string permission in globalPermssions)
        {
          Console.WriteLine(permission);
        }

        Console.WriteLine("Permissions for item " +
          item + " for " + tfs.AuthenticatedUserName);

        foreach (string permission in itemPermssions)
        {
          Console.WriteLine(permission);
        }
      }
      catch (Exception ex)
      {
        Console.WriteLine("Error: " + ex.Message);
      }

      Console.ReadLine();
    }
  }
}
```

The output of the program for displaying access control permissions is as follows:

```
Global permissions for LocalAdmin

CreateWorkspace
AdminWorkspaces
AdminShelvesets
AdminConnections
AdminConfiguration

Permissions for item
$/MSF_Agile_1/Main/HelloWorld/HelloWorld/Program.cs for LocalAdmin

Read
PendChange
Checkin
Label
Lock
ReviseOther
UnlockOther
UndoOther
LabelOther
AdminProjectRights
CheckinOther
```

Note that there's no specific security setting that controls whether a user can create a branch. The same is true for deleting branches. In order to create a branch, a user needs to have Check-out (tf:PendChange from command prompt) and Check-In (tf:Checkin from command prompt) permissions on the target folder. (The user also needs Read permission on the source folder; otherwise you won't be able to see the folder that you're trying to branch.) If you want to retire a branch permanently, remove the Read permission for the developers—this will make the branch invisible to them.

There are times when you may want to prevent direct check-ins to a branch, and only allow merge operations. For example, you may not allow developers to directly check in code to a production branch. You may want them to only merge code changes from a QA branch to a production branch. This can be achieved by creating a custom check-in policy that allows only merge operations to take place in a particular branch.

5.2.1 Understanding locks

If you need to temporarily freeze a branch (such as when working on a hotfix), consider using a lock instead of changing the permission settings. Use permissions for more durable access control settings.

There are two kinds of locks in TFVC—check-in locks and check-out locks. Check-in locks allow developers to check out a file and make changes, but prevent them from checking the file back in. Check-out locks are more restrictive. Check-out locks prevent developers from checking out files in the first place—since they can't check out a file, they won't be able to check it in either, unless the file was already checked out. If there are pending changes for a file in another workspace, you can't place a check-out lock on that file.

Locks are recursive—if you lock a folder, all subfolders and items therein will be locked as well. You need to have the necessary permission (the Lock permission setting in the Security tab) in order to lock a branch.

Keep in mind that locks belong to a workspace. If you delete the workspace, the locks will be released.

5.2.2 Using the TFSSecurity tool

You can use the TFSSecurity.exe command-line tool to manage users and permissions. For example, you can use it to find the names of individual users in server-level or project-level groups. Open a command prompt, navigate to the directory containing the TFSSecurity.exe file (located at %ProgramFiles%\Microsoft Visual Studio 2008 Team Foundation Server\Tools folder) and run the utility. For more information regarding the syntax and available options, visit the Microsoft web site at http://msdn2.microsoft.com/en-gb/library/ms252504(VS.80).aspx.

For example, to find out the users in the Project Administrators group in your project, type the following:

```
Tfssecurity /server:<tfs_server_name>
/imx n:"[Sample_Project]\Project Administrators"
```

As another example, to find out the list of valid users for your TFS server, type the following:

```
Tfssecurity /server:<tfs_server_name>
/imx n:"[SERVER]\Team Foundation Valid Users"
```

So far in this chapter, we've focused on learning about access-control policies. We now switch gears and talk abut how you can associate check-in policies with branches. This is a common requirement, since there are often different quality gates associated with various branches.

In TFVC, out-of-the-box, check-in policies are specified at the team project level, not at the branch level. But you can use TFS Power Tools to associate a policy with one or more folders. If you need more advanced capabilities (such as controlling the execution order of associated policies), you need to create a custom solution. In the next section, we discuss the Custom Path policy available in TFS Power Tools. We also create a custom solution to better manage branch-specific policies.

5.3   Using the Custom Path policy

After installing TFS Power Tools, you'll find a number of new policies available in the Add Check-in Policy dialog box (see figure 5.1). To display the dialog box, right-click a team project, click Team Project Settings, and then click Source Control; in the Source Control Settings dialog box, click the Check-in Policy tab and then click Add. One of the newly available policies is the Custom Path policy. In the Custom Path Policy configuration dialog box, you have the option to associate a single check-in policy with one or more folders in TFVC (see figure 5.2).

TIP   Before you can select a policy from the Select Child Policy drop-down, a child policy should already be added to the team project. You also need to mark the policy as disabled. Otherwise, the child policy will be executed twice. Moreover, due to a bug in TFS 2005, after adding a child policy to a team project, you need to close the Source Control Settings dialog box (click OK) and then launch the dialog box again. The newly added child policy will be available for use in the Custom Path policy.

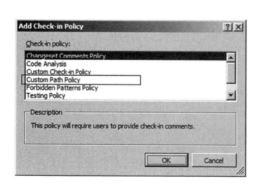

Figure 5.1   TFS Power Tools provides additional check-in policies.

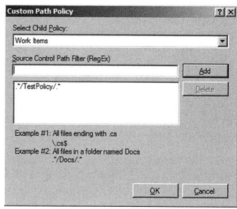

Figure 5.2   You can associate a check-in policy with specific folders using the Custom Path policy.

5.4 Creating a custom policy

In this section, we create a custom policy for associating check-in policies with branches. The motivation for creating a custom policy is to improve the user experience associated with defining, executing, and maintaining branch-specific child policies.

The Custom Path policy (available in TFS Power Tools) allows you to associate a single child policy with a folder. To associate multiple policies with one or more branches, the Custom Path policy has to be invoked multiple times. If there are many combinations of policies and branches, the Source Control Settings dialog box (in the Check-in Policy tab) becomes cluttered, and you can't tell which instance belongs to which policy and branch.

The custom policy that we create allows you to view branches and corresponding child policies in a single form. Only a single instance of the custom policy appears in the Source Control Settings dialog box (Check-in Policy tab). This approach enhances usability and makes it easier to create and maintain branch-specific policy associations.

Moreover, the Custom Path policy executes the child policies in alphabetical order, no matter which order you added them in. For example, if you specify the Work Items, Testing Policy, and Code Analysis policies, the policies will be executed in the following order:

- Code Analysis
- Testing Policy
- Work Items

This behavior is similar to the policy execution order when check-in policies are defined at the team-project level.

The custom policy that we create provides the flexibility to define the policy execution order. The policies are executed in the order that they're added. This feature gives you greater control, as sometimes it becomes necessary to execute check-in policies in a specific order, due to their logical dependencies.

Our functional approach is as follows:

- Create a custom policy that's invoked when a developer attempts to check in code. Just like the Custom Path policy in TFS Power Tools, the child policies are defined at the team-project level and marked disabled (see figure 5.3). But unlike the Custom Path policy in TFS Power Tools, only a single instance of the policy appears in the Source Control Settings dialog box (in the Check-in Policy tab), and the child policies are executed in the order they're added.
- When you add the custom policy, a dialog box is displayed where you can specify branches and associated policies (see figure 5.4). Click Add Branch to specify a branch. Click Add Policy to select the policies associated with the branch. When you click Add Policy, a dialog box is displayed containing the list of policies installed on the client machine.

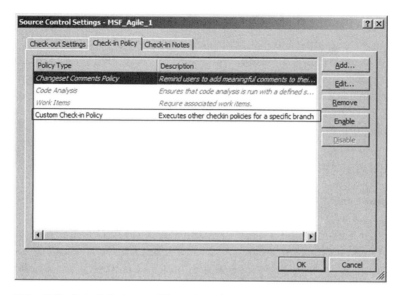

Figure 5.3   A single instance of the custom check-in policy appears in the Source Control Settings dialog box (in the Check-in Policy tab).

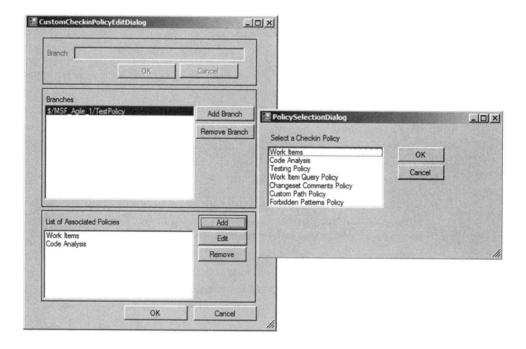

Figure 5.4   The custom policy displays branches and associated policies in a single form.

5.4.1   Understanding the core interfaces

In order to create a custom check-in policy, you need to understand two inter-faces—IPolicyDefinition and IPolicyEvaluation (see figure 5.5). When creating

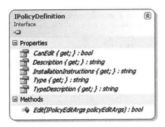
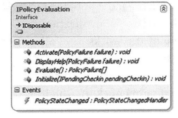

Figure 5.5
The IPolicyDefinition and IPolicyEvaluation interfaces are needed for defining a custom policy.

your custom policy class, you can either directly implement these two interfaces or simply inherit from the PolicyBase base class (see figure 5.6). The PolicyBase class provides default implementations for IPolicyDefinition and IPolicyEvaluation interfaces.

IPolicyDefinition is used when defining a policy—it contains simple properties to specify the description, installation information, and so on, as well as a method to edit the configuration options (if any) for the policy. When you install a policy for the first time, as well as when you subsequently click Edit in the Check-In Policy tab, TFVC evaluates the CanEdit property. If the value is true, the Edit method is invoked. If you have configurable properties for your custom policy, you can display your own dialog box in the Edit method so that the user can specify their values. The user-specified selections are stored as object

Figure 5.6   The PolicyBase class provides a useful base class for creating custom policies; it also contains some default implementations.

properties. These properties are serialized to storage in TFS. The framework deserial-izes the configuration properties when the policy class is instantiated during policy execution or when you click Edit in the Check-In Policy tab. That's why the policy class needs to be marked as [Serializable]. Serialization and deserialization take place behind the scenes by TFVC—you only need to mark the policy class as [Serial-izable] (and ensure that you're using serializable classes for storing the configura-tion options) and proceed normally.

IPolicyEvaluation is used when executing a policy during check-in. TFVC calls the Initialize method first, passing information about the files that are about to be checked in; the parameter type is IPendingCheckin. IPendingCheckin contains a number of useful properties, such as associated work items, check-in notes, and the changes that are ready for check-in (see figure 5.7). The pending changes are encapsulated in an object of type `IPendingCheckInPendingChanges`.

`IPendingCheckInPendingChanges` contains a number of useful properties, such as the name of the workspace, all changes available in the workspace, which changes have been marked for inclusion in the current check-in, which team projects will be affected by the current check-in (remember, you can map multiple team projects to a single workspace), and the check-in comment (see figure 5.8). You could, for example, create a policy to make sure that developers don't check in files without writing comments—a common-sense best practice for change management.

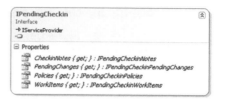

Figure 5.7   The `IPendingCheckIn` interface provides properties and methods to obtain information associated with a check-in.

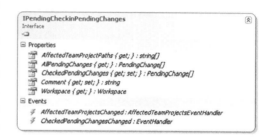

Figure 5.8   The `IPendingCheckinPending-Changes` interface provides granular information about the changes as well other relevant information.

The `Evaluate` method does the main work—it executes the policy rules. The method returns a collection of `PolicyFailure` objects (see figure 5.9) if errors are encountered during rules processing. If a nonempty `PolicyFailure` collection is returned from the `Evaluate` method, TFVC cancels the check-in and displays the errors to the user (based on the `Message` property of the `PolicyFailure` objects in the return collection). If the user double-clicks a policy failure message, TFVC calls the `Acivate` method of the corresponding `PolicyFailure` object. Note in Figure 5.9 that the `PolicyFailure` object, via its `Policy` property, knows which policy produced the error. Consequently, when the `Activate` method is invoked on a `PolicyFailure` object, the call is delegated to the `Activate` method of the actual policy object. If the user presses F1 for help, TFVC calls the `DisplayHelp` method of the `Policy-Failure` object; this call is also delegated to the `DisplayHelp` method of the corresponding policy object.

With an understanding of the basic concepts, we next look at the actual mechanics of creating a custom policy.

5.4.2   *Technical implementation*

As discussed, there are two aspects to creating a custom policy—writing code to support policy definitions, and policy execution phases. Instead of implementing the `IPolicyDefinition` and

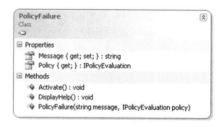

Figure 5.9   The `PolicyFailure` class contains methods and properties to display policy violations as well as to launch screens for help or remediation.

IPolicyEvaluation interfaces directly, we inherit from the PolicyBase class, which implements these interfaces and provides helpful default implementations (see listing 5.2).

When adding the policy for the first time (or editing it subsequently), the Edit method in listing 5.2 is executed. This method launches the CustomCheckinPolicy-EditDialog dialog box, where you can select branches and associated policies. The code for the CustomCheckinPolicyEditDialog dialog box is displayed in listings 5.3 and 5.4. When you click Add Policy in the CustomCheckinPolicyEditDialog dialog box, the btnAddPolicy_Click method is invoked; this method launches the PolicySelection-Dialog dialog box, where you can select the policies to associate with a particular branch. The code for the PolicySelectionDialog dialog box is displayed in listing 5.5. Note the pAddPoliciesToList method in listing 5.5; this method uses the Workstation class, located in the Microsoft.TeamFoundation.VersionControl.Client assembly, to obtain the list of installed policies and their types from TFVC. The Workstation class contains a number of other methods related to local workspaces and server mappings (see figure 5.10)—such as clearing the local workspace cache in case of a server move—which you may find useful when working with TFVC in general.

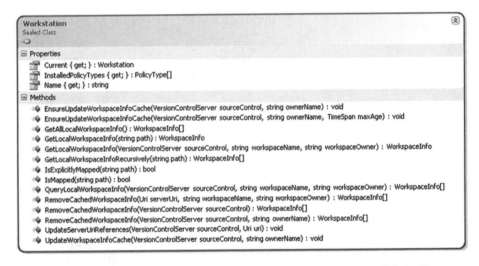

Figure 5.10 The Workstation class contains properties and methods associated with policy and workspace configuration on the machine running the Source Control Explorer.

Listing 5.2 Source code for custom check-in policy class

```
using System;
using System.Collections.Generic;
using System.Text;
using System.Windows.Forms;

using Microsoft.TeamFoundation.VersionControl.Client;

[Serializable]
```

```
public class CustomCheckinPolicy : PolicyBase
{
   // Holds the Branch Policies serialized to TFS
   public IList<BranchPolicies> _branchPolicies;

   public CustomCheckinPolicy()
   {
      _branchPolicies = new List<BranchPolicies>();
   }

   public override string Description
   {
      get { return Constants.Description; }
   }

   /// <summary>
   /// This method is invoked by the policy framework when
   /// the user creates a new check-in
   /// policy or edits an existing check-in policy.
   /// We can use this as an opportunity to
   /// display UI specific to this policy type allowing
   /// the user to change the parameters
   /// of the policy.
   /// </summary>
   public override bool Edit(IPolicyEditArgs policyEditArgs)
   {

      CustomCheckinPolicyEditDialog dialog
         = new CustomCheckinPolicyEditDialog(
         policyEditArgs.TeamProject, _branchPolicies);

      DialogResult dialogResult = dialog.ShowDialog(
         policyEditArgs.Parent);

   if (DialogResult.OK == dialogResult)
      {
         try
         {
            _branchPolicies = dialog.BranchPoliciesCollection;

            return true;
         }
         catch (Exception ex)
         {
            return false;
         }
      }
      else
      {
         return false;
      }
   }

   /// <summary>
   /// This method performs the actual evaluation.  It is
   /// called by the policy framework when the policy needs
   /// to be evaluated. In this method, we invoke
```

Create instance of CustomCheckin-PolicyDialog

Retrieve branch policies from dialog

```
/// the Initialize and Evaluate methods of
/// each policy associated with the specified branch.
/// We assume the user checks into a single branch.
/// </summary>
public override PolicyFailure[] Evaluate()
{
    List<PolicyFailure> allPolicyFailures = new
        List<PolicyFailure>();

    TeamProject teamProject =                                Get
        ((VersionControlServer)PendingCheckin.GetService(    corresponding
        typeof(VersionControlServer))).GetTeamProject(       team project
        Constants.TeamProject);

    PolicyEnvelope[] installedPolicies =          Get installed policies
        teamProject.GetCheckinPolicies();         in team project

    // **assume the user is checking into a single branch.**
    // Consequently, the server path for the first
    // item can be used.
    string serverPath =
        PendingCheckin.PendingChanges.
        CheckedPendingChanges[0].ServerItem;

    BranchPolicies branchPolicies =               Search branch policies
        pSearchPoliciesForBranch(serverPath);     for given server path

    if (branchPolicies != null)
    {
        // Evaluate each policy associated with the branch
        foreach (IPolicyDefinition policyDefinition in
            branchPolicies.AssociatedPolicies)
        {
            PolicyFailure[] policyFailures;

            //locate the corresponding policy in the
            //available policy collection for the team project
            foreach (PolicyEnvelope installedPolicyEnvelope
                in installedPolicies)
            {
                if (installedPolicyEnvelope.Policy.Type ==
                    policyDefinition.Type)
                {
                    IPolicyEvaluation policy =
                        installedPolicyEnvelope.Policy as
                        IPolicyEvaluation;
                                                            Invoke
                    if (policy != null)                     policy
                    {
                        policy.Initialize(PendingCheckin);
                        policyFailures = policy.Evaluate();

                        allPolicyFailures.AddRange(
                        policyFailures);

                    }
                }
            }
        }
```

```
        }
    }

    return allPolicyFailures.ToArray();
}

/// This string is the type of our policy. It will be
/// displayed to the user in a list
/// of all installed policy types when a user
/// creates a new policy.
public override string Type
{
    get { return Constants.Type; }
}

/// This string is a description of the policy type.
/// It will be displayed to the
/// user when he selects the policy in the
/// list of policies.
public override string TypeDescription
{
    get { return Constants.TypeDescription; }
}

/// This is a string that is stored with the policy
/// definition on the source
/// control server. If a user does not have
/// the policy plugin installed, this string
/// will be displayed.
public override string InstallationInstructions
{
    get { return Constants.InstallationInstructions; }
}
}
```

The Evaluate method in listing 5.2 determines the server path associated with the check-in and looks up the corresponding policies associated with the branch. We use a class named BranchPolicies to store the policies associated with each branch. Recall from our previous discussion that when a custom policy is added in TFVC, you get to specify which policies are associated with which branch. These choices are stored in a variable named branchPolicies as a collection of objects of type BranchPolicies. The collection is serialized and deserialized by TFVC.

The Evaluate method looks up the BranchPolicies objects associated with the current branch and determines which policies need to be evaluated. It then iterates over the policies collection; for each policy, it invokes the Intialize and Evaluate methods. The PolicyFailure collection returned from the Evaluate method of each target policy is aggregated into a composite collection and sent back to TFVC.

Listing 5.3   Source code for the Edit dialog box (private methods omitted)

```
/// *** using statements omitted for brevity ***

public partial class CustomCheckinPolicyEditDialog : Form
{
```

```
private TeamProject _teamProject;
```
Branch policies saved in TFS
```
private IList<BranchPolicies> _originalBranchPoliciesCollection;
```
```
private IList<BranchPolicies> _clonedBranchPoliciesCollection;
```
```
public IList<BranchPolicies> BranchPoliciesCollection
{
```
Updated or newly added policies
```
   get { return _clonedBranchPoliciesCollection; }
}
public CustomCheckinPolicyEditDialog(TeamProject teamProject,
   IList<BranchPolicies> installedBranchPolicies)
{
   this._teamProject = teamProject;
   this._originalBranchPoliciesCollection =
      installedBranchPolicy;
   this._clonedBranchPoliciesCollection =
      new List<BranchPolicies>();
   InitializeComponent();
   this.pCloneOriginalToClonedCollection();
   this.pInitBranchList();
   this.pEnableAddBranchControls(false);
}

#region Handler Methods

/// Handler for Add Policy button. Invoked
/// when the button is clicked.
private void btnAddPolicy_Click(object sender, EventArgs e)
{
   if (null == lstBranchList.SelectedItem)
   {
```
If no branch selected, display an error
```
      MessageBox.Show("Please select a branch
         from the list");
      return;
   }

   PolicySelectionDialog policySelectionDialog = new
      PolicySelectionDialog();
```
Show policy selection dialog box
```
   DialogResult dialogResult =
      policySelectionDialog.ShowDialog(this);

   if (dialogResult == DialogResult.OK)
   {
      if (policySelectionDialog.SelectedPolicy !=null)
      IPolicyDefinition policyDef =
        policySelectionDialog.SelectedPolicy.New();
      else
        return;
```
Retrieve selected policies from PolicySelection-Dialog
```
      if (lstBoxInstalledPolicies.Items.
         IndexOf(policyDef.Type) != -1)
      {
         MessageBox.Show("Policy already
            exists for the branch");
      }
```
Display message if policy associated with branch

```
            else
            {
               BranchPolicies branchPolicies
                  = pSearchBranchInCollection(
                  m_installedBrannchPolicyCollection,
                  lstBranchList.SelectedItem.ToString());

               if (branchPolicies != null)
               {
                  branchPolicies.AssociatedPolicies.Add(
                     policyDef);

                  lstBoxInstalledPolicies.Items.Add(
                     policyDef.Type);
               }
            }
         }
      }

      /// Handler for Branch List. This is invoked
      /// when the item selection is changed in List.
      private void lstBranchList_SelectedIndexChanged(
         object sender, EventArgs e)
      {
         object branchName = lstBranchList.SelectedItem;

         if (branchName == null) return;
         this.pSetAssociatedPoliciesInList(branchName.ToString());
      }

      /// Handler for Add Branch button.
      private void btnAddBranch_Click(object sender, EventArgs e)
      {
         this.pEnableAddBranchControls(true);
      }

      /// Handler for btnOkNewBranch button.
      private void btnOkNewBranch_Click(object sender, EventArgs e)
      {
         BranchPolicies branchPolicies =
            this.pSearchBranchInCollection(
            _clonedBranchPoliciesCollection, txtBranch.Text);

         if (branchPolicies != null)
         {
            MessageBox.Show("This branch already
               contains associated policies", "Policy Exists");
         }
         else if (pValidateBranchPath(txtBranch.Text))
         {
            BranchPolicies newBranchPolicies = new BranchPolicies();
            newBranchPolicies.BranchName = txtBranch.Text;
            _clonedBranchPoliciesCollection.Add(newBranchPolicies);

            lstBranchList.Items.Add(txtBranch.Text);

            txtBranch.Text = string.Empty;
            pEnableAddBranchControls(false);
         }
```

Search for branch in policies collection

Add to collection associated with branch

Determine if path is associated with policy

Create policy and add to collection

```csharp
     else
     {
        MessageBox.Show("Branch Path is not valid",
           "Path not valid");
     }
}

/// Handler for btnCancelNewBranch Button.
private void btnCancelNewBranch_Click(
   object sender, EventArgs e)
{
   txtBranch.Text = string.Empty;
   pEnableAddBranchControls(false);
}

/// Handler for btnRemovePolicy Button.
private void btnRemovePolicy_Click(
   object sender, EventArgs e)
{
   if (lstBoxInstalledPolicies.SelectedItem == null)
   {
      MessageBox.Show("Please select a policy
         from the list");
      return;
   }

   BranchPolicies branchPolicies = pSearchBranchInCollection(
      _clonedBranchPoliciesCollection,
      lstBranchList.SelectedItem.ToString());
      int indexPolicyDef = pSearchPolicyInBranch(
      branchPolicies, lstBoxInstalledPolicies.
      SelectedItem.ToString());

   if (indexPolicyDef != -1)
   {
      branchPolicies.AssociatedPolicies.RemoveAt(
         indexPolicyDef);
      lstBoxInstalledPolicies.Items.Remove(
         lstBoxInstalledPolicies.SelectedItem);
   }
}

/// Handler for btnRemoveBranch Button.
private void btnRemoveBranch_Click(
   object sender, EventArgs e)
{
   if (lstBranchList.SelectedItem == null)
   {
      MessageBox.Show("Select a branch from the list.");
      return;
   }

   BranchPolicies branchPolicies
      = pSearchBranchInCollection(
      _clonedBranchPoliciesCollection,
      lstBranchList.SelectedItem.ToString());

   if (branchPolicies != null)
```

```
         {
            _clonedBranchPoliciesCollection.Remove(branchPolicies);
            lstBranchList.Items.Remove(
               lstBranchList.SelectedItem);
            lstBoxInstalledPolicies.Items.Clear();
         }
      }
   }

   #endregion Handler Methods
```

Listing 5.3 does not contain any private methods or using statements, for the sake of brevity. Listing 5.4 shows only the private methods associated with the Edit dialog box.

Listing 5.4   Source code for the Edit dialog box (private methods only)

```
   /// Initializes the branch list when
   /// the form is loaded.
   private void pInitBranchList()
   {
      foreach (BranchPolicies branchPolicies in
         _clonedBranchPoliciesCollection)
      {
         lstBranchList.Items.Add(branchPolicies.BranchName);
      }
   }

   /// Searches through all branch policies in the List.
   /// If a match is found with the name of the branch,
   /// returns the corresponding branch policy.
   private BranchPolicies pSearchBranchInCollection(
      IList<BranchPolicies> branchList, string branchName)
   {
      BranchPolicies returnedPolicies = null;
      foreach (BranchPolicies branchPolicies in branchList)
      {
         if (branchPolicies.BranchName == branchName)
         {
            returnedPolicies = branchPolicies;
            break;
         }
      }

      return returnedPolicies;
   }

   /// Searches a check-in policy in a specified branch.
   /// If found, returns the index of the
   /// policy in the branch, otherwise returns -1. The search
   /// is conducted based on the input policy name.
   private int pSearchPolicyInBranch(
      BranchPolicies branchPolicies, string policyName)
   {
      int index = -1;

      if (branchPolicies == null) return index;

      for (int i = 0; i < branchPolicies.
```

```
            AssociatedPolicies.Count; i++)
    {
        if (branchPolicies.AssociatedPolicies[i].Type
           == policyName)
        {
           index = i;
           break;
        }
    }

    return index;
}


/// Sets policies associated with a specific branch.
private void pSetAssociatedPoliciesInList(string branchName)
{
    lstBoxInstalledPolicies.Items.Clear();

    BranchPolicies branchPolicies =
        pSearchBranchInCollection(
        _clonedBranchPoliciesCollection, branchName);
    if (branchPolicies != null)
    {
        foreach (IPolicyDefinition policyDef in
           branchPolicies.AssociatedPolicies)
        {
           lstBoxInstalledPolicies.Items.Add(
              policyDef.Type);
        }
    }
}

/// Enables or disables the controls for adding a branch.
private void pEnableAddBranchControls(bool enable)
{
    panel3.Enabled = enable;
    panel1.Enabled = !enable;
    panel2.Enabled = !enable;
}

/// Validates the branch path specified by the user.
private bool pValidateBranchPath(string path)
{
    VersionControlServer vcServer =
        _teamProject.VersionControlServer;
    try
    {
        Item item = vcServer.GetItem(path);
        if (item != null && item.ItemType == ItemType.Folder)
           return true;
        else
           return false;
    }
    catch (Exception ex)
    {
```

```
            return false;
        }
    }

    /// Clones branch policies from a collection of policies.
    /// This is done to keep the original collection unchanged.
    private void pCloneOriginalToClonedCollection()
    {
        foreach (BranchPolicies branchPolicies in
           _originalBranchPoliciesCollection)
        {
           _clonedBranchPoliciesCollection.Add(
               branchPolicies.Clone() as BranchPolicies);
        }
    }

    private void CustomCheckinPolicyEditDialog_Load(
        object sender, EventArgs e)
    {

    }
}
```

At this point, we've seen how the Edit dialog box works. Let's now review the code associated with the Policy Selection dialog box, which is shown in listing 5.5.

Listing 5.5   Source code for the Policy Selection dialog box

```
using System;
using System.Collections.Generic;
using System.ComponentModel;
using System.Data;
using System.Drawing;
using System.Text;
using System.Windows.Forms;

using Microsoft.TeamFoundation.VersionControl.Client;
using Microsoft.TeamFoundation.VersionControl.Controls;

public partial class PolicySelectionDialog : Form
{
    private IList<PolicyType> policyList;

    // Returns the policy selected in the Dialog
    public PolicyType  SelectedPolicy
    {
        get
        {
         if (lstBoxPolicies.SelectedIndex == -1)
          return null;
         else
          return policyList[lstBoxPolicies.SelectedIndex];
        }
    }

    public PolicySelectionDialog()
    {
        this.policyList = new List<PolicyType>();
```

```
        InitializeComponent();
        this.pAddPoliciesToList();
    }

    /// <summary>
    /// Reads installed policies from the Registry and
    /// adds them to the List Box and Collection
    /// </summary>
    private void pAddPoliciesToList()
    {
        foreach (PolicyType policy in
            Workstation.Current.InstalledPolicyTypes)
        {
            if (policy.Name != Constants.Type)
            {
                int index = lstBoxPolicies.Items.Add(
                    policy.Name);
                policyList.Insert(index, policy);
            }
        }

        if (policyList.Count == 0)
            lstBoxPolicies.Items.Add("No policies
                installed....");
    }

    private void PolicySelectionDialog_Load(
        object sender, EventArgs e)
    {

    }
}
```

5.4.3 *Installing custom policies*

In TFVC, check-in policies are evaluated in the client machine, not the server. This means that you need to install the check-in policy on every developer machine. In order to install a policy, copy the assembly to an appropriate location and update one of the following registry entries (see figure 5.11):

- HKEY_LOCAL_MACHINE\Software\Microsoft\VisualStudio\9.0\TeamFoundation\SourceControl\Checkin Policies
- HKEY_CURRENT_USER\Software\Microsoft\VisualStudio\9.0\TeamFoundation\SourceControl\Checkin Policies

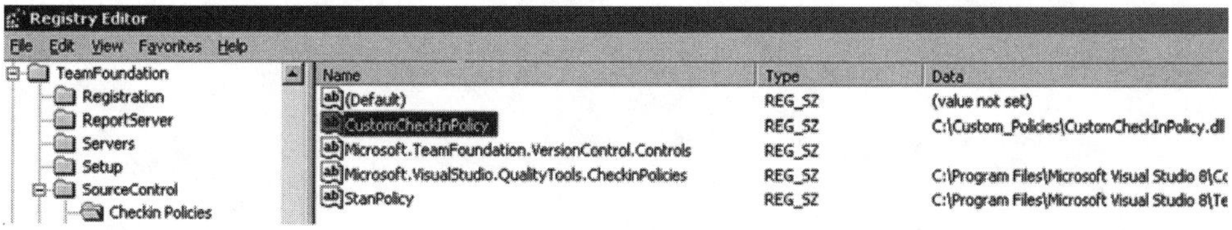

Figure 5.11   Create a registry entry for the custom policy.

Keep in mind that since the check-in policies are executed inside the IDE, there's no fool-proof guarantee that they'll be executed prior to a check-in. For example, a developer could simply uninstall a check-in policy from his machine (by deleting the corresponding registry key) and check in the code. He could also bypass the check-in policies by connecting to the TFVC application-tier machine using the TFS web services or by writing a custom program using the client-object model. Check-in policies act more as reminders for developers to follow certain procedures.

5.5   *Summary*

In this chapter, we saw how to associate access control policies and check-in policies with specific branches. We also learned how to create custom check-in policies and deploy them. This information will help you configure an appropriate branching structure for your organization and assign roles and responsibilities to various team members for maintaining it.

In the next chapter, we look at merge operations, which is complementary to branching. Once you branch a codebase, chances are high that at some point you'll need to reconcile the changes that take place in those branches. The next chapter discusses how to achieve this effectively.

Understanding merging
in version control

6

This chapter covers

- Understanding merge operations
- Comparing branch contents
- TFS events and notifications

Merging is the process of integrating changes between different branches. Merging is used to propagate changes from one branch to another. While you could propagate changes by manually editing files in a target branch—and sometimes that is the only way to achieve the desired outcome—it helps to have a tool that can detect changes and automate the routine aspects, especially when there are a large number of files involved. As a best practice, keep in mind that it's better to merge early and often so that changes that need to be merged are as small as possible. Effective merging practices are essential for sustaining parallel development.

Merging involves transferring changes from one branch to another. It's important to understand that merging doesn't mean comparing two branches and reconciling their differences. Therefore, when merging between two branches, the direction of the merge is important. As a simple example, if you create a branch from the main codeline, make changes in the branch, and then try to merge from main to branch, TFVC will inform you that there are no changes to merge. On the other hand, if you try to merge from branch to main, TFVC will show the changes that you made in the branch and help you incorporate them in the main. The target files in a merge operation are always the ones that are located at the tip of the target branch (the latest version of each file). In TFVC, you can't merge changes with a version of a target file that isn't the latest version.

In this chapter, we explore various options available in TFVC for merging related as well as unrelated branches. We talk about viewing merge candidates, reviewing merge histories, detecting and resolving merge conflicts, and rolling back merges.

In this chapter, you'll learn about the following:

- *Understanding common merge operations*—Learn about common merge operations such as viewing merge histories, viewing changes in merged files, determining merge candidates and potential conflicts, resolving merge conflicts, rolling back merges, and performing baseless merges.

- *Notifying developers about concurrent changes*—A common issue with shared repositories is the potential that somebody else could change a file that you're currently working on, and you may be unaware of that change for a long time. Unless a file is locked upon checkout (not a good idea, since it impedes productivity), there's a possibility that multiple people might modify a file that's been checked out. The sooner the users can be notified of the concurrent changes, the lesser the pain of merging. Create a custom program to notify the developers who've checked out a file about the concurrent changes that have been checked in.

6.1   *Viewing merge history*

After you merge changes from one branch to another, you'll frequently want to find out the lineage of a file—that is, exactly which version of the source file was merged with the target file. This information is useful when troubleshooting the origin of bugs and determining what changes were made to a file and why. Without the merge history, you'll have no context to debug the random-looking changes to your codebase that result from merge operations.

If you simply view the history from the TFVC user interface (right-click the target file and select View History from the context menu), you'll see something similar to figure 6.1.

The History pane at the bottom tells you that changeset number 238 was created when the file was first branched, and changeset 240 was created during a subsequent merge operation. But the information isn't detailed enough—you don't know which chagesets from the parent branch were included in either the original branch operation or the subsequent merge operation. To get the detailed history, type the following at the command prompt:

```
tf merges <full_server_path_to_target_branch>
/server:<tfs_server_name> /recursive
```

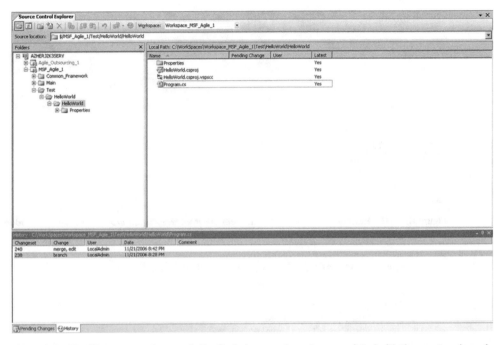

Figure 6.1 The History pane shows only the final changeset number associated with the merge or branch operation on the target branch.

In our example, the output of the command looks like the following:

```
Changeset Merged in Changeset Author        Date
--------- -------------------- --------------------- ----------
    208*            238 LocalAdmin          11/21/2006
    216             238 LocalAdmin          11/21/2006
    222             238 LocalAdmin          11/21/2006
    227             238 LocalAdmin          11/21/2006
    239             240 LocalAdmin          11/21/2006
```

The information provided by the `tf merges` command provides the necessary details to understand which changesets were incorporated in the target branch, both during the creation of the target branch and during subsequent merge operations. The same information can be obtained using the History Sidekick (see figure 6.2; sidekicks were discussed in chapter 4). The History Sidekick also displays the merge information at the file level, allowing you to see which files were modified during merge.

Another way to obtain the full history is to use TFS Power Tools. For TFS 2008, this tool can be downloaded from Microsoft web site at http://msdn.microsoft.com/en-us/tfs2008/bb980963.aspx. After installation, TFS Power Tools can be run from the command line. Selected features of TFS Power Tools are also accessible through the Visual Studio IDE. To obtain the history for a branched item, type the following at the command prompt:

```
tfpt history <path_to_target_file> /followbranches
```

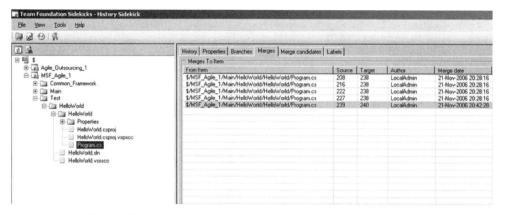

Figure 6.2   The History Sidekick shows changesets from the source branch that were included when performing branch or merge operation on the target branch.

In our example, the output looks like the following:

```
Changeset Change      User          Date        Comment
--------- ------------ ------------- ----------- --------------
240       merge, edit  LocalAdmin    11/21/2006
238       branch       LocalAdmin    11/21/2006
```

```
$/MSF_Agile_1/Test/HelloWorld/HelloWorld/Program.cs;C238 was branched
from $/MSF_Agile_1/Main/HelloWorld/HelloWorld/Program.cs;C227:
```

```
Changeset Change      User          Date        Comment
--------- ------------ ------------- ----------- --------------
227       edit         LocalAdmin    11/15/2006
222       edit         LocalAdmin    11/10/2006
216       merge, edit  LocalAdmin    11/7/2006
208       add          LocalAdmin    11/7/2006
```

Note that changeset 239 is missing from the output. If you look at the output of the `tf merges` command as well the display in the History Sidekick, you'll see that changeset 239 was a changeset in the parent branch that was merged with the child branch. (The merge operation itself was contained in changeset 240.) The output of `tfpt history` command doesn't show that changeset, since it's associated with a change that occurred in the parent branch after branching. Be aware of these subtle differences as you work with various tools.

Now that we've learned how to determine merge history, let's find out how we can view the actual changes that have occurred during a merge.

6.2   *Viewing changes*

After a merge operation, you might be interested in seeing exactly what changes were made in an individual file. This capability is especially important if you're merging changes into a stable codebase and want to understand the effect of the merge at a granular level. To see the latest changes in a file on a line-by-line basis, type the following TFS Power Tools command at the command prompt:

```
tfpt annotate <path_to_file>
```

```
Form1.cs;C580 (Annotated)
536  darren  4/21/2007   using System;
                         using System.Collections.Generic;
                         using System.ComponentModel;
                         using System.Data;
                         using System.Drawing;
                         using System.Text;
                         using System.Windows.Forms;

539  darren  4/21/2007   using MessageClassLibrary;

536  darren  4/21/2007   namespace ShowHelloWorld
                         {
                             public partial class Form1 : Form
                             {
                                 public Form1()
                                 {
                                     InitializeComponent();
                                 }

580  darren  5/11/2007       /// <summary>
                             /// this is the handler method for Show Message
                             /// </summary>
                             /// <param name="sender"></param>
                             /// <param name="e"></param>
536  darren  4/21/2007       private void button1_Click(object sender, EventArgs e)
                             {
539  darren  4/21/2007           MessageClass msgClass = new MessageClass();
536  darren  4/21/2007
580  darren  5/11/2007           //fetch message from library
539  darren  4/21/2007           string msgString = msgClass.GetMessage();
580  darren  5/11/2007
                                 //trim the message
                                 msgString = msgString.Trim();

539  darren  4/21/2007           label1.Text = msgString;

536  darren  4/21/2007       }
                             }
                         }
```

Figure 6.3   The annotation viewer provides the latest change information for each line of code.

The `annotate` command launches the annotation viewer as shown in figure 6.3. In our example, changeset 580 resulted from a merge operation. As you can see, the markings on each line inform you when a line was last changed, by whom, and via which changeset. You can click on a changeset number to get additional info about the check-in.

In TFS 2005, the annotation functionality becomes available in the IDE when you install TFS 2005 Power Tools. In TFS 2008, the annotation functionality is available in the IDE out of the box. Right-click any file in the Source Control Explorer; you'll find a new option named Annotate in the context menu (see figure 6.4).

6.3   *Comparing contents of two branches*

In TFS 2005, you can use the `tfpt treediff` command available in TFS 2005 Power Tools to compare folders. In TFS 2008, the functionality is called *Folder Diff* and is integrated into the IDE. Capabilities include comparing two server folders or a server and a local folder. The tool can also reconcile changes between a server folder and a local folder that's mapped to the server folder.

Figure 6.4   The Annotate option is available in the IDE after TFS Power Tools is installed.

In TFS 2005, to compare two folders from the command line, install TFS 2005 Power Tools, and type the following:

```
tfpt treediff <source_folder> <target_folder> /recursive
```

In TFS 2008, the Folder Diff functionality is built into the IDE. To compare two folders in Source Control Explorer, right-click a folder and select Compare from the context menu. In the Compare dialog box, specify the source and target folder names as well as the comparison type (see figure 6.5). You can compare based on the latest version,

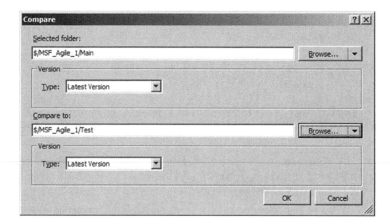

Figure 6.5   You can compare the contents of two folders in TFVC.

a label, a changeset, and so on. The comparison screen shows the differences between the selected folders (see figure 6.6). By reviewing the changes, you'll see which files have changed between the two branches. To review the changes in a specific file, right-click the file and select Compare from the context menu.

You may sometimes need to generate a change report for auditing purposes. However, if you use the IDE, you won't be able to extract the necessary data to create reports—the change information is only available onscreen. In TFS 2005, you can use the `tfpt treediff` command from the command prompt (assuming you have installed TFS 2005 Power Tools) and redirect the output to a file. In TFS 2008, you can use the `tf folderdiff` command from the command prompt and also redirect the output to a file. For more information on the `tf folderdiff` command, visit http://msdn.microsoft.com/en-us/library/bb385992.aspx.

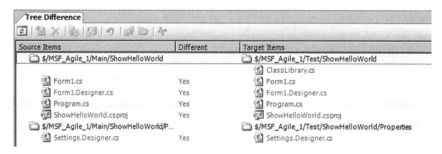

Figure 6.6   The comparison screen shows file level changes between two folders.

6.4   *Determining merge candidates and conflicts*

Before you actually perform a merge, you might want to know about the unmerged changesets between two branches, so that you can decide, for example, which changesets to merge or whether to merge changes at all. This information isn't available from the TFVC user interface. You can get information about unmerged changesets either from the History Sidekick (see figure 6.7) or by typing the following at the command prompt:

```
tf merge /candidate <path_to_source_branch>
<path_to_target_branch> /recursive
```

If you want to know which files are affected by the unmerged changesets, you can use the History Sidekick (the tree on the right pane shows which files are impacted) or type the following at the command prompt:

```
tf merge /preview <path_to_source_branch>
<path_to_target_branch> /recursive
```

The output of the command looks like the following:

```
merge, edit:
$/MSF_Agile_1/Main/HelloWorld/HelloWorld/Program.cs;C239~C241 ->
$/MSF_Agile_1/Test/HelloWorld/HelloWorld/Program.cs;C240
```

The output shows the files involved in the merge, the type of edit that will be pended, the changesets that will be merged from the source branch, and the current changeset number of the file in the target branch.

If there's a merge conflict between the source and target branches (this could happen, for example, if a file has been changed both in the source and in the target branch), the command output will look like the following:

```
Conflict (merge, edit):
$/MSF_Agile_1/Main/HelloWorld/HelloWorld/Program.cs;C239~C241 ->

$/MSF_Agile_1/Test/HelloWorld/HelloWorld/Program.cs;C242
```

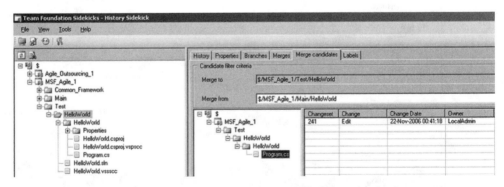

Figure 6.7   The History Sidekick shows unmerged changesets between two branches, as well as which files are affected.

6.5   *Resolving merge conflicts*

Merging and merge conflict resolution is a two-step process in TFVC (although when using the Source Control Explorer, it feels like only one single step). The first step involves checking the branch and merge history to determine version conflicts, namespace conflicts (detected during check-in), and writeable file conflicts. Microsoft calls this step *tree merge*. For more information on conflict types and available options, visit http://msdn.microsoft.com/en-us/library/ms181434.aspx.

The second step involves analyzing the actual file contents. In this step, a base version is determined based on the point of last consistency. TFVC then determines the patches needed to replicate the source and target versions. If the patches have overlapping areas, a merge screen is displayed. Microsoft calls this step *content merge*.

Merges can be initiated using the `tf merge` command. The `tf merge` command looks for tree conflicts and displays the Resolve Conflicts screen if conflicts are detected. If no tree conflicts are detected, the `tf merge` command proceeds to look for content conflicts.

You can use the Resolve Conflicts screen or the `tf resolve` command to resolve the merge conflicts. You can also use third-party tools to compare and merge files. To configure a third-party tool, bring up the Source Control Explorer, click the Tools menu, and click Options; in the Options dialog box, expand the Source Control node, click Visual Studio Team Foundation Server, and click Configure User Tools on the right pane (see figure 6.8).

If TFVC can't automatically merge the changes in the second step, it'll display the merge screen so that you can manually resolve the conflicts (see figure 6.9). To understand this screen, you need to be aware of the concept of a *base*. The base is the changeset in the source branch at the last point of consistency between the source and

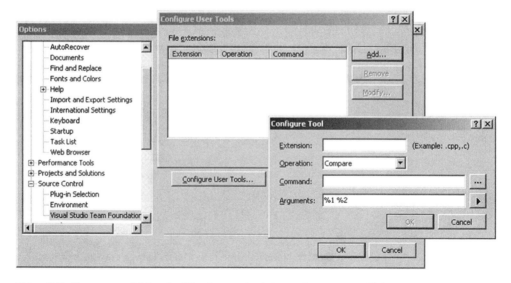

Figure 6.8   You can use third-party diff and merge tools to resolve merge conflicts.

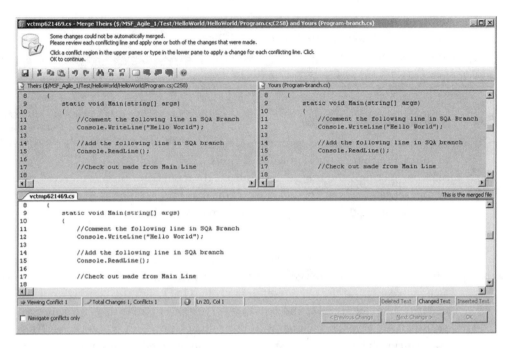

Figure 6.9   The merge screen shows the source and target files on top and the merged file at the bottom.

target branches (the branch point or the last merge point). You can view the base, as well as its differences with the source and target versions, by clicking Compare in the Resolve Version Conflict dialog box (see figure 6.10).

In the merge screen, the top-left pane marks the patches that were applied to the base to produce the source version. The top-right pane shows the patches that were applied to the base to produce the target version. The bottom pane is where you specify

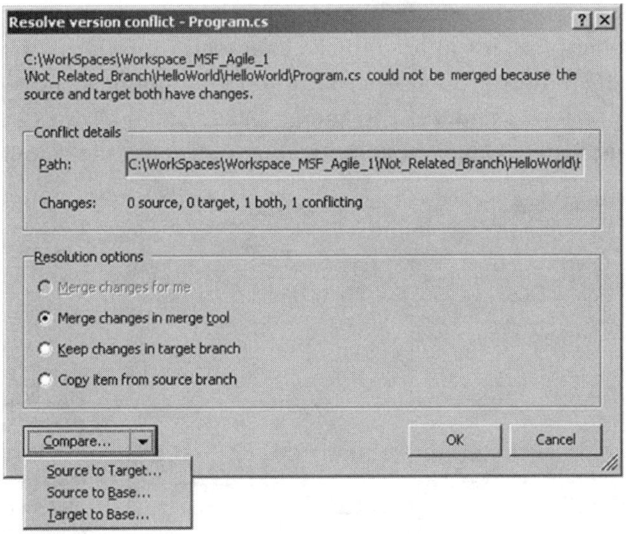

Figure 6.10   You can compare the source and target files with each other as well as with the base version.

the final merged contents of the file. You can right-click the elevated patches in the top panes and make appropriate choices (see figure 6.11) or type text directly in the bottom pane.

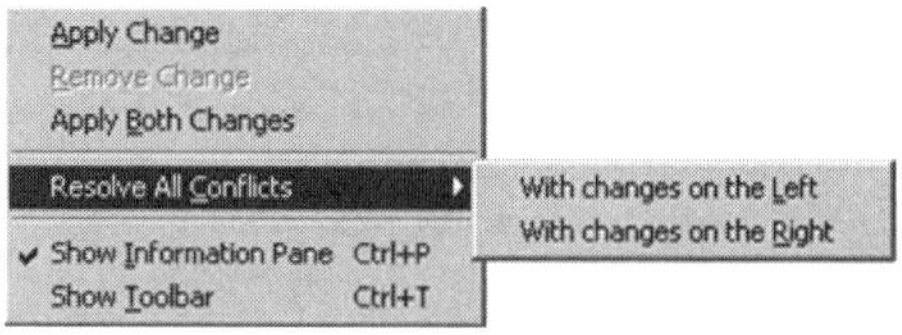

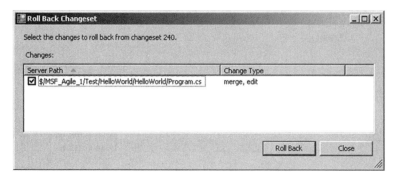

Figure 6.11   In the merge screen, you can right-click on the elevated areas of the top panes and choose various resolution options.

6.6   *Rolling back a merge*

After a successful merge, you may decide to undo the merge operation for various reasons—perhaps the merge destabilized the codebase, or you merged an incorrect changeset, and so on. In such cases, you can use TFS Power Tools to roll back the merge by typing the following at the command prompt:

```
tfpt rollback /changeset:<changeset_number_to_roll_back>
```

The `rollback` command displays a Roll Back Changeset dialog box where you can choose the individual merge target files that you want to revert to their previous states (see figure 6.12). If the changeset being rolled back isn't the latest changeset, you may need to manually resolve the conflicts—TFS Power Tools displays a merge screen if needed. One caveat associated with the rollback process (as TFS Power Tools will also warn you) is that the merge history remains unchanged; in other words, the merge history will continue to show the changeset that you've rolled back, potentially causing confusion later on. The implications include difficulties when trying to remerge the changesets (a fix is discussed next), as well as potentially misleading branch/merge reports. The good news is that the rollback shows up as an edit in the file's change history—alerting you to the fact that the file was changed after the merge operation.

A potential problem arises if a merge contains multiple changesets from the source branch and you roll back the merge operation. After the merge is rolled back, all changesets that went into the merge are undone. At this point, if you try to remerge the latest version from the source branch, TFVC will report that there are no changes to merge. Furthermore, if you try to pick changesets from the source branch and merge them to the target branch—perhaps you've identified the offending changeset(s) merged previously and want to merge back the good ones—you'll be unable to do so from the Source Control Explorer. You need to use the command-line

Figure 6.12   TFS Power Tools allows you to select the individual merged files to roll back.

interface to remerge changesets that have been rolled back. Let's walk through a representative example.

Right-click a branch or a file that you want to merge and select Merge from the context menu. In the first screen of the Source Control Merge Wizard, select Selected Changesets as the source changes to merge. In the second screen of the wizard, you'll see a list of available changesets (see figure 6.13). Note that changesets 241 and 243 are available for merging. Select both changesets and click Finish. The changesets will be merged into the target branch in changeset 244.

Let's assume that you discovered a problem with a merge operation—it destabilized your codebase. Consequently, you need to undo the merge. As discussed previously, use TFS Power Tools to roll back the merge as follows (remember, the changeset that contains the merge is numbered 244):

```
tfpt rollback /changeset:244
```

Let's assume that after troubleshooting, you found that the problem was in changeset 243, which destabilized the target codebase. Consequently, you want to remerge the changeset (number 241 in our example) and skip the offending changeset (number 243 in our example). If you try to repeat the merge operation from the Source Control Explorer, TFVC will inform you that there are no outstanding source changesets to merge. To remerge the source changesets, type the following at the command prompt:

```
tf merge /force /version:C241 <source_branch> <target_branch> /recursive
```

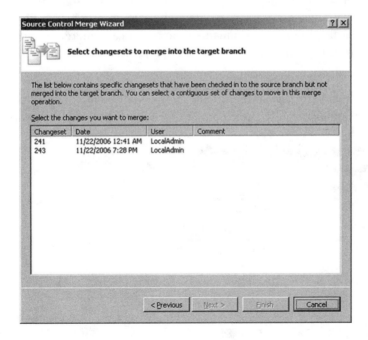

Figure 6.13 The merge wizard allows you to pick the changesets to merge.

6.7   *Understanding baseless merges*

If you ever need to merge changes between two branches that don't have a direct parent-child relationship, you need to understand the concept of *baseless merges*. A baseless merge is needed when TFVC can't find a base—a common ancestral point of consistency—between two branches. Baseless merges can't be performed from the Source Control Explorer. From the Source Control Explorer, you can only merge between branches that have direct parent-child relationships. Once you execute a baseless merge, TFVC establishes a merge history between the branches; subsequent merges between those branches can be normal merges. But the Source Control Explorer still doesn't let you merge between branches that have a merge history established by a baseless merge. You need to use the `tf merge` command to merge these branches normally (after you've created a merge history via a baseless merge).

To run a baseless merge, type the following at the command prompt:

```
tf merge <path_to_source_branch> <path_to_target_branch>
/recursive /baseless
```

The `tf merge /baseless` command displays the Resolve Conflicts dialog box, showing a version conflict for every file involved (see figure 6.14). Namespace operations such as add, delete, and rename aren't pended during a baseless merge, since TFVC can't do a direct comparison between the source and target files. Due to a bug in the Resolve Conflicts screen, the auto merge feature doesn't work as expected. If you click Auto Merge All in the Resolve Conflicts dialog box, the screen still displays the files that can be merged automatically. This is a major problem in large projects, since you'll be forced to unnecessarily inspect potentially a huge number of files. Fortunately, you can use the following command to automatically merge identical files, after the changes have been pended by the `tf merge /baseless` command:

```
tf resolve /auto:acceptmerge
```

This command will only display conflicts that can't be resolved automatically. Use the merge screen to manually resolve these conflicts (see figure 6.15). By comparing the

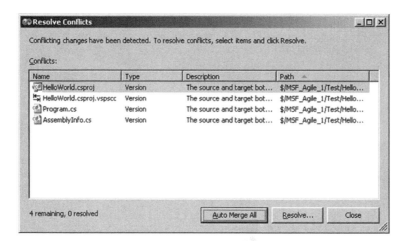

Figure 6.14   A baseless merge shows conflicts for every file.

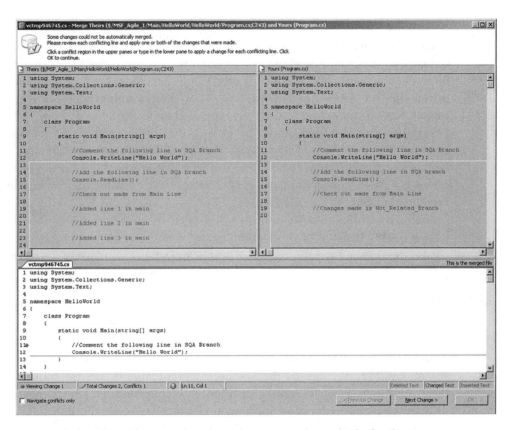

Figure 6.15   Conflicts detected during a baseless merge can be resolved using the merge screen.

source or target version with the base version, you'll realize that the base is actually the first changeset associated with the source branch. Since there's no branch or merge history between the two branches, in order to find a base version during a baseless merge, TFVC goes back to the root of the source branch and refers to it as the base.

What happens if you try to do a baseless merge between two branches that have a direct parent-child relationship? Does it take the last point of consistency (the last source changeset version that was branched or merged with the target) between the two branches or does it go all the way back to the root of the source branch? As it turns out, TFVC chooses the root of the source branch (the first changeset in the source branch) as the base version if you do a baseless merge between parent-child branches.

At this point, we've reviewed some common merge operations. We now switch gears and discuss another real-life problem that arises when working with any source code management system—how to get notified when someone modifies and commits a file that you're currently working on.

6.8   *Notifying developers about concurrent changes*

A common scenario when working in a large team is that other people might change the files you're working on. Imagine three people checking out a file—the file is checked out to them concurrently. If one person makes a change and checks in the file, the other two have no idea that their working copies are now stale. Depending on the extent and nature of the changes, the longer they wait before integrating everybody's changes, the greater the difficulty. It would be best to be aware of the concurrent changes as soon as possible, so that conflict resolution can be initiated without delay. By default, this isn't possible in TFVC. In this section, we create a custom application to notify developers if the files they're working with become outdated.

In order to design a solution, we first need to understand how the TFS event engine works. Armed with this knowledge, we create a custom web service to receive check-in events and to send emails to developers who've concurrently checked out a particular file.

6.8.1   *The TFS event engine*

In order to detect check-ins, we need to leverage the capabilities of the event engine built in to TFS. The TFS event engine is based on an extensible publisher-subscriber model. Various tools (for example, the work item tracking system, the version control system, and so forth) register their respective event types in TFS. Subscribers register their interests in selected events using a loosely coupled model. The TFS event engine delivers the events to the subscribers via emails or SOAP method calls.

You can view the events registered by the version control system by invoking the `GetRegistrationEntries` method of the TFS registration service (Registration.asmx). By default, the test page can only be viewed on the application tier machine. Invoke the `GetRegistrationEntries` method specifying `VersionControl` as the tool ID, as shown in figure 6.16 (or leave the tool ID blank to view the registration entries associated with all tools in TFS). Figure 6.17 shows the output of this method call. Note that there's an event named `CheckinEvent` defined by the version control system; you can also see the schema associated with the event. This is the event we plan to trap in order to monitor the check-ins that take place in TFVC.

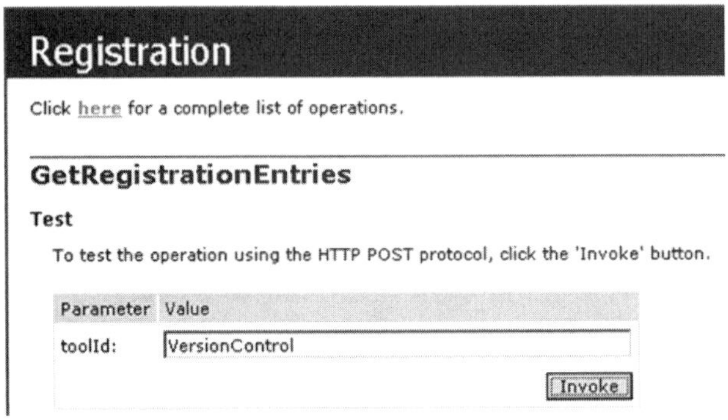

Figure 6.16   Invoke the `GetRegistrationEntries` method with the tool ID for the version control system to view the associated registration properties.

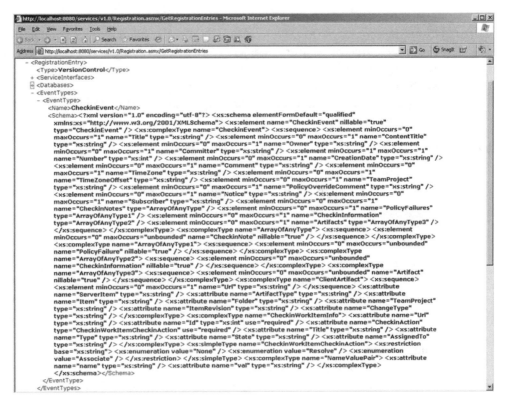

Figure 6.17   The schema associated with the `CheckinEvent`

Tools raise events by calling the `FireAsyncEvent` or `FireBulkAsyncEvents` method of the event service (EventService.asmx). The event service exposes various methods for raising events as well as subscribing to them (see figure 6.18). The event service is a wrapper around the `Microsoft.TeamFoundation.Server.Event` class located in the Microsoft.TeamFoundation.Server.dll assembly.

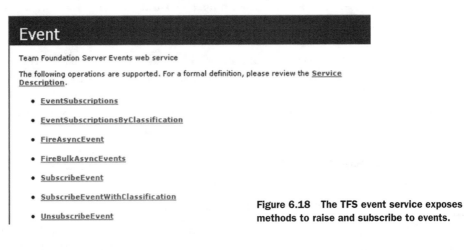

Figure 6.18   The TFS event service exposes methods to raise and subscribe to events.

To subscribe to TFS events, you can programmatically call the `SubscribeEvent` or `SubscribeEventWithClassification` method of the event service. (Don't call the TFS web services directly; use the TFS object model.) Alternatively, you can use the BisSubscribe.exe utility. Internally, BisSubscribe invokes the `SubscribeEvent` method of the TFS event service (via the `IEventService` interface of the TFS object model).

Now that we have a basic understanding of the TFS event engine, let's learn how to create a web service to receive and process check-in events.

6.8.2   *Technical review: implementing an event receiver web service*

Begin by subscribing to `CheckinEvent`; this event is raised when a new changeset is checked in to TFVC. Use the BisSubscribe utility to subscribe to `CheckinEvent`, as follows:

```
Bissubscribe /eventType CheckinEvent /address
<checkin_notification_service_url>
/deliveryType Soap /server <your_tfs_server>
```

Replace the `<checkin_notification_service_url>` tag with the URL of the custom web service that receives the check-in events and notifies the developers who have one or more of the files (contained in the changeset) checked out. Replace the `<your_tfs_server>` tag with the name of your TFS server.

The source code for implementing the check-in notification service is displayed in listings 6.1 and 6.2. Keep in mind that the user account associated with the web service needs to have appropriate permissions to access TFS (since the web service queries TFS to get a list of users who've checked out the target files). The general technical approach is as follows:

- Parse the input parameter named `eventXml` and determine the names of the files that were checked in. This action takes place in the private method named `pGetCheckedInItems`.
- Use the `QueryPendingSets` method (of the `Microsoft.TeamFoundation.VersionControl.Client.VersionControlServer` class) to determine if there are any pending sets associated with the files that have been checked in. The pending sets represent outstanding check-outs. Obtain the list of users who own the pending sets. This action takes place in the private method named `pGetMailingList`.
- Send out emails to the list of users who own the pending sets. To create the mail body, you can use the CheckInEvent.xsl and TeamFoundation.xsl stylesheets that TFS itself uses. These files are located in the %ProgramFiles%\Microsoft Visual Studio 2008 Team Foundation Server\Web Services\Services\v1.0\Transforms folder. You can also use a custom stylesheet.

Listing 6.1   Code for check-in notification service (private methods omitted)

```
//*** using statements omitted for brevity ***

[WebService(Namespace = "http://tempuri.org/")]
```

```
[WebServiceBinding(ConformsTo = WsiProfiles.BasicProfile1_1)]
public class Service : System.Web.Services.WebService
{
    public Service ()
    {
    }

    [SoapDocumentMethod(Action =
        "http://schemas.microsoft.com/TeamFoundation/2005/06/
        Services/Notification/03/Notify", RequestNamespace =
        "http://schemas.microsoft.com/TeamFoundation/2005/
        06/Services/Notification/03")]
    [WebMethod]
    public void Notify(string eventXml, string tfsIdentityXml)
    {
        XmlDocument eventXmlDoc = new XmlDocument();        Load
        eventXmlDoc.LoadXml(eventXml);                      received XML
        XmlElement eventData = eventXmlDoc.DocumentElement;

        List<string> checkedInItems =           Extract checked-in
            this.pGetCheckedInItems(eventData);  items from XML

        string tfsUrl = this.pGetTfsUrl(tfsIdentityXml);   <-- Extract TFS URL

        List<Identity> mailingList =                        Get users who
            this.pGetMailingList(checkedInItems, tfsUrl);   have pending edits

        if (mailingList.Count != 0)
        {                                                        Create body
            string mailBody = this.pGetMailBody(eventXml);   <-- of email

            this.pSendMail(mailingList, mailBody);   <-- Send email
        }
    }
}
```

Now that we've seen the overall structure of the web service, let's review the details (see listing 6.2).

Listing 6.2 Code for check-in notification service (private methods only)

```
    /// This method sends mail to target users
    private void pSendMail(List<Identity> mailingList,
                    string mailBody)
    {
        SmtpClient client = new SmtpClient(                      Create SMTP
            ConfigurationManager.AppSettings["SMTPHost"]);       client using
        client.Port = Convert.ToInt32(                          values from
            ConfigurationManager.AppSettings["SMTPPort"]);       config file

        // Create the mail message
        using (MailMessage message = new MailMessage())
        {
            message.From = new MailAddress(
                ConfigurationManager.AppSettings[
                "MailSenderAddress"],                     Specify
                ConfigurationManager.AppSettings[         sender info
                "MailSenderName"]);
```

```
    foreach (Identity user in mailingList)
    {
        message.To.Add(new MailAddress(
        user.MailAddress, user.DisplayName));
    }
```
Specify recipient info

```
    message.Subject =
        ConfigurationManager.AppSettings[
        "MailSubject"];
```
Specify email subject

```
    message.Body =
        ConfigurationManager.AppSettings[
        "MailInitPart"] + "<br />";
    message.Body += mailBody;
```
Create body of email

```
    message.IsBodyHtml = true;

    client.Send(message);
```
⟵ Send email

```
  }
}

/// Parses received XML and converts to HTML
private string pGetMailBody(string eventXml)
{
    XslCompiledTransform xsl = new XslCompiledTransform();
    xsl.Load(Server.MapPath(
        ConfigurationManager.AppSettings["MailXSL"]));
```
Load XSL file

```
    XPathDocument xpathDocument =
        new XPathDocument(new StringReader(eventXml));

    MemoryStream stream = new MemoryStream();
    xsl.Transform(xpathDocument,
        new XmlTextWriter(stream, Encoding.UTF8));
```
Perform transformation

```
    return Encoding.UTF8.GetString(stream.ToArray());
}

/// This method determines the users who have
/// checked out file(s) that have just been checked in.
private List<Identity> pGetMailingList(
    List<string> checkedInItems, string tfsUrl)
{
    TeamFoundationServer tfs =
        new TeamFoundationServer(tfsUrl);
```
Get reference to TFS

```
    VersionControlServer vcServer
        = tfs.GetService(typeof(VersionControlServer)) as
        VersionControlServer;
```
Get reference to TFVC

```
    IGroupSecurityService gss
        = tfs.GetService(typeof(IGroupSecurityService)) as
        IGroupSecurityService;
```
Get reference to IGroupSecurityService

```
    List<Identity> mailingList = new List<Identity>();
```
⟵ Holds target users

```
    PendingSet[] pendingSets = vcServer.QueryPendingSets(

        checkedInItems.ToArray(),
        RecursionType.None, null, null);
```
Get pending sets for checked-in items

```
    foreach (PendingSet pendingSet in pendingSets)
```

```
    {
        Identity user = gss.ReadIdentity(
            SearchFactor.AccountName, pendingSet.OwnerName,
            QueryMembership.None);
        if (!mailingList.Contains(user) &&
            user.MailAddress != string.Empty)
        {
            mailingList.Add(user);
        }
    }

    return mailingList;
}

/// Parses the TeamFoundationServer(tfs) url from
/// parameter string.
private string pGetTfsUrl(string tfsIdentityXml)
{
    XmlDocument tfsXmlDoc = new XmlDocument();
    tfsXmlDoc.LoadXml(tfsIdentityXml);

    return tfsXmlDoc.DocumentElement.GetAttribute("url");
}

/// Parse eventData XmlElement to find out
/// the server path of the items that were
/// checked-in in the current Changeset
private List<string> pGetCheckedInItems(
    XmlElement eventData)                              Holds
{                                                     checked-in
    List<string> items = new List<string>();   <———   items

    XPathNavigator navigator = eventData.CreateNavigator();
    XPathNodeIterator xPathItems =
        navigator.Select("/CheckinEvent/Artifacts
        /Artifact[@ServerItem!='']/@ServerItem");

    foreach (XPathItem tempItem in xPathItems)
    {
        items.Add(tempItem.Value);
    }

    return items;
}
}
```

6.9 *Summary*

In this chapter, we learned how to determine the changes between two folders and view merge candidates, how to resolve merge conflicts, how to view merge history, how to roll back a merge, and how to perform a baseless merge. We also learned how to leverage the TFS event engine and notify developers if concurrent changes occur in the code files that they're working on.

In the next chapter, we look at how to use Team Build. After all, the ultimate goal of creating and organizing source code is to generate assemblies that can be executed in target machines. We review the high-level concepts involved in creating builds and then drill down into some specific issues.

Understanding
Team Build

7

This chapter covers

- Team Build under the hood
- Creating a source code submission service
- Distributed builds

The act of creating executable builds is the culmination of all the work that goes into the software development process. As such, this often-neglected step requires careful attention in order to deliver high-quality software to customers. Given the complexities of enterprise software—co-development by geographically distributed teams and dependencies on myriad external components, systems, and services—it's become even more important to frequently create dependable builds. Furthermore, given the availability of multiple platforms and processors (for example, 64-bit machines), the executables may need to be tweaked for target runtime environments. To create efficient and error-free builds, you also need to optimally configure the build machines with appropriate hardware, operating systems, service packs, compilers, and so on. After the build binaries are generated from the source files, a battery of build verification tests (BVTs) needs to be run to determine software quality. Builds validate the business requirements, assumptions, and expectations. From a process point of view, the automated build step needs to be an integral part of your software development methodology, not just an afterthought.

Recognizing the importance of producing reliable builds, larger organizations create dedicated build teams. Many smaller organizations also realize the importance of the build manager role and assign a full-time or part-time person to it. No matter how large or small your build team happens to be, the build team needs to have independent machines, mandates, and management. Their goal is to independently retrieve the appropriate source files (from potentially multiple source control systems in large organizations or in distributed scenarios); compile the code in the correct order (based on project dependencies) using appropriate compilers, compiler options, and versioning strategies; take remedial actions in case of exceptions; deploy the generated binaries in a test environment; run the BVTs; and take proper action in case of test failures. Depending upon your development methodology, a build could take place every time a changeset is checked into the source control system (as in continuous integration), at specified intervals, or as needed.

Team Build provides powerful tools to create an automated build process. You can create build projects using a wizard, directly from Team Explorer. Behind the scenes, Team Build generates an MSBuild project file and invokes MSBuild to perform the actual build. You can customize the build project file to override default targets and properties with your own implementation, create new targets and properties to meet your needs, or hook into the build process at various points to invoke custom logic. You can also tailor the overall build process for your unique scenario. For instance, you can create custom tasks to programmatically implement your custom logic in your favorite language. In addition to compiling the source code via MSBuild, Team Build downloads the latest files from Team Foundation version control (TFVC), labels the source files, stamps corresponding work items with the build number, produces build reports, and performs other housekeeping tasks. In this chapter, we look at selected business needs and how they can be achieved by extending Team Build. The goal is to create a build process that's automated, reliable, repeatable, and maintainable.

In chapter 2, we discussed the major Team Build–related changes in TFS 2008. In this chapter, we dive into specific build-related issues and learn how to solve them using Team Build. As such, the material is problem-specific and context-sensitive. The walkthroughs and code samples provide technical information regarding selected real-life problems. By learning how to solve such practical problems, you'll gain a deeper insight into the inner workings of Team Build. This knowledge will be helpful as you attempt to solve problems in your own organization.

This chapter doesn't provide beginner-level information on Team Build. We assume that you already know how to use Team Build and are attempting to solve specific build-related problems in the real world.

The specific issues that we discuss include stamping the generated assemblies based on a consistent numbering scheme, building from specified labels instead of the tip of a codeline, setting up a service to accept code from contributors and commit to a shared repository (after validating that the code meets certain quality criteria), building source code from multiple TFS machines, and so on. As you'll discover, some of the issues are more complex than they might appear at first glance.

In this chapter, you'll learn about the following:

- *Overview of Team Build*—You'll learn about the architecture of Team Build, the structure of the build project file, the order of target execution, and how to determine build success and failure.
- *Creating builds from labeled source files*—You may want to create builds from points other than the tip of a codeline. Being able to created builds from labeled sources is a common requirement. We discuss how to accomplish this in TFS.
- *ClickOnce deployment*—ClickOnce facilitates deployment of smart client applications by providing support for web-based delivery, automatic incremental downloads, version rollback, and code access security.
- *Creating a source code submission service*—Checking source code directly into a shared repository carries the risk of destabilizing the work of a large number of developers. We create an intermediate service that accepts source code submissions, builds the source, runs critical verification checks on the build, and finally commits the source code to the shared repository, provided the necessary quality bars are passed.
- *Desktop builds*—Desktop builds enable developers to create ad hoc local builds using the same build script that the build team uses, while minimizing interactions with TFS. Using a standard build script helps improve quality and efficiency.
- *TFS and distributed builds*—If the solution being built depends on source files that are located in multiple TFS servers, then you need to create a process for downloading sources from diverse locations and assembling them in the build machine, prior to launching the final build step. We discuss several scenarios and strategies.

In the next section, we review how build systems are typically configured depending on the size of a company.

7.1   Company types and build issues

Since there's no one-size-fits-all build process, you need to configure Team Build to suit your organizational practices. The good news is that Team Build is highly customizable. Once you understand the structure of the build script, you can modify the build file and alter its default behavior. For more advanced tasks, you can create custom tasks and perform virtually anything that can be done via custom programming.

7.1.1   Small companies

If you work for a small company, you may not have a dedicated build team in your organization. Nevertheless, you need to give selected people—development, SQA, or other teams, depending on qualifications and training—the responsibility to create public builds. These public builds are formally tested and released. Developers shouldn't be creating public builds at random or using local builds from their workstations for formal SQA or production purposes. If you create builds haphazardly, you'll eventually face the following difficulties:

- When a bug is reported, or a patch needs to be sent out, you won't be able to correlate a specific build with the corresponding source files. You'll face greater problems if the code churn has been considerable since the build was created. For servicing the release, you need to know which source files went into a specific build so you can make incremental changes.

- When you try to determine which requirements or fixes were included in which builds, you'll be lost. Human memory or disconnected artifacts don't serve efficiently when you attempt to dig up this information. This information is important when deciding which build to test and release, especially under intense deadline pressure.

- You'll find it hard to ensure that the appropriate build type was used (debug/release type or processor-specific optimizations) and that the supporting assemblies, databases, environment variables, or configuration files were chosen correctly.

7.1.2 Large companies

If you belong to a large company, you have developers checking in code from multiple locations. Some of the distributed locations may be situated in different time zones. Your main concerns in this situation are as follow:

- Ensuring that the checked-in code doesn't "break" the build in the main codeline. This means that the submitted code must not only compile but pass necessary build verification tests.

- Ensuring that the code meets the quality criteria such as adherence to coding standards, code review requirements, code coverage rate via automated unit tests, and so on.

Although some of these checks may seem redundant, they're highly recommended for large teams. Otherwise, you won't be able to maintain efficiency and quality in your software development process. For example, you wouldn't want a single check-in to break a public build and bring everybody's work to a halt. You also wouldn't want a developer to unwittingly introduce grave errors—destabilizing not only his particular component but also other dependant pieces of the software. In such cases, the offending check-in should be detected "at the gate" and prevented from making its way into the main codeline. TFS makes this possible with a little custom programming.

7.1.3 Large companies with distributed TFS

If you have multiple TFS servers deployed in your organization (perhaps connected via a WAN link), you need to think about the location of the build machines in relation to the TFS application-tier machines. Should the build machines be local (connected to the corresponding application-tier machines via a LAN) or remote (connected to the corresponding application-tier machines via a WAN)? What kind of bandwidth exists between the TFS application-tier machines and the build machines? Is the connection over VPN or simple Internet? Do you have proxy servers installed in distributed locations? Since there's no one-size-fits-all solution, you need to consider the pros and cons associated with each configuration. In this chapter, we look at the factors that'll be part of your decision-making process.

7.2   *An overview of Team Build*

Team Build is a collection of distributed components and services that facilitate creating public builds. Before Team Build was released, many developers created local builds using Visual Studio and shipped the output binaries to customers. Although a number of third-party products were available for creating public builds, many companies either weren't aware of the concept or found it difficult to integrate yet another disparate product into the development lifecycle.

Team Build enables you to create public builds from Visual Studio (via Team Explorer). Using a wizard-driven interface, you can create build scripts to download source code from TFVC into a build machine, compile the code, run build verification tests, perform static code analysis, gather code coverage information, and associate relevant work items with the build. You can also label the source tree to indicate which files were included in the build, copy the assemblies to a drop location, create a new work item in case of build failure, create build reports, generate build notifications, and so on.

7.2.1   *Architecture*

Team Build is based on a distributed architecture, as shown in figure 7.1. The client tier includes Team Explorer (the build types are located under the Team Build node)

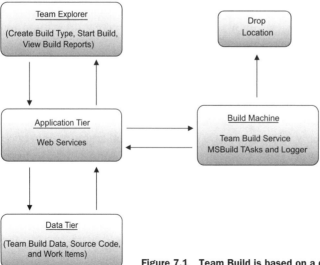

Figure 7.1   Team Build is based on a distributed architecture.

and a command-line utility (TfsBuild.exe). The application tier consists of a number of web services that enable the client tier (or custom programs) to start, stop, and delete builds as well as perform other build-related functions. The application tier communicates with a Windows service (the Team Build service) located in a build machine. The Team Build service executes the build scripts using MSBuild. The data tier stores build-related information in relational tables and also makes the data available for reporting purposes via an analytical database (the Team System cube).

7.2.2 The build project file

When you create a new Team Build type from Team Explorer, Team Build creates an XML-based build project file named TFSBuild.proj. (In TFS 2008, some build settings are stored in the database instead of the TFSBuild.proj file.) The TFSBuild.proj file conforms to the MSBuild schema. The MSBuild schema file is named Microsoft.Build.xsd and is located in %FrameworkDir%; it includes the %FrameworkDir%\MSBuild\Microsoft.Build.Commontypes.xsd file, which in turn includes the %FrameworkDir%\MSBuild\Microsoft.Build.Core.xsd file. Review the MSBuild schema files to understand how properties, items, tasks, and targets are constructed in MSBuild.

The TFSBuild.proj file imports the Microsoft.TeamFoundation.Build.targets file (located in %ProgramFiles%\MSBuild\Microsoft\VisualStudio\v8.0\TeamBuild directory for TFS 2005 or %ProgramFiles%\MSBuild\Microsoft\VisualStudio\TeamBuild directory for TFS 2008). The targets defined in the Microsoft.TeamFoundation.Build.targets file orchestrate the build process. A target represents a collection of tasks.

7.2.3 Target execution order

The first target that's executed in the Microsoft.TeamFoundation.Build.targets file is called EndToEndIteration. But the EndToEndIteration target itself doesn't contain any tasks—it invokes other targets using the DependsOnTargets attribute. Before a target is run, the dependencies specified in the target's DependsOnTargets attribute are executed. The dependencies of the EndToEndIteration target are specified in the EndToEndIterationDependsOn property (see listing 7.1 for TFS 2005 and listing 7.2 for TFS 2008). The targets defined in EndToEndIterationDependsOn in turn have their own dependencies—creating a nested dependency structure.

Listing 7.1 The entry point and target execution sequence in TFS 2005

```
<PropertyGroup>
 <EndToEndIterationDependsOn>
  BeforeEndToEndIteration;
  BuildNumberOverrideTarget;
  InitializeEndToEndIteration;
  Clean;
  TeamBuild;
  DropBuild;
  AfterEndToEndIteration;
 </EndToEndIterationDependsOn>
</PropertyGroup>
```

```
<!-- Entry point: this target is invoked on the build machine
 by the build agent -->
<Target Name="EndToEndIteration"
       Condition=" '$(IsDesktopBuild)'!='true' "
       DependsOnTargets="$(EndToEndIterationDependsOn)" />
```

Listing 7.2 The entry point and target execution sequence in TFS 2008

```
<PropertyGroup>
 <EndToEndIterationDependsOn>
  CheckSettingsForEndToEndIteration;
  InitializeBuildProperties;
  BeforeEndToEndIteration;
  BuildNumberOverrideTarget;
  InitializeEndToEndIteration;
  InitializeWorkspace;
  TeamBuild;
  DropBuild;
  AfterEndToEndIteration;
 </EndToEndIterationDependsOn>
</PropertyGroup>
<!-- Entry point: this target is invoked on the build machine
 by the build agent -->
<Target Name="EndToEndIteration"
       Condition=" '$(IsDesktopBuild)'!='true' "
       DependsOnTargets="$(EndToEndIterationDependsOn)" />
```

At runtime, the targets are invoked according to the order of their dependencies. Assuming a build is successful, the targets in the Microsoft.TeamFoundation.Build.targets file are executed in the order specified in listing 7.3 for TFS 2005, or listings 7.4 and 7.5 for TFS 2008. Notice that the execution sequence varies depending upon the value of the CleanCompilationOutputOnly property. If this property is true, only the output assemblies are deleted, leaving the source files intact. If this property is false, the source files as well as the output assemblies are deleted. However, do not modify the CleanCompilationOutputOnly property directly—use IncrementalGet and IncrementalBuild properties to control what gets deleted during the build process.

Listing 7.3 Target execution order for a successful build in TFS 2005

```
 1.  BeforeEndToEndIteration
 2.  BuildNumberOverrideTarget
 3.  InitializeEndToEndIteration
 4.  BeforeClean
 5.  CoreClean
 6.  AfterClean
 7.  Clean
 8.  InitializeBuild
 9.  InitializeWorkspace
10.  BeforeGet
11.  CoreGet
12.  AfterGet
13.  BeforeLabel
14.  CoreLabel
15.  AfterLabel
```

```
16.  PreBuild
17.  BeforeCompile
18.  CoreCompile
19.  AfterCompile
20.  Compile
21.  GetChangeSetsAndUpdateWorkItems
22.  PostBuild
23.  BeforeTest
24.  CoreTest
25.  AfterTest
26.  Test
27.  PackageBinaries
28.  TeamBuild
29.  BeforeDropBuild
30.  CoreDropBuild
31.  CopyLogFiles
32.  AfterDropBuild
33.  DropBuild
34.  AfterEndToEndIteration
35.  EndToEndIteration
```

Listing 7.4   Target execution order for TFS 2008 (CleanCompilationOutputOnly != true)

```
1.   CheckSettingsForEndToEndIteration
2.   InitializeBuildProperties
3.   BeforeEndToEndIteration
4.   BuildNumberOverrideTarget
5.   InitializeEndToEndIteration
6.   BeforeInitializeWorkspace
7.   CoreInitializeWorkspace
8.   AfterInitializeWorkspace
9.   BeforeClean
10.  CoreCleanAll
11.  AfterClean
12.  InitializeBuild
13.  BeforeGet
14.  CoreGet
15.  AfterGet
16.  BeforeLabel
17.  CoreLabel
18.  AfterLabel
19.  BeforeCompile
20.  ComputeConfigurationList
21.  CoreCompile
22.  BeforeCompileConfiguration
23.  ResolveSolutionPathsForEndToEndIteration
24.  CoreCompileConfiguration
25.  BeforeCompileSolution
26.  CoreCompileSolution
27.  AfterCompileSolution
28.  AfterCompileConfiguration
29.  AfterCompile
30.  BeforeGetChangesetsAndUpdateWorkItems
31.  CoreGetChangesetsAndUpdateWorkItems
32.  AfterGetChangesetsAndUpdateWorkItems
33.  BeforeTest
```

```
34. CoreTest
35. RunTest
36. BeforeTestConfiguration
37. ResolveTestFilesForEndToEndIteration
38. CoreTestConfiguration
39. AfterTestConfiguration
40. AfterTest
41. GenerateDocumentation
42. PackageBinaries
43. BeforeDropBuild
44. CoreDropBuild
45. AfterDropBuild
46. AfterEndToEndIteration
```

Listing 7.5   Target execution order for TFS 2008 (CleanCompilationOutputOnly == true)

```
1.  CheckSettingsForEndToEndIteration
2.  InitializeBuildProperties
3.  BeforeEndToEndIteration
4.  BuildNumberOverrideTarget
5.  InitializeEndToEndIteration
6.  BeforeInitializeWorkspace
7.  CoreInitializeWorkspace
8.  AfterInitializeWorkspace
9.  InitializeBuild
10. BeforeGet
11. CoreGet
12. AfterGet
13. BeforeLabel
14. CoreLabel
15. AfterLabel
16. BeforeClean
17. ComputeConfigurationList
18. CoreCleanCompilationOutput
19. ResolveSolutionPathsForEndToEndIteration
20. AfterClean
21. BeforeCompile
22. CoreCompile
23. BeforeCompileConfiguration
24. CoreCompileConfiguration
25. BeforeCompileSolution
26. CoreCompileSolution
27. AfterCompileSolution
28. AfterCompileConfiguration
29. AfterCompile
30. BeforeGetChangesetsAndUpdateWorkItems
31. CoreGetChangesetsAndUpdateWorkItems
32. AfterGetChangesetsAndUpdateWorkItems
33. BeforeTest
34. CoreTest
35. RunTest
36. BeforeTestConfiguration
37. ResolveTestFilesForEndToEndIteration
38. CoreTestConfiguration
39. AfterTestConfiguration
40. AfterTest
```

```
41. GenerateDocumentation
42. PackageBinaries
43. BeforeDropBuild
44. CoreDropBuild
45. AfterDropBuild
46. AfterEndToEndIteration
```

In case of a build failure due to compilation error, the target execution order is the same until the `CoreCompile` target is executed. After that point, the target execution order changes (see listing 7.6 for TFS 2005 and listing 7.7 for TFS 2008).

Listing 7.6   Target execution order for a failed build in TFS 2005

```
1.  BeforeEndToEndIteration
2.  BuildNumberOverrideTarget
3.  InitializeEndToEndIteration
4.  BeforeClean
5.  CoreClean
6.  AfterClean
7.  Clean
8.  InitializeBuild
9.  BeforeGet
10. BeforeLabel
11. Label
12. AfterLabel
13. InitializeWorkspace
14. CoreGet
15. AfterGet
16. PreBuild
17. BeforeCompile
18. CoreCompile
19. BeforeOnBuildBreak
20. GetChangeSetsOnBuildBreak
21. BeforeDropBuild
22. CoreDropBuild
23. CopyLogFiles
24. AfterDropBuild
25. DropBuild
26. CreateWorkItem
27. AfterOnBuildBreak
28. OnBuildBreak
```

Listing 7.7   Target execution order for a failed build in TFS 2008

```
1.  CheckSettingsForEndToEndIteration
2.  InitializeBuildProperties
3.  BeforeEndToEndIteration
4.  BuildNumberOverrideTarget
5.  InitializeEndToEndIteration
6.  BeforeInitializeWorkspace
7.  CoreInitializeWorkspace
8.  AfterInitializeWorkspace
9.  BeforeClean
10. CoreCleanAll
11. AfterClean
12. InitializeBuild
```

```
13. BeforeGet
14. CoreGet
15. AfterGet
16. BeforeLabel
17. CoreLabel
18. AfterLabel
19. BeforeCompile
20. ComputeConfigurationList
21. CoreCompile
22. BeforeCompileConfiguration
23. ResolveSolutionPathsForEndToEndIteration
24. CoreCompileConfiguration
25. BeforeCompileSolution
26. CoreCompileSolution
27. SetBuildBreakProperties
28. BeforeOnBuildBreak
29. BeforeGetChangesetsOnBuildBreak
30. CoreGetChangesetsOnBuildBreak
31. AfterGetChangesetsOnBuildBreak
32. BeforeDropBuild
33. CoreDropBuild
34. AfterDropBuild
35. BeforeCreateWorkItem
36. CoreCreateWorkItem
37. AfterCreateWorkItem
38. CoreOnBuildBreak
39. AfterOnBuildBreak
```

7.2.4   *Customizing targets*

You can customize the predefined targets (as well as add custom targets) to configure
the build process to suit your needs. To learn about the targets that may be overridden
in the build script, refer to http://msdn2.microsoft.com/en-us/library/aa337604
(VS.80).aspx for TFS 2005 and http://msdn2.microsoft.com/en-us/library/aa337604.
aspx for TFS 2008. TFS 2008 offers more customizable targets compared to TFS 2005.

You can also customize the properties defined in the build script. To learn about the
properties that may be overridden, refer to http://msdn2.microsoft.com/en-us/
library/ aa337598(VS.80).aspx for TFS 2005 and http://msdn2.microsoft.com/
en-us/library/aa337598.aspx for TFS 2008. Moreover, you can create new custom properties. The values of the custom properties can be assigned directly or derived from
other elements in the build project file. The values can also be passed externally at runtime in one of two ways:

- *Using environment variables*—Environment variables that are available to the
  Team Build service account (the account under which the Team Build service
  runs) are also available for you to use in the build project file. If you define a
  new environment variable, restart the Team Build service in order for the variable to be available in the build project file. Environment variables appear as
  properties in the build script.

- *Using the MSBuild response file*—You can set the values for your custom variables by
  using /p:<variable name>=<variable value> notation in the TFSBuild.rsp file.

7.2.5 *Detecting the reason for build failure*

In TFS 2005, there's no out-of-the-box property available in the build script to indicate whether a build failed due to a compilation problem or due to a BVT failure.

To determine the compilation status in TFS 2005, you can create a custom property in the `AfterCompile` target (see listing 7.8); the `AfterCompile` target is executed only if source files were compiled successfully.

Listing 7.8 Custom property to indicate compilation status in TFS 2005

```
<Target Name="AfterCompile">
  <CreateProperty Value="true">
    <Output TaskParameter="value"
        PropertyName="CompilationSuccessful" />
  </CreateProperty>
</Target>
```

To determine the compilation status in TFS 2008, you can use the `BuildBreak` property defined in the Microsoft.TeamFoundation.Build.targets file. This property is set to `true` (in the `SetBuildBreakProperties` target) if compilation fails. If compilation fails, execution jumps first to the `SetBuildBreakProperties` target and then on to the `OnBuildBreak` target. The `AfterCompile` target isn't executed if compilation fails.

To determine the BVT status in TFS 2005, you can create a custom task to detect whether the tests were successful. Based on the output of the custom task, you can ascertain the reason for build failure—if all BVTs passed and the build still failed, it must be due to a compilation error. The custom task to detect test status can be placed in the `AfterTest` target. The `AfterTest` target is executed only if there are no compilation errors.

To determine the BVT status in TFS 2008, you can customize the build script and simply use the built-in `TestSuccess` property (see listing 7.9). The `TestSuccess` property is set by Team Build in the `CoreTest` target.

Listing 7.9 Obtaining BVT status in TFS 2008 using a built-in property

```
<Target Name="AfterTest">
  <GetBuildProperties
    TeamFoundationServerUrl="$(TeamFoundationServerUrl)"
    BuildUri="$(BuildUri)">
    <Output TaskParameter="TestSuccess" PropertyName="TestSuccess" />
  </GetBuildProperties>
</Target>
```

TFS 2008 introduces a new build result named *Partially Succeeded*. A build is marked Partially Succeeded if compilation is successful but one or more BVTs fail (or some other kind of failure occurs). If both compilation and BVTs are successful, the build is marked *Succeeded*.

7.2.6 *Build directories*

At runtime, Team Build downloads the source code files from TFVC and builds the specified solution(s). During this process, a number of subfolders are created under the root folder specified in the `BuildDirectory-Path` property in the build project file (see figure 7.2).

In TFS 2005, the root build directory can also be specified from the Build *<Team_Project_Name>* dialog box when a build is started from Team Explorer. In TFS 2008, the build directory is a property associated with a build agent and can't be specified when queuing a new build.

The subfolders that are created are as follow:

Figure 7.2   A sample directory structure created by Team Build for compiling the source code

- *<root_build_directory>\<team_project_name>\<build_type>\Sources in TFS 2005 and $(Temp)\<team_project_name>\<build_definition>\Sources in TFS 2008*—Contains the downloaded source files from TFVC. This directory name is available in the `SolutionRoot` property (defined in the Microsoft.TeamFoundation.Build.targets file). The solution file being built is placed in a subdirectory under this directory. The name of the solution file is defined in the TFSBuild.proj file and is available in the `SolutionToBuild` item. The `SolutionToBuild` item can contain one or more solutions to be built.

- *<root_build_directory>\<team_project_name>\<build_type>\BuildType in TFS 2005 and $(Temp)\<team_project_name>\<build_definition>\BuildType in TFS 2008*—Contains the downloaded build project file (TFSBuild.proj), MSBuild response file (TFSBuild.rsp), and workspace mapping file (WorkspaceMapping.xml). The workspace mapping file is present in TFS 2005 only. This directory name is available in the `MSBuildProjectDirectory` property (predefined).

- *<root_build_directory>\<team_project_name>\<build_type>\Binaries in TFS 2005 and $(Temp)\<team_project_name>\<build_definition>\Binaries in TFS 2008*—Contains the assemblies generated by the build process. If your solution contains multiple projects, the output binaries of all projects are placed in this directory. This directory name is available in the `BinariesRoot` property (defined in the Microsoft.TeamFoundation.Build.targets file). But the assemblies aren't directly placed in this directory; they're placed in a subdirectory. The name of the subdirectory depends on the platform—`%(ConfigurationToBuild.PlatformToBuild)`—and flavor—`%(ConfigurationToBuild.FlavorToBuild)`—specified in the TFSBuild.proj file. By convention, if the platform isn't "Any CPU," then the actual output directory is `$(BinariesRoot)\%(ConfigurationToBuild.PlatformToBuild)\%(ConfigurationToBuild.FlavorToBuild)`. If the platform is "Any CPU," then the actual output directory is `$(BinariesRoot)\%(ConfigurationToBuild.FlavorToBuild)`. In either case, the full name of the output directory is available in the `OutDir` property (defined in the Microsoft.TeamFoundation.Build.targets file).

When specifying the build directory, if you have deeply nested files with long file-names, be careful to avoid the 260-character limit for fully qualified file names in Windows. For more information, refer to http://msdn.microsoft.com/en-us/library/aa365247.aspx. In chapter 2, we talked about how to configure build directories associated with build agents to stay under this limit.

After compilation, the output binaries (and the build log file) are copied to a subdirectory under the drop location specified (in the DropLocation property) in the build project file. In TFS 2008, the drop location is a property of the build definition and is stored in the database. The drop location can also be specified when queuing a new build in TFS 2008. The name of the subdirectory is generated from the current build number. The full drop directory can be derived from $(DropLocation)\ $(BuildNumber). This is why if you have multiple build types with potentially the same build numbers, you should either create a build numbering convention to avoid potential conflicts (for example, prefix the build numbers with the build types) or create a separate folder for each build type.

It's worthwhile to note that some output assemblies may be placed in the drop location even if the compilation fails. This is because the target responsible for copying the binaries to the drop location (the CoreDropBuild target and the Copy task contained therein) is executed even if there are compilation errors. Consequently, the binaries generated during the build process (which could be an incomplete set in the event of a compilation failure in a solution containing multiple projects) are placed in the drop location.

7.2.7 *Coupling between TFS and build machines*

A build machine accepts build requests from a single TFS application-tier machine only. You can configure the machine name using the registry or the TFSBuildService.exe.config file. If using the registry, modify the AllowedTeamServer attribute at the following registry entry for TFS 2005 (see figure 7.3):

```
HKEY_USERS\<build_service_account_id>\Software\Microsoft\
VisualStudio\8.0\TeamBuild
```

For 2008, the registry entry (for the Team Build service account) is

```
HKCU\Software\Microsoft\VisualStudio\9.0\TeamBuild
```

You can also open the TFSBuildService.exe.config file and edit the AllowedTeam-Server key (this is the recommended approach). This file is located in the %Program Files%\Microsoft Visual Studio 9.0\Common7\IDE\PrivateAssemblies folder.

Whether you modify the registry entry or the configuration file (the value in the .config file overwrites the value in the registry), keep in mind that a build machine can accept build requests from a single TFS server, although a TFS server machine can execute builds on multiple build machines.

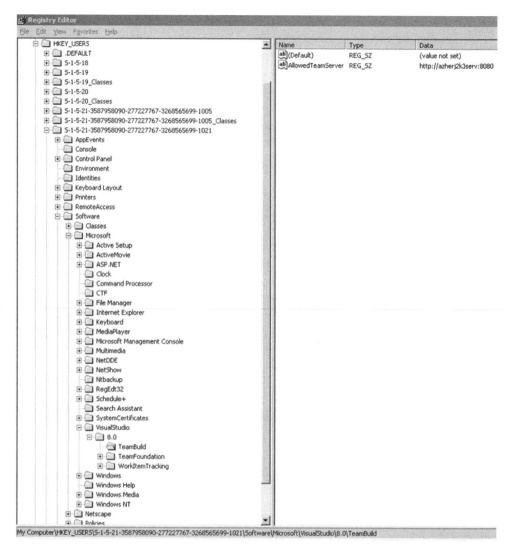

Figure 7.3   Modify the `AllowedTeamServer` attribute to specify a new Team Foundation Server binding for a build machine.

7.2.8   *Associating changesets and related work items*

If a build succeeds, Team Build invokes the `GetChangeSetsAndUpdateWorkItems` target to obtain the list of associated changesets and optionally update the `Microsoft.VSTS.Build.IntegrationBuild` field in the related work items with the successful build number. The work items are only updated if the `UpdateAssociatedWorkItems` property is set to `true` in the build project file (by default, the property is set to `true`). On the other hand, if a build fails, Team Build invokes the `GetChangeSetsOnBuildBreak` target to fetch the list of associated changesets, but the related work items aren't updated.

Instead, Team Build executes the `CreateWorkItem` target to create a new work item indicating build failure. (The default work item type is Bug; this can be changed by modifying the `WorkItemType` property in the TFSBuild.proj file.) The `Microsoft.VSTS.Build.FoundIn` field of the new work item is set to the failed build number.

Both the `GetChangeSetsAndUpdateWorkItems` target and the `GetChangeSetsOnBuildBreak` target execute the `GenCheckinNotesUpdateWorkItems` task to obtain the list of associated changesets and optionally update the related work items. The algorithm for this task is as follows:

1 Analyze the labels associated with the last successful build (of the same build type) and the current build to determine which changesets occurred after the previous label, up through and including the current label.

2 For each changeset, determine the related work items.

In TFS 2005, if there are no previous successful builds of the current build type, then all outstanding changesets are associated with the current build. In TFS 2008, this logic has been modified; if there are no previous successful builds of the current build type, then no changesets are associated with the current build.

Due to the complex logic required to determine the associated changesets, the `GenCheckinNotesUpdateWorkItems` task could potentially become expensive if a lot of changesets are involved. You can bypass the `GenCheckinNotesUpdateWorkItems` task by setting `SkipPostBuild` to `true` in the TFSBuild.proj file.

You can cut down the number of associated changesets (and related work items) by modifying the workspace mapping information so that only the required TFVC folders (corresponding to the solutions being built) are mapped. To do so, edit the WorkspaceMapping.xml file in TFS 2005, or use the Workspace tab in the Build Definition dialog box in TFS 2008. Alternatively, you can customize the build script and narrow the scope of the labels so that only the files that are needed for the build get included in the labels.

In TFS 2008, the workspace mapping information can be edited from the user interface, simplifying its maintenance. In TFS 2005, you need to edit it manually. There's no published schema for the WorkspaceMapping.xml file and its structure can be confusing. The rules for editing the WorkspaceMapping.xml file are as follow (reproduced from Buck Hodges's blog with permission):

- The `ServerItem` should be a valid server path.
- The server paths must all be in the same team project.
- A server path can either be mapped or cloaked.
- The local path for a mapped server item (specified via `LocalItem`) needs to be a legal local path, but is otherwise completely ignored.
- Don't specify local paths for cloaked mappings.
- All cloaked paths must be children of mapped paths. Cloaking is just a means of avoiding getting parts of an otherwise mapped tree.

7.3   *Creating builds from labeled source files*

By default, Team Build fetches the latest version of the source code files from TFVC. But for various reasons, you may need to build sources from labeled points in the codeline other than the tip. For example, if your codebase has an active mainline, the developers may label the set of files that need to go into a particular build. After labeling, they continue to work in the same branch. Another reason to do this would be to reproduce a previous build. In both cases, you need to build based on a label, although the techniques may be different. In this section, we look at both scenarios.

7.3.1   *Creating a new build from a label*

Before getting into the details of the required changes, let's review how Team Build downloads the source code files by default. The CoreGet target defined in the Microsoft.TeamFoundation.Build.Targets file is responsible for fetching the source files from TFVC. The CoreGet target executes the Get task. The Get task has an attribute named Version; by default, the value of this attribute is T (for *Tip*), which causes the Get task to download the latest source files. The Version attribute can also take a label name, among other options. (Other choices include fetching source files based on a changeset number, a specific date, or a workspace version.) When specifying a label with the Version attribute, the label name needs to be prefixed with an L.

The procedure for downloading files based on a label varies depending on whether you're using TFS 2005 or TFS 2008. For TFS 2005, in the TFSBuild.proj file, set the Skip-Get property to true and override the AfterGet target as shown in listing 7.10.

Listing 7.10   Downloading source code based on a label in TFS 2005

```
<PropertyGroup>

   <BuildFromLabelNumber>
      Label_Ready_for_Release_2.0.0.0
   </BuildFromLabelNumber>

   <SkipGet>true</SkipGet>

</PropertyGroup>

<Target Name="AfterGet"
   Condition=" '$(IsDesktopBuild)'!='true'">

   <Get
      Condition=" '$(BuildFromLabelNumber)'!='' "
      Workspace="$(WorkspaceName)"
      Recursive="$(RecursiveGet)"
      Version="L$(BuildFromLabelNumber)"
      Force="$(ForceGet)" />
</Target>
```

For TFS 2008, in the TFSBuild.proj file, simply set the GetVersion property to the label name, as shown in listing 7.11. No need to override any targets.

Listing 7.11 Downloading source code based on a label in TFS 2008

```
<PropertyGroup>

  <BuildFromLabelNumber>
    Label_Ready_for_Release_2.0.0.0
  </BuildFromLabelNumber>

  <GetVersion>L$(BuildFromLabelNumber)</GetVersion>

</PropertyGroup>
```

7.3.2 *Reproducing a previous build from a label*

You may need to reproduce a previous build for a variety of reasons. For example, maybe you received a bug report from a client concerning a previous version and you can't locate the binaries generated earlier. Or you might need to create a new build, based on old files, in order to reproduce a reported bug in an old release. Alternatively, you may suspect that a previous build was somehow incorrect (perhaps it used an incorrect satellite assembly version) and need to create a new set of build binaries.

When reproducing a previous build, you may want to stamp the binaries with a new build number or reuse an old build number. Your choice will depend on the circumstances associated with reproducing the build. For example, perhaps you lost the previous assemblies that were shipped (maybe due to hardware failure), and now want to send the same assemblies (bearing the same build number) to another client. In this case, do you want to create a new build and execute the associated actions such as creating a new label for the source files, updating the associated work items, creating new work items in case of build failure, and so on? Or would you rather just compile the previously labeled code, run the tests, and skip the default associated actions?

If you want to create a new build and execute the default associated actions (labeling the source files, associating changesets and work items with the build), follow the process outlined in section 7.3.1. On the other hand, if you want to reproduce an old build (based on a previous label) and skip some of the default actions, set the Skip-Label and SkipPostBuild properties to true in the build script. Setting SkipLabel to true prevents Team Build from labeling the source files. (The build script will crash if you try to apply the same label name twice; remember, we're using a previous build number, and therefore, by default, we'll end up with the same label name again.) Setting SkipPostBuild to true prevents Team Build from associating changesets and work items with the build.

You can also use the AssemblyInfo task to autogenerate the build number. To do so, update a reference AsssemblyInfo.cs file with an autoincremented integer build number and copy it to the build location. The AssemblyInfo task is covered in detail in the next chapter.

Using the properties associated with the AssemblyInfo task, specify the version information. The build script for reproducing a previous build is shown in listing 7.12. In this example, the build is reproduced without labeling the source files again or associating changesets and work items with the build again. Note that we introduced a custom property named `ReproducePreviousBuild` to indicate whether we're reproducing a previous build.

Listing 7.12   Reproducing a previous build in TFS 2008

```xml
<?xml version="1.0" encoding="utf-8"?>
<Project DefaultTargets="DesktopBuild"
   xmlns="http://schemas.microsoft.com/
   developer/msbuild/2003">
   <!-- Do not edit this -->
   <Import
      Project="$(MSBuildExtensionsPath)\Microsoft\
      VisualStudio\v9.0\TeamBuild\
      Microsoft.TeamFoundation.Build.targets" />
   <Import
      Project="$(MSBuildExtensionsPath)\Microsoft\
      AssemblyInfoTask\Microsoft.VersionNumber.targets"/>
      <ProjectExtensions>
         <Description>
         </Description>
         <BuildMachine>BUILD_MACHINE_NAME</BuildMachine>
      </ProjectExtensions>
   <PropertyGroup>
      <TeamProject>TEAM_PROJECT_NAME</TeamProject>
      <BuildDirectoryPath>C:\Build</BuildDirectoryPath>
      <DropLocation>\\BUILD_MACHINE_NAME\Drop</DropLocation>
      <RunTest>false</RunTest>
      <WorkItemFieldValues>Symptom=build break;
         Steps To Reproduce=Start the build using Team Build
      </WorkItemFieldValues>
      <RunCodeAnalysis>Default</RunCodeAnalysis>
      <UpdateAssociatedWorkItems>
         true
      </UpdateAssociatedWorkItems>
      <!-- Title for the work item created on
      build failure -->
      <WorkItemTitle>Build failure in build:</WorkItemTitle>
      <!-- Description for the work item created
         on build failure -->
      <DescriptionText>
         This work item was created by Team
         Build on a build failure.
      </DescriptionText>
      <!-- Text pointing to log file location
         on build failure -->
      <BuildlogText>The build log file is at:</BuildlogText>
      <!-- Text pointing to error/warnings file location
         on build failure -->
      <ErrorWarningLogText>
         The errors/warnings log file is at:
      </ErrorWarningLogText>
   </PropertyGroup>
   <ItemGroup>
```

```
      <SolutionToBuild Include="$(SolutionRoot)\Main\
         TestReproduceBuild\TestReproduceBuild.sln" />
   </ItemGroup>
   <ItemGroup>
      <ConfigurationToBuild Include="Debug|Any CPU">
         <FlavorToBuild>Debug</FlavorToBuild>
         <PlatformToBuild>Any CPU</PlatformToBuild>
      </ConfigurationToBuild>
   </ItemGroup>
   <ItemGroup>
      <MetaDataFile Include=" ">
         <TestList> </TestList>
      </MetaDataFile>
   </ItemGroup>
   <ItemGroup>
   </ItemGroup>
   <PropertyGroup>
      <!-- If you want to build from a label, specify the
         label name in the BuildFromLabelNumber property-->
      <BuildFromLabelNumber>
         BuildNumber_2.0.61.0
      </BuildFromLabelNumber>
      <!-- The ReproducePrevBuild property indicates whether
         we want to create a new build from a label
         or re-generate an old build -->
      <ReproducePreviousBuild>true</ReproducePreviousBuild>
      <!-- Set the GetVersion property to the label name -->
      <GetVersion>L$(BuildFromLabelNumber)</GetVersion>
   </PropertyGroup>

   <!-- set SkipLabel and SkipPostBuild to true if
      re-generating an old build -->
   <PropertyGroup>
      <SkipLabel Condition=
         " '$(ReproducePreviousBuild)'=='true'>
         true
      </SkipLabel>
      <SkipPostBuild Condition=
         " '$(ReproducePreviousBuild)'=='true' ">
         true
      </SkipPostBuild>
   </PropertyGroup>

   <PropertyGroup>
      <!-- Directory of the reference AssemblyInfo.cs file -->
      <ReferenceAssemblyInfoFileDir>
         C:\Build\RefAssemblyInfo
      </ReferenceAssemblyInfoFileDir>

      <!-- Directory where the AssemblyInfo.cs file will
         reside during build.
         The reference AssemblyInfo.cs file will be copied
         to this directory before compilation. -->
      <AssemblyInfoFileBuildDir>
         $(SolutionRoot)\Main\TestReproduceBuild\Properties
      </AssemblyInfoFileBuildDir>
```

```xml
    <!-- Build Number and Label Number will be
        prefixed with the string specified here. -->
    <BuildNumberPrefix>BuildNumber_</BuildNumberPrefix>
</PropertyGroup>

<!--Include the Reference AssemblyInfo.cs file.
    The AssemblyInfoFiles property is used by the
    AssemblyInfo task -->
<ItemGroup>
     <!--Point to the reference location if creating
        a new build-->
     <AssemblyInfoFiles Condition=
        " '$(ReproducePreviousBuild)'!='true' " Include=
        "$(ReferenceAssemblyInfoFileDir)\AssemblyInfo.*"/>
     <!--Point to the source code directory if reproducing
        a previous build-->
     <AssemblyInfoFiles Condition=
        " '$(ReproducePreviousBuild)'=='true' " Include=
        "$(AssemblyInfoFileBuildDir)\AssemblyInfo.*"/>
</ItemGroup>

<!-- The IntermediateAssembly item is required for forcing
    the execution of the UpdateAssemblyInfoFiles target -->
<ItemGroup>
     <IntermediateAssembly Include=
     "$(SolutionRoot)\dummy.dll"/>
</ItemGroup>

<!--Properties for controlling the
    Assembly Version Number -->
<PropertyGroup>
     <AssemblyMajorVersion>2</AssemblyMajorVersion>
     <AssemblyMinorVersion>0</AssemblyMinorVersion>
     <AssemblyBuildNumber>0</AssemblyBuildNumber>
     <AssemblyRevision>0</AssemblyRevision>
     <AssemblyBuildNumberType>
        NoIncrement
     </AssemblyBuildNumberType>
     <AssemblyBuildNumberFormat></AssemblyBuildNumberFormat>
     <AssemblyRevisionType>NoIncrement</AssemblyRevisionType>
     <AssemblyRevisionFormat></AssemblyRevisionFormat>
</PropertyGroup>

<!-- Properties for controlling the File Version Number -->
<PropertyGroup>
     <AssemblyFileMajorVersion>2</AssemblyFileMajorVersion>
     <AssemblyFileMinorVersion>0</AssemblyFileMinorVersion>
     <AssemblyFileBuildNumber>61</AssemblyFileBuildNumber>
     <AssemblyFileRevision>0</AssemblyFileRevision>

<!-- AutoIncrement the build number if *not* reproducing
    a previous build -->
     <AssemblyFileBuildNumberType Condition="
        '$(ReproducePreviousBuild)'!='true' " >
        AutoIncrement
     </AssemblyFileBuildNumberType>

<!-- Specify the build number in this file if reproducing
    a previous build -->
```

```xml
      <AssemblyFileBuildNumberType Condition="
         '$(ReproducePreviousBuild)'=='true' " >NoIncrement
      </AssemblyFileBuildNumberType>
      <AssemblyFileBuildNumberFormat>
      </AssemblyFileBuildNumberFormat>
      <AssemblyFileRevisionType>
         NoIncrement
      </AssemblyFileRevisionType>
      <AssemblyFileRevisionFormat></AssemblyFileRevisionFormat>
   </PropertyGroup>

   <!-- Override BuildNumberOverrideTargetDependsOn property
      to execute the UpdateAssemblyInfoFiles
      target which updates the reference AssemblyInfo file -->
   <PropertyGroup>
      <BuildNumberOverrideTargetDependsOn>
         UpdateAssemblyInfoFiles
      </BuildNumberOverrideTargetDependsOn>
   </PropertyGroup>

   <!-- Override the BuildNumberOverrideTarget target to
      customize the build number, if we are
      creating a new build -->
   <Target Name = "BuildNumberOverrideTarget"
      Condition=" '$(IsDesktopBuild)'!='true' and
      '$(ReproducePreviousBuild)'!='true' "
      DependsOnTargets="$(BuildNumberOverrideTargetDependsOn)">
      <!-- Create a property with the name "BuildNumber" to
         customize the build number. The value for the
         BuildNumber property is constructed from
         BuildNumberPrefix and MaxAssemblyFileVersion
         properties. The MaxAssemblyFileVersion is
         output from the AssemblyInfo task (
         executed in the UpdateAssemblyInfoFiles
         target in Microsoft.VersionNumber.targets file) -->
      <CreateProperty
         Value=
         "$(BuildNumberPrefix)$(MaxAssemblyFileVersion)">
         <Output TaskParameter="Value"
         PropertyName="BuildNumber"/>
      </CreateProperty>
   </Target>

   <!--Override the CoreCompileDependsOn property to copy
      the reference AssemblyInfo file
      to the build location, before compilation. -->
   <PropertyGroup>
      <CoreCompileDependsOn Condition="
         '$(ReproducePreviousBuild)'!='true' ">
         CopyAssemblyInfoFile
      </CoreCompileDependsOn>

   <!-- If reproducing a previous build, remove the readonly
      attribute of the downloaded AssemblyInfo file,
      prior to running the AssemblyInfo task-->
      <CoreCompileDependsOn Condition="
         '$(ReproducePreviousBuild)'=='true' ">
         RemoveReadOnlyAttribute
```

```
            $(CoreCompileDependsOn)
          </CoreCompileDependsOn>
        </PropertyGroup>

        <!--Copy reference AssemblyInfo.cs file to build location,
          if we are creating a new build -->
        <Target Name="CopyAssemblyInfoFile"
          Condition=" '$(IsDesktopBuild)'!='true' and
          '$(ReproducePreviousBuild)'!='true' " >
          <Exec Command="attrib $(AssemblyInfoFileBuildDir)\
          assemblyinfo.cs -r"/>
          <Copy
            SourceFiles="@(AssemblyInfoFiles)"
            DestinationFolder="$(AssemblyInfoFileBuildDir)" />
        </Target>

        <!--Remove the read-only attribute of the downloaded
          AssemblyInfo file-->
        <Target Name="RemoveReadOnlyAttribute"
          Condition=" '$(IsDesktopBuild)'!='true' and
          '$(ReproducePreviousBuild)'=='true' " >
          <Exec Command="attrib $(AssemblyInfoFileBuildDir)\
            assemblyinfo.cs -r"/>
        </Target>

        <!--Set standard modification times -->
        <Target Name="AfterDropBuild"
          Condition=" '$(IsDesktopBuild)'!='true' " >
          <CreateItem Include=
            "$(DropLocation)\$(BuildNumber)\**\*.*" >
            <Output ItemName="FilesToTouch"
              TaskParameter="Include" />
          </CreateItem>

          <Touch
            Time="12:00:00"
            Files="@(FilesToTouch)" >
            <Output TaskParameter="TouchedFiles"
              ItemName="FilesTouched"/>
          </Touch>

        </Target>
      </Project>
```

In this section, we learned how to create a new build based on a label in TFVC. Let's now switch gears and discuss how to extend Team Build to support ClickOnce deployment. The goal is to automatically publish an application at a designated ClickOnce deployment location as part of the build process.

7.4   *Deploying ClickOnce*

ClickOnce is a new technology available in .NET Framework 2.0 that allows you to easily install Windows Presentation Foundation, Windows Forms, or console applications. ClickOnce applications are self-contained and self-updating. For example, you can publish your application to a web site and users can run the application simply by clicking on a link on the site. (In addition to a web server, you can publish the application to a file server or a CD-ROM.) Users have the option of installing the application on their local machines (offline mode) or running the application from a sandboxed temporary location (online mode). Updates may be automatically downloaded from the web site. For more information on ClickOnce deployment, visit http://msdn. microsoft.com/en-us/library/t71a733d.aspx.

7.4.1 Configuring ClickOnce

Begin by configuring ClickOnce for your solution. On the Project menu, click Properties; then click the Publish tab on the properties form (see figure 7.4). Specify the

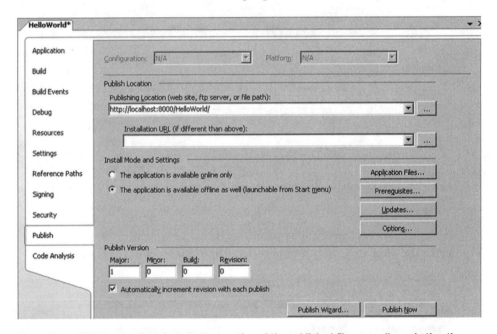

Figure 7.4 ClickOnce options include the location of the published files as well as whether the application is available online or offline.

publishing location, installation mode, update policy, version number, and so on. Click the Security tab to specify the security settings (see figure 7.5) or leave the default as a full-trust application. You can also use certificates to identify the author of the application (click the Signing tab).

Once you've configured the options, click Publish Now (in the Publish tab) to publish the application to the designated location. This will add the ClickOnce-related entries to the project file (.csproj file) as shown in listing 7.13. The published application web page is shown in figure 7.6.

Note that the publish version number is independent of the assembly version number or the file version number specified in the AssemblyInfo.cs file. This disconnect

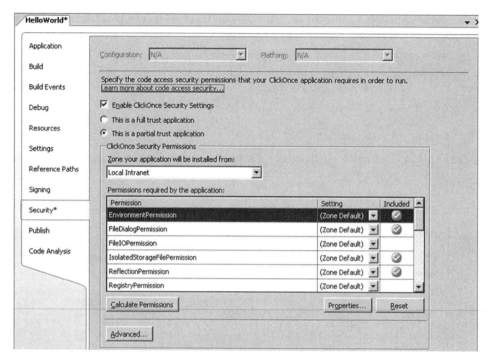

Figure 7.5   The ClickOnce security screen contains options to specify the security requirements of the application.

creates a potential traceability problem. In the next section, we demonstrate a way to make the publish version number identical to the assembly version number.

Figure 7.6   Published application web page

Listing 7.13   ClickOnce elements added to the .csproj file

```
<PropertyGroup>
    <SignManifests>true</SignManifests>
    <TargetZone>LocalIntranet</TargetZone>
    <GenerateManifests>true</GenerateManifests>
```

```
    <ManifestCertificateThumbprint>
        A37F9B055AE9EFFFF8D163F9F25787B1415BAA06
    </ManifestCertificateThumbprint>
    <ManifestKeyFile>
        Hello_World_TemporaryKey.pfx
    </ManifestKeyFile>
    <IsWebBootstrapper>true</IsWebBootstrapper>
    <PublishUrl>http://localhost:8000/Hello_World/</PublishUrl>
    <Install>true</Install>
    <InstallFrom>Web</InstallFrom>
    <UpdateEnabled>true</UpdateEnabled>
    <UpdateMode>Foreground</UpdateMode>
    <UpdateInterval>7</UpdateInterval>
    <UpdateIntervalUnits>Days</UpdateIntervalUnits>
    <UpdatePeriodically>false</UpdatePeriodically>
    <UpdateRequired>false</UpdateRequired>
    <MapFileExtensions>true</MapFileExtensions>
    <ApplicationVersion>1.0.0.%2a</ApplicationVersion>
    <BootstrapperEnabled>true</BootstrapperEnabled>
  </PropertyGroup>
  <ItemGroup>
    <BootstrapperPackage Include="Microsoft.Net.Framework.3.5">
        <Visible>False</Visible>
        <ProductName>.NET Framework 3.5</ProductName>
        <Install>true</Install>
    </BootstrapperPackage>
  </ItemGroup>
```

7.4.2   *Extending Team Build to incorporate ClickOnce*

The "standard" way to incorporate ClickOnce deployment in a build project file is to include the solution name in the `SolutionToPublish` element (instead of including the solution name in the usual `SolutionToBuild` element), as follows:

```
<SolutionToPublish
    Include="$(SolutionRoot)\Test\HelloWorld\HelloWorld.sln" />
```

Although this technique correctly generates the necessary files (including the deployment manifest and application manifest), the problem is that the publish version number is generated independent of the assembly version number (per settings in the Publish tab, as shown in figure 7.4).

To make the publish version number the same as the assembly version number, follow these steps:

1 Revert the changes and delete the `SolutionToPublish` entry that was shown previously. Include the solution name in the `SolutionToBuild` element, as usual.

2 Use the `AssemblyInfo` task in the build script and override the `AfterCompile` target, as shown in listing 7.14. Note that we set the `ApplicationVersion` property to the `MaxAssemblyVersion` property. The `MaxAssemblyVersion` property contains the assembly version number of the output assembly. (`MaxAssemblyVersion` is an output property of the `AssemblyInfo` task.) The `AssemblyInfo` task is discussed in detail in the next chapter.

Listing 7.14 ClickOnce elements added to the build script

```
<Target Name="AfterCompile">

  <MSBuild
  Condition=" '@(SolutionToBuild)'!='' "
  Projects="@(SolutionToBuild)"
  Properties="Configuration
   =%(ConfigurationToBuild.FlavorToBuild);
   Platform=%(ConfigurationToBuild.PlatformToBuild);
   SkipInvalidConfigurations=true;
   VCBuildOverride=$(MSBuildProjectDirectory)\
   TFSBuild.vsprops;FxCopDir=$(FxCopDir);
   OutDir=$(OutDir);PublishDir=$(OutDir);
   ReferencePath=$(ReferencePath);
   TeamBuildConstants=$(TeamBuildConstants);
   $(CodeAnalysisOption);ApplicationVersion=
   $(MaxAssemblyVersion);PublishUrl=
   $(DeploymentServerUrl);InstallUrl=$(DeploymentServerUrl)"

  Targets="Publish" />
</Target>
```

Executing the `Publish` target of the `MSBuild` task (as shown in listing 7.14) creates the necessary output files in the drop location. You could also use the `PublishDir` property to create the files in another location. But `MSBuild` doesn't create the application launch web page, which is named publish.htm by default. Consequently, we need to create a custom task to modify an existing publish.htm file (created by Visual Studio) and change the version number.

7.4.3 *Creating a custom task to configure deployment files*

In this section, we create a custom task named `UpdateClickOnceLaunchPage` to modify the publish.htm file generated by Visual Studio (see Listing 7.15).

Listing 7.15 Modifying the ClickOnce application launch page

```
using System;
using System.IO;
using System.Text;

using Microsoft.Build.Utilities;
using Microsoft.Build.Framework;

namespace TeamBuild.TeamBuildTasks
{
    public class UpdateClickOnceLaunchPage : Task
    {

        private ITaskItem _publishTemplateFile;

        [Required]
        public ITaskItem PublishTemplateFile
        {
            set { _publishTemplateFile = value; }
        }
```

```csharp
private string _stringToReplace;

[Required]
public string StringToReplace
{
   set { _stringToReplace = value; }
}

private string _assemblyVersion;

[Required]
public string AssemblyVersion
{
   set { _assemblyVersion = value; }
}

private string _outputFileCreationDirectory;

[Required]
public string OutputFileCreationDirectory
{
   set { _outputFileCreationDirectory = value; }
}

/// Overridden method. This method is executed
/// when the task is called by MSBuild.
public override bool Execute()
{
   try
   {
      base.Log.LogMessage("Template file: " +
         _publishTemplateFile.ItemSpec);
      string content = string.Empty;

      using (StreamReader reader = new
         StreamReader(_publishTemplateFile.ItemSpec))
      {
         content = reader.ReadToEnd();
         reader.Close();
      }

      string outputPublishFile =
       _outputFileCreationDirectory + "\\Publish.htm";

      using (StreamWriter writer = new
         StreamWriter(outputPublishFile))
      {
         content = content.Replace(_stringToReplace,
            _assemblyVersion);

         writer.Write(content);

         base.Log.LogMessage("Publish file created:
            " + outputPublishFile, null);
         writer.Close();
      }

      return true;
   }
   catch (Exception ex)
   {
```

Read contents of template file

Replace template string with assembly version

```
                        base.Log.LogError(ex.Message, null);
                        return false;
                    }
                }
            }
        }
```

We now override the `AfterDropBuild` target and execute the `UpdateClickOnce-LaunchPage` task to generate the correct publish.htm file in the drop location. After the file is created, copy all the files from the drop location to the publish location. Listing 7.16 shows the overridden `AfterDropBuild` target in the build project file.

Listing 7.16   Overriding `AfterDropBuild` to execute the custom task

```
<Target Name="AfterDropBuild"
    Condition=" '$(IsDesktopBuild)'!='true' " >
    <!-- Create ClickOnce publish html file -->
    <UpdateClickOnceLaunchPage
    PublishTemplateFile="@(TemplateFile)"
    StringToReplace ="{AssemblyVersion}"
    AssemblyVersion="$(MaxAssemblyVersion)"
    OutputFileCreationDirectory=
    "$(DropLocation)\$(BuildNumber)\
    %(ConfigurationToBuild.FlavorToBuild)" />
    <CreateItem Include="$(DropLocation)\$(BuildNumber)\**\*.*" >
        <Output ItemName="FilesToTouch" TaskParameter="Include" />
    </CreateItem>
    <!-- Set standard modification time -->
        <Touch
            Time="12:00:00"
            Files="@(FilesToTouch)" >
            <Output TaskParameter="TouchedFiles"
            ItemName="FilesTouched"/>
        </Touch>

<!-- Create ClickOnce files Item -->
    <CreateItem Include="$(DropLocation)\$(BuildNumber)\
        %(ConfigurationToBuild.FlavorToBuild)\**\*.*" >
        <Output ItemName="ClickOnceFiles"
            TaskParameter="Include" />
    </CreateItem>

<!-- Copy ClickOnce related files to the publish directory -->
    <Copy
        SourceFiles="@(ClickOnceFiles)"
        DestinationFiles="@(ClickOnceFiles ->'
        $(PublishDir)\%(RecursiveDir)%(Filename)%(Extension)')"
        ContinueOnError="true" />

</Target>
```

7.4.4   *Configuring ClickOnce using Team Build tasks*

For the sake of completeness, it's worth knowing that you can set up a ClickOnce deployment using Team Build tasks only. Although it's simpler to follow the technique outlined in this section—using Visual Studio to initially configure the ClickOnce options and then executing the Publish target using MSBuild—you could do all of this using pure code. MSBuild offers the GenerateBootStrapper, GenerateApplicationManifest, and GenerateDeploymentManifest tasks (for more information, visit http://msdn.microsoft.com/en-us/library/7z253716.aspx) to create a bootstrapper setup.exe program, generate the application manifest, and create the deployment manifest, respectively.

7.5 A source code submission service

In this section, we create a simple process for evaluating check-ins and making sure that they pass the necessary quality criteria before committing the code to a codeline in TFVC. You can customize this system to meet your requirements. The simple process described here serves as a proof of concept (see figure 7.7). The next version of TFS is expected to have a feature called *Gated Check-in* that will offer similar functionality.

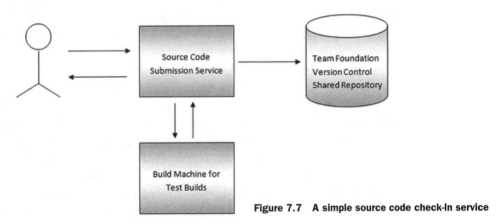

Figure 7.7 A simple source code check-In service

The overall strategy is as follows:

1 A developer creates a shelveset containing the modified code files and work item associations.
2 The developer logs in to the source code submission web site and enters the name of the shelveset, the name of the team project, the name of the target branch, and other information regarding the intended check-in.
3 The submission service verifies conformance with check-in policies, creates a test build, and runs appropriate build verification tests. If the tests pass, the code is checked into the target branch in TFVC. If an error occurs at any stage, the service rejects the submitted code and notifies the developer.

The details of the steps are described in the following sections.

7.5.1 Step 1—Create a shelveset for code submission

When a developer is ready to commit his changes, he uploads the modified files to TFVC in a shelveset. When creating the shelveset, the developer makes sure that the Evaluate

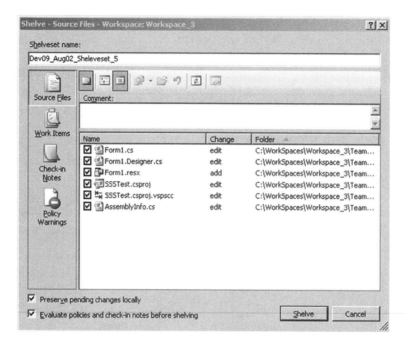

Figure 7.8 The Evaluate Policies and Check-in Notes Before Shelving check box should be selected when creating shelvesets for code submission.

Policies and Check-in Notes Before Shelving check box (in the Shelve-Source Files dialog box) is selected; see figure 7.8. This option causes the check-in policies and notes to be evaluated during the shelveset creation process. The policy evaluation step helps ensure software quality and consistency with your corporate standards.

In TFVC, there's no way to require a developer to select this option when creating a shelveset. Additionally, there's no way to ensure that the custom policies that you've created are actually installed on a developer's machine. Consequently, your only recourse is to provide adequate training to your developers so that they follow this process whenever a shelveset is created for code submission. Additionally, you should try to run as many checks as possible on the server side.

7.5.2   *Step 2—Submit change information via submission web site*

Once a shelveset is created, the developer logs in to the source code submission web site and provides information regarding the code changes. This information includes the name of the shelveset, the name of the team project, the name of the solution, and so on (see figure 7.9).

In our simple example, the requests submitted via the web site are processed immediately. This means that other requests are blocked while a build is executed. In real life, you'd want to enhance the following factors:

Figure 7.9   Provide shelveset and other relevant information via the code submission web site to kick off the source code submission service.

- Implement a durable queuing mechanism using Microsoft Message Queue (MSMQ) so that the incoming requests are persisted and processed in sequence. This feature will also help survive a web site crash or restart.
- Assign a priority to incoming requests so that certain code changes can be processed preferentially.
- Use a bank of build machines to speed up the build process.
- Provide status information regarding the current state of a particular request and its position in the processing pipeline.

7.5.3 *Step 3—Process requests using the submission service*

The submitted requests are processed by the source code submission service. The steps involved are shown in figure 7.10. As mentioned previously, in real life, you should consider setting up a build farm and process multiple requests in parallel. In a large project, the time required to create a build and to run the build verification tests is much longer than the time required to check in a set of code files. Using multiple build machines significantly speeds up the code submission process.

In the parallel build scenario, if there are incompatible changes in the shelvesets that are built in parallel, those conflicting changes could be checked in to the shared repository undetected. For example, suppose there are two submitted shelvesets—shelveset 1 and shelveset 2. Assume shelveset 2 conflicts with shelveset 1.

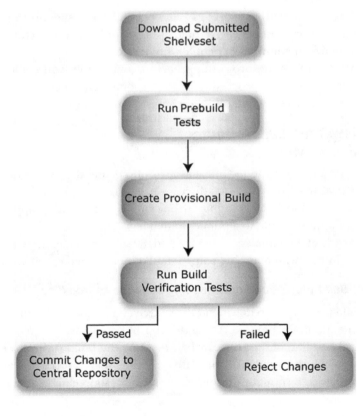

Figure 7.10
Source code submission request-handling process

If building in sequence (on a single build machine), the conflict between shelveset 1 and shelveset 2 will be detected when creating a test build for shelveset 2. Consequently, shelveset 2 won't be checked in.

But if building in parallel (on multiple build machines), assume machine 1 builds shelveset 1, and in parallel, machine 2 builds shelveset 2. Since machine 2 doesn't know anything about shelveset 1, it'll commit shelveset 2 to TFVC (assuming the test build succeeds). Machine 1 will also commit shelveset 1 to TFVC (assuming the test build succeeds) since it doesn't know anything about shelveset 2. But since shelveset 2 conflicts with shelveset 1, this process will result in a codeline in TFVC that can't be built anymore. The conflict will probably be detected when you try to build the next shelveset.

Moreover, even if there are no conflicts between shelveset 1 and shelveset 2, there could be incompatibilities between them that might require a manual merge. In the parallel build scenario, assuming machine 1 has already committed shelveset 1, when machine 2 attempts to commit shelveset 2, it might encounter a merge conflict that can't be resolved automatically.

You need to devise custom solutions to resolve these problems. For example, in case of a build failure in TFVC, you could undo each check-in until a stable point is reached where the codeline can be built again, and reject the subsequent check-ins. In case of a merge conflict that can't be resolved automatically, you could simply reject the corresponding shelveset, asking the developer to reconcile with the latest codebase and resubmit her changes.

You could also take various steps to mitigate the possibility of issues arising due to concurrent test builds. For example, by setting up an appropriate branching structure, you could minimize the number of people who need to check in code to a particular branch. Furthermore, as the project approaches completion, you could switch from parallel processing to serial processing of code submissions, thereby increasing the stability of the codebase. The tradeoff is efficiency versus accuracy.

7.6   Technical review: creating the source code submission service

In this section, we look at some the technical aspects of creating the source code submission service. Recall from our previous discussion that this service will review the code submitted by developers (by creating ad hoc builds and running appropriate BVTs) before committing the code to a public branch in TFVC.

The full source code of the submission web site and the submission service is available for download from http://www.manning.com/TeamFoundationServer2008inAction.

7.6.1   Creating a Team Build project and downloading baseline source files

Create a Team Build project file to download the source code associated with the solution. The build type should include executing the appropriate BVTs.

Create an initial baseline build manually by executing the build project file. This important step populates the build directory with a baseline set of source files and creates the necessary folders. By initially downloading the latest source files from TFVC to the build directory, you synchronize the files in TFVC and in the build directory. Assuming you're using a single build machine (as in our example), you don't need to download the full set of source files prior to generating every build. After the initial download, the submission service keeps the files in sync. In large projects, downloading thousands of files from TFVC could become expensive. Of course, if you use multiple build machines, you need to synchronize each machine with the latest code in TFVC prior to processing each submission.

Modify the build project file as shown in listing 7.17. The changes are as follow:

- Skip downloading the source code. By default, the build project file deletes the existing source files from the build directory and downloads the full set of files from TFVC prior to creating a build. But this step can have significant performance overhead in large projects. Since the source code submission service manages what gets uploaded to TFVC, the service can keep the build directory in sync with TFVC, avoiding the need to download the source files repeatedly. But if you're using multiple build machines, you can't skip this step. You need to either download the latest files from TFVC or come up with another mechanism to incrementally update the build machines so that all machines contain the latest file prior to creating test builds.
- Skip labeling the source files. Since we're creating throwaway test builds with code that hasn't yet been checked in, the labels are unnecessary (and in fact, erroneous).
- Skip the post-build tasks such as updating work items. These steps are also unnecessary for test builds.

> **Listing 7.17 Changes in the build script for creating test builds**

```
<PropertyGroup>
  <SkipGet>true</SkipGet>
  <SkipClean>true</SkipClean>
  <SkipLabel>true</SkipLabel>
  <SkipPostBuild>true</SkipPostBuild>
  <SkipInitializeWorkspace>true</SkipInitializeWorkspace>
</PropertyGroup>
```

7.6.2 *Downloading the shelveset*

The source code submission service downloads the shelveset that was submitted by the developer. Download the shelveset directly into the build directory (see listing 7.18). If the build directory is located on a separate machine (where Team Build is running), use a UNC path and ensure that the account the submission service is running under can write to the destination folder. We can always undo the changes if the code doesn't compile or if the BVTs fail, restoring the build directory to its original condition.

Another point to note is that when you executed the build project file in the previous step, a workspace was automatically created in the build location. The name of the TFS-generated workspace follows this pattern:

```
<Build Machine Name>_<Team Project Name>_<Build Type Name>
```

TIP To view a list of all workspaces along with their local working folders, type the following at the command prompt:

```
tf workspaces /owner:* /format:detailed / server:<tfs_server_name>
```

Replace *<tfs_server_name>* with the name of your Team Foundation Server. For more information, visit http://msdn2.microsoft.com/en-us/library/54dkh0y3.aspx.

Listing 7.18 Downloading the submitted shelveset to the build directory

```
///The following method fetches the workspace
///associated with the build directory. If a workspace
///does not exist, a new one is created
private Workspace pCreateWorkspace(string teamProject)
   {
      string buildDirSolutionRoot =
         Configurations.BuildDirUncPath +
         Path.DirectorySeparatorChar
         + teamProject + Path.DirectorySeparatorChar
         + Configurations.GetBuildTypeForTeamProject(
         teamProject) + Path.DirectorySeparatorChar
         + "Sources";                                          Create path to directory

      Workspace ws;
      try
      {
         ws = _vcServer.GetWorkspace(buildDirSolutionRoot);    Get workspace mapped to build dir
      }
      catch (Exception e)
      {
         // If no workspace is mapped then create a
         // workspace and map on that path.

         string workspaceName = Environment.MachineName + "_"
            + teamProject + "_" +
            Configurations.GetBuildTypeForTeamProject(
            teamProject)
            + "_" + "Shelveset";                               Construct workspace name

         ws = _vcServer.CreateWorkspace(workspaceName,
            Configurations.TfsUserName);                       Create workspace

         ws.Map("$/" + teamProject, buildDirSolutionRoot);     Map workspace
      }

      return ws;
   }

   ///the following method downloads the shelveset to the build
   ///location. The workspace contains the necessary mappings.
   private Shelveset pDownloadShelveset(Workspace workspace,
         out PendingChange[] shelvesetChanges, ShelvesetInfo shelveset)
   {
      Shelveset submittedShelveset = null;

      shelvesetChanges = null;

      //assuming that each file in the shelveset is mapped
```

```
//in the local workspace
submittedShelveset =
    workspace.Unshelve(shelveset.ShelvesetName,
        shelveset.ShelvesetOwner, null, out
        shelvesetChanges);

return submittedShelveset;
}
```

7.6.3   *Running prebuild checks*

Once the code is downloaded from the shelveset, before launching the build process, run appropriate checks to make sure that the code changes meet the quality criteria. These prebuild checks help ensure that code submission policies are being followed. But to a large extent, you're dependent on the cooperation of the developer—you can't be certain that the code check-in policies were actually executed on the developer's machine prior to uploading the files to the shelveset (see section 7.5.1). In TFVC, the code check-in policies can't be executed outside of Visual Studio. Since it's not realistic to expect the Visual Studio development environment to be installed on the build machine, you can't be certain that the check-in policies were actually executed prior to creating the shelveset. But you can still conduct a number of verifications such as the following (the implementation is left to the reader):

- Check whether any policy was violated. Check the `PolicyOverrideComment` property of the `Shelveset` class to determine whether any policy was overridden. If a policy violation is detected during creation of a shelveset, VSTS displays a warning window (see figure 7.11). The developer can only check in the code by providing a reason in the dialog box. The reason is captured in the `Policy-OverrideComment` property of the `Shelveset` class.

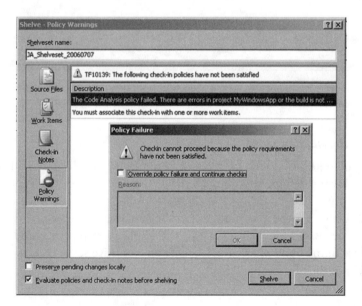

Figure 7.11   VSTS displays a warning dialog box if a policy violation is detected.

- Check whether the check-in notes contain appropriate values. By default, the check-in notes contain the names of the code reviewer, security reviewer, and performance reviewer (see figure 7.12). You can define additional check-in notes for the team project using the Source Control Settings dialog box. Instead of simply checking for nonblank values in the check-in note fields (as we do in the sample code), you can check whether the code was reviewed by people assigned to various roles—perhaps by members of the tech lead group, or people from specific feature or domain teams. (For example, security review may need to be performed by people who have particular skills in the security domain.) You can also customize the check-in notes and ask specific questions, such as whether unit testing was conducted, what code coverage percentage was achieved with unit testing, and so forth. You can then take appropriate action based on the answers provided.

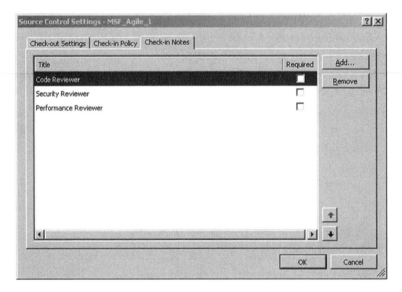

Figure 7.12   The default check-in notes help ensure that the submitted code was peer reviewed; you can also add custom check-in notes.

7.6.4   *Launching the build process*

Execute the build project file to generate a test build (see listing 7.19). As discussed earlier, modify the default build project file so that the source code isn't fetched again from TFVC (refer back to listing 7.18). Use the well-defined Team Foundation Server object model to invoke the build controller in the application tier machine (as opposed to accessing the web service in the application tier machine or calling the build service in the build machine). Execute an extensive set of BVTs to ensure the stability and integrity of the code base.

Listing 7.19   Code for launching Team Build to generate a test build

```
/// the build project file (TFSBuild.proj) should have
/// the following attributes set
///   <SkipGet>true</SkipGet>
///   <SkipClean>true</SkipClean>
///   <SkipLabel>true</SkipLabel>
///   <SkipPostBuild>true</SkipPostBuild>
///   <SkipInitializeWorkspace>true</SkipInitializeWorkspace>///
//Create the controller object
Proxy.BuildController controller =
   (Proxy.BuildController)_tfsServer.GetService(
   typeof(Proxy.BuildController));
Proxy.BuildStore store =
   (Proxy.BuildStore)_tfsServer.GetService(
   typeof(Proxy.BuildStore));
Proxy.BuildParameters buildParams =
   new Proxy.BuildParameters();

buildParams.TeamFoundationServer = buildparam_TfsServer;
buildParams.TeamProject = buildparam_TeamProject;
buildParams.BuildType = buildparam_BuildType;
buildParams.BuildDirectory = buildparam_BuildDir;
buildParams.BuildMachine = buildparam_BuildMachine;

//now start the build
string buildUri = controller.StartBuild(buildParams);
bool buildComplete = false;

Proxy.BuildData bd;
BuildConstants.BuildStatusIconID status;
//wait till the build completes
do
{
   //sleep for a sec and poll.
   try
   {
      System.Threading.Thread.Sleep(1000);
   }
   catch (Exception) {
   //deal with exceptions as appropriate
   }

   //fetch build results
   bd = store.GetBuildDetails(buildUri);
   status = (BuildConstants.BuildStatusIconID)bd.BuildStatusId;

   buildComplete = (status ==
   BuildConstants.BuildStatusIconID.BuildSucceeded ||
   status == BuildConstants.BuildStatusIconID.BuildFailed ||
   status == BuildConstants.BuildStatusIconID.BuildStopped) &&

} while (!buildComplete);
```

7.6.5 *Evaluating build results*

After the test build is completed, inspect the status of the build. If the build is successful, commit the submitted source files to the TFVC repository. When uploading the files, also update the work item associations so that TFVC knows which work items are affected by the committed changeset. The CheckIn method of the Workspace class has an overloaded version that allows you to specify the name of the author, check-in notes, work item associations, and so on (see listing 7.20). If the test build has failed, undo the changes from the temporary workspace and revert the files in the build directory to their previous states. A build will be unsuccessful if there's a compilation error or if any of the BVTs fail.

Listing 7.20   Evaluating the build result and checking code in to TFVC

```
/// <summary>
/// Performs the post build tasks.
/// </summary>
private string pPerformPostBuildTasks(Workspace workspace,
   PendingChange[] shelvesetChanges,
   Shelveset submittedShelveset,
   BuildConstants.BuildStatusIconID status,
   string developerMailAddress)
{
   //step 4: check build status.
   //
   // If build failed:
   //     i.   undo changes from local workspace
   //     ii.  put a clean set of files in build directory,
   //          if build failed
   //     iii. send notification email to developer
   //
   // If build succeeded:
   //     i.   check in the changes to TFVC
   //     ii.  delete shelveset

   if (status ==
      BuildConstants.BuildStatusIconID.BuildSucceeded)
   {
      // build succeeded
      // check in changes to TFVC;
      workspace.CheckIn(shelvesetChanges,
         submittedShelveset.OwnerName,
         "Checked-in by Code Submission Service",
         submittedShelveset.CheckinNote,
         submittedShelveset.WorkItemInfo, null);

      // Delete shelveset
      _vcServer.DeleteShelveset(submittedShelveset.Name,
         submittedShelveset.OwnerName);
      // create a success email if needed
      // return success message
      return Configurations.SuccessMessage;
   }
   else
   {
```

```
            // build failed
            // undo changes from local workspace
            workspace.Undo(shelvesetChanges);
            //generate notification email
            this.pGenerateEmail (Configurations.FailureMessage,
                developerMailAddress);
            // return failure message
            return Configurations.FailureMessage;
        }
    }
```

7.7   *Desktop builds*

One of the best practices associated with build management is for all developers—local as well as remote—to use the same build script to the maximum extent possible. While everybody won't have the right to modify the master build scripts—the central build team is usually responsible for maintaining them—developers should try to use the same scripts for generating builds. Minor customizations may be necessary to run them in local environments. Additionally, there are times—such as when the central team wants to build all components and feature teams are only interested in a single component for the sake of efficiency—when various parties need to tweak the build script. But these changes are usually peripheral in nature and the core logic is left unchanged. That's why the build script should be treated just like any other piece of shared source code. When you create a new build type, VSTS automatically checks in the build script to TFVC for shared access and maintenance.

If a developer needs to create a local build, she may use the shared build script and create a desktop build. A desktop build doesn't fetch the source code from TFVC or label the set of source files. But a desktop build creates the build binaries using the same MSBuild project file that Team Build uses. You may need to download the latest related source code manually from one or more TFS machines prior to creating a desktop build, unless you're building local work-in-progress code only.

To create a desktop build, execute the build project file using MSBuild. Download the build script from TFVC, open a Visual Studio Command Prompt window, and type the following:

```
MSBuild TFSBuild.proj
```

A desktop build is created when using this syntax because in the TFSBuild.proj file, the DefaultTargets attribute of the Project element is specified to be the Desktop-Build target, as follows:

```
<Project DefaultTargets="DesktopBuild"
    xmlns="http://schemas.microsoft.com/developer/msbuild/2003">
```

When running the MSBuild command-line program, you can specify additional optional parameters to run BVTs, perform code analysis, and so on. For example, to skip the BVTs—which a developer might do if his local machine isn't configured for testing—type the following:

```
MSBuild TFSBuild.proj /property:RunTest=false
```

For a complete list of available MSBuild command line options, visit the Microsoft web site at http://msdn2.microsoft.com/en-us/library/ms164311.aspx.

Keep in mind the difference between creating a desktop build and a local build from the Visual Studio IDE. Desktop builds are much more powerful. In a desktop build, you run the same build script that Team Build uses to create production builds. You can run BVTs, gather code coverage information, perform static code analysis, execute custom tasks, and customize the build process per your requirements. Also, using desktop builds, you can build multiple solutions; this isn't possible using the build feature of Visual Studio.

The difference between a desktop build and a build created using Team Build is that a desktop build minimizes interaction with TFS. As discussed, a desktop build doesn't retrieve source code from TFVC, doesn't update existing work items or create new work items (in case of build failure), doesn't label the source files, and doesn't log events in TFS databases. Using this strategy, the TFS server is updated only when the central build team creates "official" builds using Team Build.

In the next section, we look at the scenario where source files are located in multiple TFS servers and the central build team needs to create a public build. Given the prevalence of globally distributed development teams, it's worthwhile to discuss the various strategies for integrating code changes from distributed locations. We begin with a review of the major components of the build sub-system and their interactions.

7.8   *TFS and distributed builds*

In this section, we discuss how to create a build from multiple TFS servers. As discussed, TFS is based on a distributed architecture. The major pieces are shown in figure 7.13. From a networking point of view, in order to support a remote build machine, the following ports need to be open (refer to http://msdn.microsoft.com/en-us/library/ms252473.aspx for more information regarding the ports used by TFS):

- Port 8080 on the application tier machine needs to be accessible from the build machine. This port is used to fetch source code from TFS, associate work items and changesets with the build, log build events, and so on.

- Port 9191 on the build machine should be available to receive .NET remoting calls (for TFS 2005) or WCF calls (for TFS 2008) from the TFS application-tier machine. This port is used by the build controller on the application-tier machine to communicate with the build service (a Windows service) running on the build machine. The communications include starting and stopping a build, checking whether a build is completed, and so forth.

Depending on the number of source code files that need to be transferred between the TFS application-tier machine and the build machine, as well as the speed of the connection between them, consider installing a proxy server in the remote build location. The proxy server caches the source files locally instead of downloading them from TFVC every time a get request is made. The proxy server should be connected to the build machine via a high-speed LAN connection, since both machines are in the

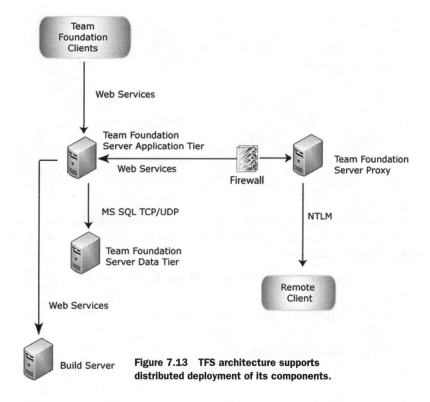

Figure 7.13　TFS architecture supports distributed deployment of its components.

remote build location. The proxy server requires a trusted connection to the TFS application-tier machine. In TFS 2005, this is possible only by establishing a VPN link between the proxy server and the TFS application-tier machine. Once you set up the proxy server and start satisfying the get requests from the local cache, you'll be able to significantly decrease the volume of traffic between the TFS application-tier machine and the remote build machine. The traffic associated with other build-related interactions is usually not of much concern.

You need to carefully think about your team structure, system configuration, and project requirements when setting up a build lab in a distributed TFS scenario. You need to come up with an optimum strategy based upon your organizational structure, project requirements, and TFS configuration. Let's look at a few scenarios.

7.8.1 Scenario: central build machine

In this configuration, the build machine is located on the main site and the TFS machines are located in distributed locations (see figure 7.14). The central build team is responsible for collecting source code from distributed locations and creating the build binaries. Teams in the distributed locations don't create official builds.

To implement this strategy, you need to be able to fetch source code from multiple TFS machines prior to compilation. A proxy server should be installed to speed up the download process. But downloading source code from multiple TFS machines isn't

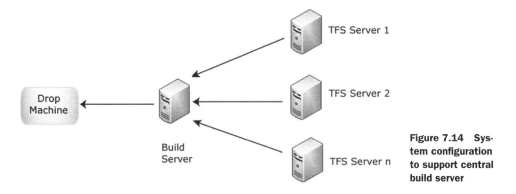

Figure 7.14   System configuration to support central build server

supported out-of-the-box in Team Build. By default, a Team Build project can download source code only from a single TFS application-tier machine. Consequently, you need to do one of the following:

- Download source code from multiple TFS machines manually or using an automated process.
- Modify the default build project file to download source code from multiple TFS machines.

MODIFYING THE TEAM BUILD PROJECT FILE

To download source files that are located in multiple TFS machines, you need to override the `BeforeGet` target and execute the `DeleteWorkspaceTask` and `CreateWorkspaceTask` tasks. Specify the URL of the TFS server(s) in the `TeamFoundationServerUrl` attribute. Both `DeleteWorkspaceTask` and `CreateWorkspaceTask` take the `TeamFoundationServerUrl` attribute to point to the machine containing the source code. Use the `Get` task (in the `BeforeGet` target) to download the source code from multiple TFS machines into the workspaces (created by the `CreateWorkspaceTask` task). You also need to override the `BeforeCompile` and `AfterCompile` targets as appropriate (based on the dependencies) and invoke the `MSBuild` task to actually compile the code.

7.8.2   *Scenario: distributed build machines*

In this configuration, each distributed TFS location has its own build team responsible for creating binaries for their respective subsystems (see figure 7.15). Upon creation, the latest build binaries are placed in a shared location or uploaded to TFVC on the main site. The central build team downloads the necessary code from the main TFS machine, grabs the assemblies generated from distributed locations, and creates a final production build.

The build scripts running in the distributed locations can be customized to automatically transmit the generated assemblies when distributed builds are created. For example, you can override the `AfterDropBuild` target in the build project file to automatically copy the binaries to a remote network share, upload via FTP, or check the output assemblies in the main TFS machine.

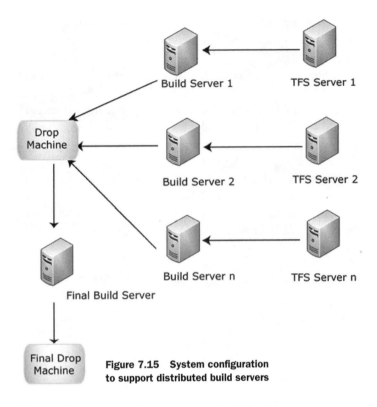

Figure 7.15 System configuration to support distributed build servers

This configuration makes sense in the following cases:

- When a proxy server hasn't been set up and bandwidth is a problem relative to the volume of source files that need to be downloaded to a central build machine from distributed locations.
- When the central build team doesn't have permission to download source code from distributed TFS machines given the trust requirement between domains or organizational constraints.
- When there's something unique about the build environment or skills required (for example, building BizTalk applications) that the remote build team is uniquely equipped to handle.

7.9 Summary

In this chapter, we looked at some common business needs, and we extended Team Build to meet those objectives. We saw that since Team Build creates and executes MSBuild project files, we have a lot of flexibility in customizing the build process. Businesses face a new set of realities today—globally distributed teams, dependence on interoperable third-party solutions, and regulatory requirements. Development organizations are asked to ensure auditability, consistency, dependability, and transparency of the software development processes. Since the build process generates the executables that get shipped to the customers or deployed in production environments, the integrity of the build process is of utmost concern. You need to design a dependable process with real-life issues in mind and execute the process with the highest fidelity every time.

We created an end-to-end custom process for submitting source files via a shelve-set, creating a test build, validating the test build, and finally checking in the files to the main codeline. Such a process improves code quality, ensures integrity of the production codebase, and guards against accidental build breaks. Variations of this system exist in large organizations, and they're of proven value when you have a large number of contributors and there's a lot of code churn.

In the next chapter, we use Team Build to solve a real-life problem—how to automatically generate meaningful and unique build numbers and associate them with the output binaries. Although on the surface, this might seem like a trivial problem, you'll discover that there's more to consider than what appears at first glance.

7.10 References

Hashimi, Sayed Y. and Sayed I. *Deploying .NET Applications.* Apress, 2006.

Versioning assemblies using Team Build

This chapter covers

- Versioning concepts
- Versioning Windows applications
- Versioning web applications

One basic thing you can do to streamline your build process is identify each build with a unique and meaningful number that's stamped on generated assemblies. In a streamlined build process, generating this unique identifying number needs to be centrally coordinated. Otherwise, if you use an ad hoc approach, you'll run into operational difficulties trying to apply a consistent numbering scheme across multiple projects and solutions. For effective troubleshooting and traceability, it's imperative that the generated assemblies are stamped with a unique identifier that can be easily traced back to a system build number.

By default, the build number generated by Team Build is different from the version number stamped on the output assemblies. The build number generated by Team Build is based on the current date and time. The version number stamped on the generated assemblies is based on the contents of the AssemblyInfo.cs (or

AssemblyInfo.vb) file. If these two numbers aren't synchronized, you'll have a hard time tracing problems in deployment environments back to the corresponding source files.

In this chapter, you'll learn about the following:

- *Versioning Windows applications*—When building Windows applications, learn how to increment the build number field in the assembly version or the file version. Our goal is to synchronize the build number created by Team Build with the file version number stamped in the assemblies.

- *Versioning web applications*—Versioning web applications in TFS isn't as straightforward as you might expect. Learn the steps necessary to stamp web applications with unique version numbers.

8.1   Assembly versioning background

Assemblies in .NET contain two numbers for versioning purposes (see figure 8.1):

- *Assembly version number*—Used to bind to assemblies with "strong" names. A *strong name* consists of an assembly's name, version number, culture, and public key. Private assemblies (usually installed in application directories), which aren't strongly named, aren't referenced by assembly version numbers. As a general rule, the assembly version number shouldn't be altered during the build process unless you're introducing major changes. Changing the assembly version number will cause other programs that reference your strong-named assemblies to stop working. Strong-named assemblies that have the same file name but different assembly version numbers are considered to be totally different by the .NET runtime.

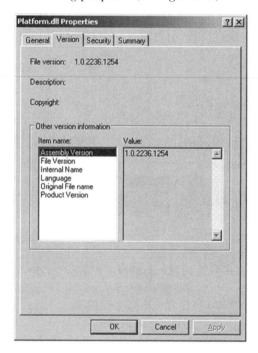

Figure 8.1   Assemblies contain assembly and file version numbers.

- *File version number*—Used to track different versions of a file. File version numbers aren't used by external programs for binding purposes. If you're making simple nonbreaking changes, increment the file version every time you create a new build.

Both the assembly version number and the file version number have the following format:

```
<major_version>.<minor_version>.<build_number>.<revision>
```

The description of each element is as follows:

- *Major_version*—Indicates major releases in a product's lifecycle. An assembly with a different major version number isn't expected to maintain backward compatibility.
- *Minor_version*—Indicates incremental feature improvements. An assembly with a different minor version number is generally expected to preserve backward compatibility.
- *Build_number*—Incremented every time a new build is made.
- *Revision*—Used for a variety of purposes—to indicate a service pack number, a bug number (in case of a hotfix that fixes a particular bug), or any other reference number deemed appropriate by the release team. In some companies, once a release candidate is decided, the build number is frozen; the revision field represents an incrementing rebuild number, for each build up to the release as well as for post-release servicing.

In C# applications, assembly and file versions are specified in a file named Assembly-Info.cs. Listing 8.1 shows an example.

Listing 8.1 Assembly and file versions are specified in AssemblyInfo.cs

```
[assembly: AssemblyVersion("3.0.0.0")]
[assembly: AssemblyFileVersion("3.0.20.0")]
```

As another example, the assembly version number for TFS 2005 assemblies was 8.0.0.0. This number remained unchanged in TFS 2005 SP1, preserving backward compatibility. The assembly version number for TFS 2008 assemblies was incremented to 9.0.0.0.

Some organizations use the yyMMdd format in the build number field and increment the revision field for each build (think about continuous integration). But starting January 1, 2007, it hasn't been possible to use the yyMMdd format in the build number field of the assembly version number. The maximum value that can exist in the build number field in the assembly version number is 65,535. (The yyMMdd value became 70,101 on January 1, 2007). This issue is discussed in more detail later.

We suggest using an automatically increasing integer in the file version number's build number field to uniquely identify each routine build. The assembly version number should only be changed for release builds after careful consideration of how the change will impact end users.

The reasons for using an integer as the build number are as follow:

- In this day of globally distributed teams, using a date to indicate the build number creates confusion due to differences in time zones. The date can differ based on geographical locations.
- If you use up both the build number and revision fields to represent a build, you won't have any other field left to add other reference information, such as a service pack or a hotfix number. When releasing maintenance patches, you might want to keep the build number unchanged and increment the revision number.

8.2   *Versioning Windows applications*

When you build a Windows application using Team Build, the assembly version number and the file version number of the generated assemblies are set based on the contents of the project's AssemblyInfo.cs file. This default approach, which involves using the same AssemblyInfo.cs file for local as well as release builds, has the following problems:

- The version numbers are hard-coded in the AssemblyInfo.cs file. In order to assign a new version number to a generated assembly, you need to check out the AssemblyInfo.cs file from TFVC, make appropriate modifications, and check the file back in again prior to kicking off a build. If a solution consists of multiple projects, you'll have to perform this operation for every AssemblyInfo.cs file in each project. In continuous integration or automated nightly build scenarios, this becomes cumbersome.

- The person or team responsible for creating the build may not have permissions to modify the source code each time a build needs to be created. The branch hosting the production code may have a strict change management policy, making ad-hoc changes by the build team difficult or impossible. Consequently, if the build team modifies a project's AssemblyInfo.cs file to streamline the version information, they may not be able to upload the modified file in TFVC in the same location.

- The version number used by the developers internally could be different from the version number published to external parties. If the build team changes the AssemblyInfo.cs file in TFVC, it might confuse the developers who are using their own version numbers for identification and referencing purposes. When developers create local builds (via Visual Studio IDE or desktop builds via MSBuild), the version numbers specified in their local AssemblyInfo.cs files are stamped on the binary output files. As discussed, if the build team wishes to generate a different set of version numbers, they'll need to create a different AssemblyInfo.cs file.

- If your organization takes a "delay signing" approach to stamping the build binaries, only a few people probably have access to the organization's private keys. An organization's private keys are a closely guarded secret. The development team members probably don't know the private keys for creating strong-named assemblies; they know the public keys only. The developers create internal builds using the public keys. The full key information is known only to a few people in the central release team. In a typical scenario, when creating local builds, the development team members add the public key information to the AssemblyInfo.cs file. When creating official release builds, the central release team adds the public and private key information to the AssemblyInfo.cs file. (Alternatively, the central release team could use the strong name tool—sn.exe—to add private key information to the generated assemblies.) Consequently, the two versions of the AssemblyInfo.cs file may be different, since the development version may contain the name of the public key file and the release version may contain the name of the public and private key file.

The best approach is to generate the appropriate version numbers during the build process itself. Since the build team (or a designated person, in a small company) owns the process and the mechanics associated with creating a build, it's best to give them the responsibility and tools to manage assembly versioning. Based on the nature of the build (daily, weekly, milestone, internal, external), the build team should be able to specify the appropriate version numbers. The build team shouldn't be dependent on the development team for the purpose of versioning assemblies.

I feel strongly that unique version numbers should be assigned to generated assemblies and tied back to labeled source code files. Failure to do so creates untold miseries in real life.

8.3   *Customizing Team Build to support assembly numbering*

You can extend Team Build to implement automatic assembly versioning. This can be done in several ways. Here's one possible approach:

1   Specify the nonvolatile portions of the version numbers in the build project file (TFSBuild.proj). Recall from our earlier discussion that a version number consists of four parts—major version, minor version, build number, and revision number. Typically the build number that exists in the file version number (not in the assembly version number) is incremented each time a new build is made. Consequently, file version number changes in every build. But you can specify the major version, minor version, and revision number fields in the file version number in the build project file, since these fields are relatively static. The assembly version number is usually more stable. As discussed, changing the assembly version number for strong-named assemblies breaks other assemblies that depend on it. Therefore, you can specify the entire assembly version number, which is typically updated for milestone or release builds only, in the build project file.

2   Create a reference AssemblyInfo.cs file to store the latest version numbers. As discussed, our strategy is to autoincrement only the build number (in the file version number) in each build. The revision number is updated only in special cases, such as when indicating a patch number. The file version number is updated with the new build number and stored in the reference AssemblyInfo.cs file. As discussed, the values for the entire assembly version number as well as the major version, minor version, and revision fields in the file version number are specified in the build script (since they don't typically change in every build).

3   Create a custom task (or use a third-party task) to read the fixed portions of the file version number from the build script and to write them to the reference AssemblyInfo.cs file. The build number is read from the reference AssemblyInfo.cs file, incremented, and then written back to the same file. Consequently, the reference AssemblyInfo.cs file contains the complete set of updated version numbers prior to generating a build.

4   Copy the reference AssemblyInfo.cs file to the appropriate location prior to compilation of the code so that the generated assemblies are stamped with the correct version numbers. If there are multiple projects in the solution, the reference AssemblyInfo.cs file should be copied to the appropriate folder for each project

The approach is depicted in figure 8.2.

After a build is created, you might want to upload the reference AssemblyInfo.cs file to TFVC for archiving purposes, along with other artifacts used in the build process (if any). The upload location of the reference AssemblyInfo.cs file may be different from the folder containing the development version of the AssemblyInfo.cs file. The upload folder for the reference AssemblyInfo.cs file is administered by the central build team, not the development team. Recall from our previous discussion that the Assembly-Info.cs file used by the development team could be different from the one used by the build team. Consequently, these files should be located in different folders, since the access control permissions are typically administered at the folder level.

8.3.1 Technical approach

In this section, we dive into the technical details involved in extending Team Build to support automatic assembly versioning. We break up the process in a series of steps, as described in the following sections.

STEP 1—DOWNLOAD ASSEMBLYINFOTASK

Instead of creating a custom task for incrementing version numbers, download a freely available component named `AssemblyInfoTask` from MSDN Code Gallery at http://code.msdn.microsoft.com/AssemblyInfoTaskvers (see figure 8.3).

`AssemblyInfoTask` can manipulate `Assembly-Version`, `AssemblyFileVersion`, and other entries in an AssemblyInfo.cs (or AssemblyInfo.vb) file, saving you hours of routine programming. You can use `AssemblyInfoTask` to update both assembly and file version numbers. You can also use it to sign assemblies.

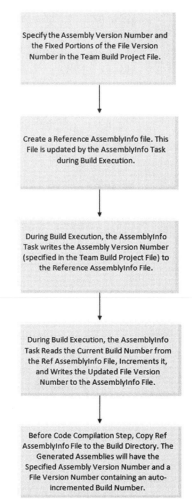

Figure 8.2   Steps involved in stamping build binaries with auto-generated build numbers

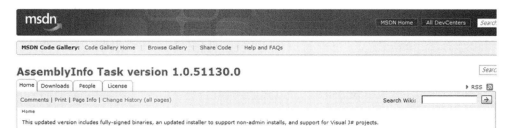

Figure 8.3 `AssemblyInfoTask`, available in the MSDN Code Gallery, allows you to customize assembly and file version information.

STEP 2—INSPECT THE MICROSOFT.VERSIONNUMBER.TARGETS FILE

After installing the component, you'll see a new target file named Microsoft.Version-Number.targets (usually located in the %ProgramFiles%\MSBuild\Microsoft\Assembly-InfoTask directory). The content of this file is presented in listing 8.2. Although we won't be changing this file, it's instructive to review its contents and understand how it works.

Listing 8.2   Microsoft.VersionNumber.targets file

```xml
<?xml version="1.0" encoding="utf-8"?>
<!-- This targets file includes all the necessary information to
    automatically increment build numbers as part of
    a regular build process. To use it simply include it in your
    project file after any other includes. The typical
    include line looks like this:

    <Import Project="$(MSBuildExtensionsPath)\Microsoft\
        AssemblyInfoTask\Microsoft.VersionNumber.targets"/>
-->
<Project xmlns="http://schemas.microsoft.com/
    developer/msbuild/2003">
    <!-- Properties for controlling the Assembly Version -->
    <PropertyGroup>
        <AssemblyMajorVersion>1</AssemblyMajorVersion>
        <AssemblyMinorVersion>0</AssemblyMinorVersion>
        <AssemblyBuildNumber></AssemblyBuildNumber>
        <AssemblyRevision></AssemblyRevision>
        <AssemblyBuildNumberType>
            DateString
        </AssemblyBuildNumberType>
        <AssemblyBuildNumberFormat>
            yyMMdd
        </AssemblyBuildNumberFormat>
        <AssemblyRevisionType>
            AutoIncrement
        </AssemblyRevisionType>
        <AssemblyRevisionFormat>00</AssemblyRevisionFormat>
    </PropertyGroup>

    <!-- Properties for controlling the Assembly File Version -->
    <PropertyGroup>
        <AssemblyFileMajorVersion>1</AssemblyFileMajorVersion>
        <AssemblyFileMinorVersion>0</AssemblyFileMinorVersion>
        <AssemblyFileBuildNumber></AssemblyFileBuildNumber>
        <AssemblyFileRevision></AssemblyFileRevision>
        <AssemblyFileBuildNumberType>
            DateString
        </AssemblyFileBuildNumberType>
        <AssemblyFileBuildNumberFormat>
            yyMMdd
        </AssemblyFileBuildNumberFormat>
        <AssemblyFileRevisionType>
            AutoIncrement
        </AssemblyFileRevisionType>
        <AssemblyFileRevisionFormat>
            00
        </AssemblyFileRevisionFormat>
    </AssemblyFileRevisionFormat>
```

```
</PropertyGroup>

<!-- Properties for controlling COM visibility -->
<PropertyGroup>
    <AssemblyComVisible></AssemblyComVisible>
    <AssemblyGuid></AssemblyGuid>
</PropertyGroup>

<!-- Properties for controlling extended
    assembly attributes -->
<PropertyGroup>
    <AssemblyCompany></AssemblyCompany>
    <AssemblyConfiguration></AssemblyConfiguration>
    <AssemblyCopyright></AssemblyCopyright>
    <AssemblyCulture></AssemblyCulture>
    <AssemblyDescription></AssemblyDescription>
    <AssemblyProduct></AssemblyProduct>
    <AssemblyTitle></AssemblyTitle>
</PropertyGroup>

<!-- Properties for controlling
    key signing through assemblyinfo files -->
<PropertyGroup>
    <AssemblyIncludeSigningInformation>
        false
    </AssemblyIncludeSigningInformation>
    <AssemblyDelaySign>false</AssemblyDelaySign>
    <AssemblyKeyFile></AssemblyKeyFile>
    <AssemblyKeyName></AssemblyKeyName>
</PropertyGroup>

<!-- The items that get processed by the task -->
<ItemGroup>
    <AssemblyInfoFiles Include="**\AssemblyInfo.*"/>
</ItemGroup>

<!-- Import the task -->
<UsingTask AssemblyName="AssemblyInfoTask,
    Version=1.0.51130.0, Culture=neutral,
    PublicKeyToken=31bf3856ad364e35"
    TaskName="AssemblyInfo"/>

<!-- Re-define CoreCompileDependsOn to
    ensure the assemblyinfo files are updated
    before compilation. -->
<PropertyGroup>
    <CoreCompileDependsOn>
        $(CoreCompileDependsOn);
        UpdateAssemblyInfoFiles
    </CoreCompileDependsOn>
</PropertyGroup>
<!-- The target that acutally does all
    the work. The inputs are the same as
    the CoreCompileDependsOn target
    (with the addition of @(AssemblyInfoFiles)
    to ensure that we only ever update the AssemblyInfo
    files if a compile is actually going to take place.
    The outputs are the AssemblyInfoFiles that
    were passed in for update. -->
```

```
<Target Name="UpdateAssemblyInfoFiles"
   Inputs="$(MSBuildAllProjects);
   @(Compile);
   @(ManifestResourceWithNoCulture);
   $(ApplicationIcon);
   $(AssemblyOriginatorKeyFile);
   @(ManifestNonResxWithNoCultureOnDisk);
   @(ReferencePath);
   @(CompiledLicenseFile);
   @(EmbeddedDocumentation);
   @(CustomAdditionalCompileInputs);
   @(AssemblyInfoFiles)"
   Outputs="@(AssemblyInfoFiles);
   @(IntermediateAssembly)">
   <AssemblyInfo AssemblyInfoFiles=
      "@(AssemblyInfoFiles)"
      AssemblyMajorVersion="$(AssemblyMajorVersion)"
      AssemblyMinorVersion="$(AssemblyMinorVersion)"
      AssemblyBuildNumber="$(AssemblyBuildNumber)"
      AssemblyRevision="$(AssemblyRevision)"
      AssemblyBuildNumberType="$(AssemblyBuildNumberType)"
      AssemblyBuildNumberFormat=
         "$(AssemblyBuildNumberFormat)"
      AssemblyRevisionType="$(AssemblyRevisionType)"
      AssemblyRevisionFormat="$(AssemblyRevisionFormat)"
      AssemblyFileMajorVersion="$(AssemblyFileMajorVersion)"
      AssemblyFileMinorVersion="$(AssemblyFileMinorVersion)"
      AssemblyFileBuildNumber="$(AssemblyFileBuildNumber)"
      AssemblyFileRevision="$(AssemblyFileRevision)"
      AssemblyFileBuildNumberType
         ="$(AssemblyFileBuildNumberType)"
      AssemblyFileBuildNumberFormat
         ="$(AssemblyFileBuildNumberFormat)"
      AssemblyFileRevisionType="$(AssemblyFileRevisionType)"
      AssemblyFileRevisionFormat
         ="$(AssemblyFileRevisionFormat)"
      ComVisible="$(AssemblyComVisible)"
      AssemblyGuid="$(AssemblyGuid)"
      AssemblyCompany="$(AssemblyCompany)"
      AssemblyConfiguration="$(AssemblyConfiguration)"
      AssemblyCopyright="$(AssemblyCopyright)"
      AssemblyCulture="$(AssemblyCulture)"
      AssemblyDescription="$(AssemblyDescription)"
      AssemblyProduct="$(AssemblyProduct)"
      AssemblyTitle="$(AssemblyTitle)"
      AssemblyIncludeSigningInformation
         ="$(AssemblyIncludeSigningInformation)"
      AssemblyDelaySign="$(AssemblyDelaySign)"
      AssemblyKeyFile="$(AssemblyKeyFile)"
      AssemblyKeyName="$(AssemblyKeyName)">
      <Output TaskParameter="MaxAssemblyVersion"
         PropertyName="MaxAssemblyVersion"/>
      <Output TaskParameter="MaxAssemblyFileVersion"
         PropertyName="MaxAssemblyFileVersion"/>
   </AssemblyInfo>
  </Target>
</Project>
```

Note that `AssemblyBuildNumberFormat` and `AssemblyFileBuildNumberFormat` are specified in yyMMdd format. If you use `AssemblyInfoTask` as-is, it fails from January 1, 2007, onward. This is because the build number field in the assembly version number (defined using the `AssemblyVersion` attribute in AssemblyInfo.cs file) is an unsigned 16-bit integer; the maximum value it can store is 65,535. The date January 1, 2007, in yyMMdd format becomes the number 070101. Since this is greater than 65,535, the build crashes. One other quirk is that the build number field in the file version number (defined using the `AssemblyFileVersion` attribute in Assembly-Info.cs file) doesn't have this limitation. In any case, the workaround is to use an alternate format for assembly versions, such as ddMMyy. A better alternative, which we describe later in the chapter, is to use a fixed number for assembly versions. This is a best practice anyway, since the assembly version number should remain relatively stable during the course of the development cycle.

TIP   You can more easily analyze the contents of a target file using a tool such as the MSBuild Sidekick from Attrice Corporation (http://www.attrice.info/msbuild/); see figure 8.4.

Note in listing 8.2 that the property `CoreCompileDependsOn` is overridden and the target `UpdateAssemblyInfoFiles` is injected. `CoreCompileDependsOn` is an empty property defined in the Microsoft.TeamFoundation.Build.targets file. The targets specified in `CoreCompileDependsOn` are executed prior to code compilation. Consequently, the `UpdateAssemblyInfoFiles` target is executed before the project is compiled. This target executes the AssemblyInfo task to read and update the version information in the AssemblyInfo.cs file.

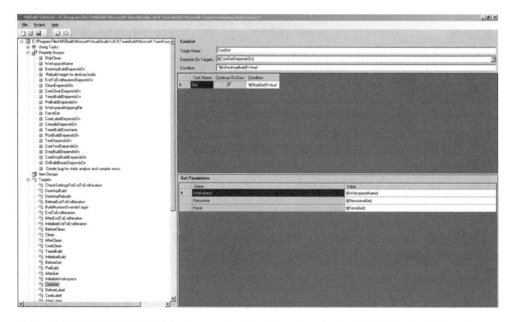

Figure 8.4   The MSBuild Sidekick allows you to visualize and customize MSBuild project files using a graphical user interface.

STEP 3—IMPORT THE MICROSOFT.VERSIONNUMBER.TARGETS FILE IN YOUR BUILD PROJECT

Hook the custom target (UpdateAssemblyInfoFiles) into the execution flow of the build process. This is achieved by importing Microsoft.VersionNumber.targets into your build project. Add the line shown in listing 8.3 to your build project file. This import statement should be added after the import statement for Microsoft.Team-Foundation.Build.targets. The MSBuild parsing process overrides previous declarations with later ones.

Listing 8.3 Import this file in your build script to execute the custom target

```
<Import Project
  ="$(MSBuildExtensionsPath)\Microsoft\
  AssemblyInfoTask\Microsoft.VersionNumber.targets"/>
```

STEP 4—MODIFY THE TEAM BUILD PROJECT FILE

Modify the build project file to tweak the behavior of AssemblyInfoTask to suit the recommended build process. This involves the following customization areas:

- Override some of the AssemblyInfo task-related properties (such as Assembly-MajorVersion, AssemblyMinorVersion, AssemblyFileMajorVersion, Assembly-FileMinorVersion, and so on) in the build script instead of changing the Microsoft.VersionNumber.targets file. The reason for this is because you're likely to reuse the Microsoft.VersionNumber.targets file for multiple build types. Since different build types could have different version numbers, it makes sense to localize the changes in individual build project files (TFSBuild.proj).

- Override the BuildNumberOverrideTarget to supply a custom build number. To assign a new build number to the current build, the task that is invoked in Build-NumberOverrideTarget should have an output property called BuildNumber. In our case, to create a custom build number, execute the UpdateAssemblyInfo-Files target (defined in Microsoft.VersionNumber.targets). Recall that the UpdateAssemblyInfoFiles target updates the reference AssemblyInfo.cs file and generates new assembly and file version numbers. Among other output properties, the UpdateAssemblyInfoFiles target returns two properties named Max-AssemblyVersion and MaxAssemblyFileVersion. These properties contain the current version numbers as generated by the AssemblyInfo task. Populate BuildNumber with the value obtained from MaxAssemblyFileVersion (along with appropriate build type-specific prefix).

- Note in listing 8.2 that in the Microsoft.VersionNumber.targets file, the UpdateAssemblyInfoFiles target is already specified to run inside Core-CompileDependsOn. Since we're invoking UpdateAssemblyInfoFiles inside the BuildNumberOverrideTarget target, we need to prevent it from being executed also in CoreCompileDependsOn. In the TFSBuild.proj file, override CoreCompileDependsOn so that the UpdateAssemblyInfoFiles target isn't executed. Instead, override the CoreCompileDependsOn property to copy the updated reference AssemblyInfo.cs file to the build location prior to code compilation. Create a new target named CopyAssemblyInfoFile and invoke it from CoreCompileDependsOn.

8.3.2   *Technical Implementation*

At this point, we have a good idea about the solution strategy. By following this process, you'll be able to stamp the generated assemblies with appropriate version information. Next, we look at the specific changes that need to be made to the build project file (TFSBuild.proj).

Override AssemblyInfo task-related properties

Note in listing 8.2 that the `AssemblyInfo` task, by default, creates a build number in yyMMdd format and autoincrements the revision number. As discussed earlier, I prefer using an automatically incrementing integer as the build number and reserving the revision number for other purposes.

Listing 8.4 shows the changes that need to be made in the build project file. For information on various properties and their valid values, refer to the help file that ships with the `AssemblyInfo` task.

> **Listing 8.4   Modifying the build script to increment the build number**

```
<PropertyGroup>
    <AssemblyMajorVersion>2</AssemblyMajorVersion>
    <AssemblyMinorVersion>0</AssemblyMinorVersion>
    <AssemblyBuildNumber>0</AssemblyBuildNumber>
    <AssemblyRevision>0</AssemblyRevision>
    <AssemblyBuildNumberType>
        NoIncrement
    </AssemblyBuildNumberType>
    <AssemblyBuildNumberFormat></AssemblyBuildNumberFormat>
    <AssemblyRevisionType>NoIncrement</AssemblyRevisionType>
    <AssemblyRevisionFormat></AssemblyRevisionFormat>
</PropertyGroup>

<!-- Properties for controlling the Assembly File Version -->
<PropertyGroup>
    <AssemblyFileMajorVersion>2</AssemblyFileMajorVersion>
    <AssemblyFileMinorVersion>0</AssemblyFileMinorVersion>
    <AssemblyFileBuildNumber></AssemblyFileBuildNumber>
    <AssemblyFileRevision>0</AssemblyFileRevision>
    <AssemblyFileBuildNumberType>
        AutoIncrement
    </AssemblyFileBuildNumberType>
    <AssemblyFileBuildNumberFormat>
    </AssemblyFileBuildNumberFormat>
    <AssemblyFileRevisionType>
        NoIncrement
    </AssemblyFileRevisionType>
    <AssemblyFileRevisionFormat></AssemblyFileRevisionFormat>
</PropertyGroup>
```

The changes described in listing 8.4 will cause the `UpdateAssemblyInfoFiles` target to behave as follows:

- Write the assembly major version, assembly minor version, assembly build number, and assembly revision specified in the build script to the reference AssemblyInfo.cs file.

- Write the file major version, file minor version, and file revision specified in the build project file to the reference AssemblyInfo.cs file.
- Increment the file build number specified in the reference AssemblyInfo.cs file and write the new value back to the same file (the reference AssemblyInfo.cs file could be uploaded to TFVC in a location managed by the central build team).

SPECIFY THE REFERENCE ASSEMBLYINFO.CS FILE

Specify the location of the reference AssemblyInfo.cs file by overriding the Assembly-InfoFiles item (see listing 8.5 and figure 8.5).

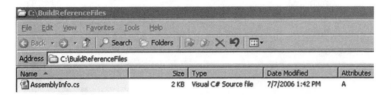

Figure 8.5
Create a reference AssemblyInfo.cs file for capturing the current assembly version information.

Listing 8.5   Override AssemblyInfoFiles to specify location of AssemblyInfo.cs

```
<ItemGroup>
  <AssemblyInfoFiles
     Include="C:\BuildReferenceFiles\AssemblyInfo.*"/>
</ItemGroup>
```

OVERRIDE THE BUILDNUMBEROVERRIDETARGET TARGET

The BuildNumberOverrideTarget is available for specifying custom build numbers. In the Microsoft.TeamFoundation.Build.targets file, this target has an empty implementation. We want to override this target in our build project file. Consistent with the best practice for overriding targets, create a property named BuildNumber-OverrideTargetDependsOn and specify the property name in BuildNumberOverride-Target's DependsOnTargets attribute. This modification causes the targets specified in the BuildNumberOverrideTargetDependsOn property to be executed before the target is invoked.

Modify the BuildNumberOverrideTargetDependsOn property in the build script to call the UpdateAssemblyInfoFiles target (see listing 8.6). Note that we create a property named BuildNumber inside the BuildNumberOverrideTarget target. In addition to other uses, this property is used in the CoreLabel target (defined in the Microsoft.TeamFoundation.Build.targets file) to label the source files (see figure 8.6). The BuildNumber property is created based on the value of the MaxAssemblyFileVersion property. MaxAssemblyFileVersion is an output property that belongs to the AssemblyInfo task (refer to listing 8.2 presented earlier).

Note that when creating the build number, we use a prefix specified in the Build-NumberPrefix property. This custom property provides an opportunity to label the source files differently, depending on whether it's an integration build, nightly build, milestone build, release build, and so on.

Moreover, in TFS 2005, the build numbers need to be unique across the TFS server—regardless of the build machine or team project involved. (This limitation has

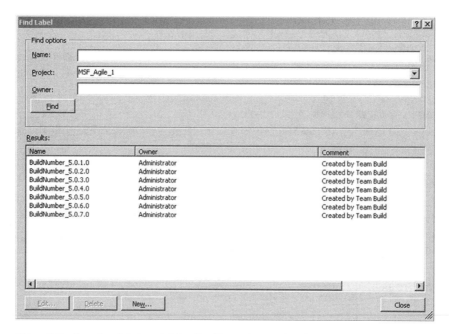

Figure 8.6   A custom label containing the file version number for identifying the source files that went into a specific build.

been removed in TFS 2008.) This means that if you've created a build numbered 1.0.20.0 in a particular team project, you can't create another build using the same number, even if the build is for another team project (assuming the team projects belong to the same TFS server). Using a prefix helps prevent build number conflicts and enables you to better organize the builds.

Listing 8.6   Override `BuildNumberOverrideTarget` to specify a custom build number

```
<!—Override the BuildNumberOverrideTargetDependsOn
    property to execute the UpdateAssemblyInfoFiles target which
    updates the reference AssemblyInfo file -->
<PropertyGroup>
    <BuildNumberOverrideTargetDependsOn>
        UpdateAssemblyInfoFiles
    </BuildNumberOverrideTargetDependsOn>
</PropertyGroup>

<!--The BuildNumberOverrideTarget target is overridden
    to customize the build number-->
<Target Name = "BuildNumberOverrideTarget"
    Condition=" '$(IsDesktopBuild)'!='true' "
    DependsOnTargets="$(BuildNumberOverrideTargetDependsOn)">

    <!-- Create a property with the name "BuildNumber" to
        customize the build number. The value for the
        BuildNumber property is constructed from
```

```
        BuildNumberPrefix and MaxAssemblyFileVersion
        properties. The MaxAssemblyFileVersion is output
        from the AssemblyInfo task
        (executed in the
        UpdateAssemblyInfoFiles target in Microsoft.
        VersionNumber.targets file)
    -->
    <CreateProperty
        Value="$(BuildNumberPrefix)$(MaxAssemblyFileVersion)">
        <Output TaskParameter="Value"
        PropertyName="BuildNumber"/>
    </CreateProperty>
  </Target>
```

TIP   You can view all labels and associated detailed information by typing the
following line at the Visual Studio command prompt:

```
C:\Program Files\Microsoft Visual Studio 8\VC>tf labels
/server:<tfs_server_name> /owner:* /format:detailed
```

If you don't want to view the detailed information, skip the /format switch.

The /owner switch is necessary if the account used by Team Build service is different
from the account you're using to run the tf command. If the accounts are different,
you won't be able to see the labels created by Team Build unless you specify the
/owner:* switch (or the specific owner name in the switch).

Copy the reference AssemblyInfo.cs file to the build location

In the previous sections, we used the AssemblyInfo task to insert appropriate version
numbers into the reference AssemblyInfo.cs file. Now we need to copy this file to the
build location (such as to the C:\Build\MSF_Agile_1\Test_Assembly_Versioning_
WinAppSources\TestWinApp\Properties folder in our build machine; see figure 8.7). If
the solution contains multiple projects, the reference AssemblyInfo.cs file should be
copied to the appropriate folder for each project. During compilation, the version information contained in the file is stamped on the build binaries.

But there's a problem with this approach. The files that are downloaded from
TFVC in the build directories happen to be read-only. Consequently, turn off the read-
only attribute of the autodownloaded AssemblyInfo.cs file prior to overwriting it with
the reference AssemblyInfo.cs file (see listing 8.7).

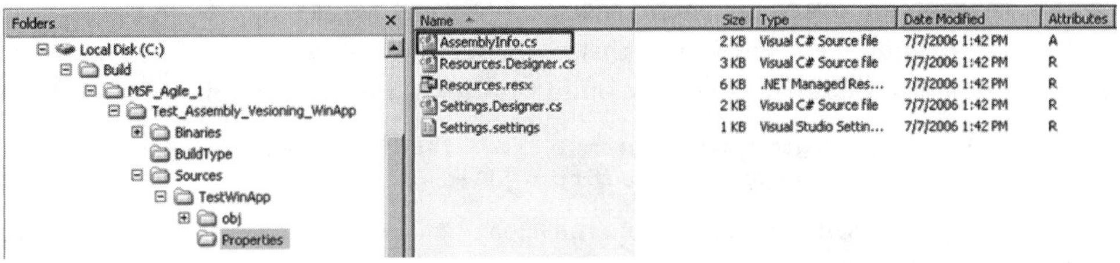

**Figure 8.7   Copy the AssemblyInfo.cs file to the build location to generate the correct version
information.**

The following steps are involved in copying the reference AssemblyInfo.cs file:

- Create a new target named `CopyAssemblyInfoFile` to encapsulate the operations required for removing the read-only attribute and copying the reference AssemblyInfo.cs file.

- Override the `CoreCompileDependsOn` property and add the `CopyAssemblyInfo-File` target. The value of `CoreCompileDependsOn` is defined as null in the Microsoft.TeamFoundation.Build.targets file. But in the Microsoft.VersionNumber.targets file, the `CoreCompileDependsOn` property is modified to include the `UpdateAssemblyInfoFiles` target (see listing 8.2). Consequently, overriding the `CoreCompileDependsOn` property in the build script (and calling only the `CopyAssemblyInfoFile` target from it) prevents the `UpdateAssemblyInfoFiles` target from being called during execution of `CoreCompileDependsOn`. This process may sound complicated, but is actually quite straightforward.

Listing 8.7 shows how to achieve these goals.

Listing 8.7   Overriding `CoreCompileDependsOn` in the build script

```
<!-- Re-define CoreCompileDependsOn to ensure the reference
   assemblyinfo.cs file is copied to the build location
   before compilation -->
<PropertyGroup>
   <CoreCompileDependsOn>
     CopyAssemblyInfoFile
   </CoreCompileDependsOn>
</PropertyGroup>

<!--Copy reference AssemblyInfo.cs file to build location-->
<Target Name="CopyAssemblyInfoFile"
   Condition=" '$(IsDesktopBuild)'!='true' " >
   <Exec Command="attrib &quot;$(AssemblyInfoFileBuildDir)\
   assemblyinfo.cs&quot; -r"/>
   <Copy
      SourceFiles="@(AssemblyInfoFiles)"
      DestinationFolder="$(AssemblyInfoFileBuildDir)" />
</Target>
```

In TFS 2008, you can also use the `OverwriteReadOnlyFiles` property of the `Copy` task to overwrite the read-only files.

FORCE EXECUTION OF THE UPDATEASSEMBLYINFOFILES TARGET

It turns out that even after all this work, the functionality of the `AssemblyInfo` task still doesn't work. If you check the build log file, you'll find the following message:

```
Skipping target "UpdateAssemblyInfoFiles" because all output files are up-
to-date with respect to the input files
```

The system is informing you that the `UpdateAssemblyInfoFiles` target wasn't executed. This is because the output files (as specified in the `Outputs` attribute of the `Update-AssemblyInfoFiles` target) aren't older than the input files (as specified in the `Inputs` attribute of the `UpdateAssemblyInfoFiles` target). Targets in MSBuild have `Inputs` and `Outputs` attributes to support incremental builds. Based on the file timestamps of the associated input and output files, a target may be executed or skipped. For more information about creating incremental builds, visit http://msdn2.microsoft.com/en-us/library/ms171483.aspx.

To force the execution of the `UpdateAssemblyInfoFiles` target, add the code shown in listing 8.8 to the build project file.

Listing 8.8 Forcing execution of the `UpdateAssemblyInfoFiles` target

```
<ItemGroup>
  <IntermediateAssembly Include="$(SolutionRoot)\
    dummy.dll"/>
</ItemGroup>
```

TIP You can dig deeper into the problems encountered during the build process by inserting the following switch in the TFSBuild.rsp file (the MSBuild response file). For TFS 2005, type

```
/verbosity:diag
```

For TFS 2008, type

```
/flp:verbosity=diag
```

This command-line option causes MSBuild to produce a more verbose build log file containing execution details.

HARMONIZE ACCESS AND MODIFICATION TIMES

For the sake of consistency, set the modification time of the generated binaries to standard values. This can be done using the predefined `Touch` task in MSBuild. The code snippet in listing 8.9 shows how to override the `AfterDropBuild` target and standardize the modification times of the build binaries using the `Touch` task (see figure 8.8).

Listing 8.9 Setting the modification time of generated binaries to standard values

```
<Target Name="AfterDropBuild"
   Condition=" '$(IsDesktopBuild)'!='true' " >
   <CreateItem Include="$(DropLocation)\
     $(BuildNumber)\**\*.*" >
     <Output ItemName="FilesToTouch" TaskParameter=
       "Include" />
   </CreateItem>
   <Touch
     Time="12:00:00"
     Files="@(FilesToTouch)" >
     <Output TaskParameter="TouchedFiles" ItemName=
       "FilesTouched"/>
   </Touch>
</Target>
```

The `Touch` task has an input parameter named `Time` that you can use to specify the standard modification time for the build binaries. If you don't specify this parameter, the current time is used.

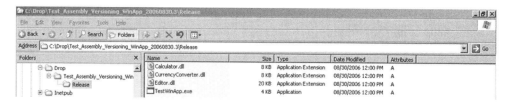

Figure 8.8   Use the `Touch` task to standardize the modification times of the generated assemblies.

8.4   Versioning web applications

Versioned assemblies for web applications need to be created for all but trivial projects. The reasons for this are the same as for Windows applications. Without a methodical version numbering strategy, you'll lose the ability to determine what changes were included in which versions, which source files went into which build, which version of the software is currently deployed at a client site, and which files to ship for client-specific incremental updates. A random version numbering system creates confusion, causes deployment problems, and results in reduced customer satisfaction.

8.4.1   Building web sites

By default, the assembly versioning mechanism in ASP.NET 2.0 is less than optimal. Let's review the options available for building a web site (see figure 8.9).

Figure 8.9   Build options available for building web sites in ASP.NET 2.0

- *Build Web Site*—This option creates a set of compiled assemblies for UI pages, the contents of the App_Code directory, and other elements of the web site. The source files (some autogenerated) as well as the compiled binaries are placed in the %WINDIR%\Microsoft.NET\Framework\v2.x.xxxx\ Temporary ASP.NET Files directory (for example, C:\WINDOWS\Microsoft.NET\Framework\v2.0.50727\Temporary ASP.NET Files\website\ bb143155 directory on my machine). This option is primarily used to check whether your web site code compiles without any errors; it's not suitable for creating binaries for deployment.

- *Publish Web Site*—This option removes source code files, optionally removing the HTML markup code from .aspx files as well, and creates a set of binaries for deployment purposes (see figure 8.10 for available options).

Let's look at some of the options available in the Publish Web Site dialog box:

- *Allow This Precompiled Site to be Updatable*—If this check box is selected, the .as*x files are left as-is with their markup HTML code unchanged. If this check box is cleared, the HTML code inside the .as*x files is compiled into binary files. Moreover, a .compiled file is generated for each .as*x file that contains the mapping between a page's virtual path and the compiled assembly.

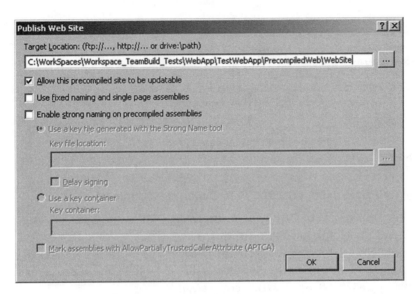

Figure 8.10   Available options during publishing a web site

- *Use Fixed Naming and Single Page Assemblies*—If this check box is selected, a separate assembly is created for each .as*x file in the site and the names of the compiled binaries remain unchanged when the code is republished. If this check box is cleared, a separate assembly is created for each directory in the site and the names of the generated assemblies change every time the code is republished.

The behavior of the Publish Web Site option isn't suitable for enterprise deployment scenarios, for the following reasons:

- Every time you publish the web site, unless the Use Fixed Naming and Single Page Assemblies check box is selected, the names of the generated assemblies change. This makes it impossible to incrementally update web sites.
- If you select the Use Fixed Naming and Single Page Assemblies option, a separate assembly is generated for each .as*x file. In a large web site with lots of UI pages, you end up with a large number of assembly files, making maintenance and deployment difficult.
- There's no way to put all code in a single assembly.
- There's no support for automatically incrementing the version number during build.

To assign specific assembly and file version information to all binaries generated during the publish operation, insert the code shown in listing 8.10 in the web.config file. The code assumes that the reference AssemblyInfo.cs file containing the intended assembly and file information is located in the C:\BuildReferenceFiles folder.

Listing 8.10   Code to stamp all generated assemblies with version information

```
<system.codedom>
    <compilers>
        <compiler language="c#;cs;csharp" extension=".cs"
            type="Microsoft.CSharp.CSharpCodeProvider, System,
            Version=2.0.3600.0, Culture=neutral,
            PublicKeyToken=b77a5c561934e089" warningLevel="1"
            compilerOptions=
            "C:\BuildReferenceFiles\AssemblyInfo.cs" />
    </compilers>
</system.codedom>
```

8.4.2   *Building web sites using VS 2005 Web Deployment Projects*

Visual Studio 2005 Web Deployment Projects (WDP) is an add-in for facilitating the deployment of ASP.NET 2.0 web sites. You can learn more about it at http://msdn.microsoft.com/en-us/library/aa479568.aspx. WDP creates an MSBuild project file to handle compilation and deployment-related tasks. It also offers options to customize the web.config file based on build configuration, create virtual directories, create a single output assembly, and so on.

Figure 8.11   The Add Web Deployment Project option is available under the Build menu after installing the Visual Studio 2005 Web Deployment Projects (WDP) add-in.

After installing WDP, you'll get a new option, Add Web Deployment Project, under the Build menu (see figure 8.11). You'll get the same option if you right-click the web site name in Solution Explorer. During installation, WDP installs a tool named aspnet_merge.exe for merging multiple source assemblies into a single target assembly. WDP also installs a set of tasks and a targets file named Microsoft.WebDeployment.targets under the MSBuild directory (in the %ProgramFiles%\MSBuild\Microsoft\WebDeployment\v8.0 directory). The target file is executed when you build the web deployment project.

When you add a WDP project to the solution containing your web site, WDP creates a MSBuild project file with the extension .wdproj. The .wdproj file imports the Microsoft.WebDeployment.targets file and contains various build-related settings. You can customize the .wdproj file to tailor the build process per your requirements.

When creating a solution for your web site, create a blank solution first. Then add your web site project, followed by a web deployment project. The reason for this is because when you create a new web project, VS 2005 creates the solution file in your My Documents\Visual Studio 2005\Projects directory. The solution file (*.sln) retains a reference to the physical path of the project file. As a result, if you try to bind the solution to the source control, you'll receive a warning message, as shown in figure 8.12. If you ignore the message and check in the code anyway, the build process will fail when you try to compile the solution using Team Build. This is because the physical path specified in the solution file doesn't exist in the build machine (unless

Figure 8.12
TFVC displays a
warning when the web
application solution file
contains a nonrelative
path to project files.

you create it yourself) and Team Build won't be able to locate the source files during compilation. To resolve this problem, create a blank solution first and then add the web site and web deployment projects. VS 2005 will insert a relative path instead of an absolute path into the solution file.

You can specify various options related to the creation of output assemblies in the web deployment project's property pages (see figure 8.13). For more information regarding the options, as well as to learn more about WDP, refer to the article "Using Web Deployment Projects with Visual Studio 2005," available from the Microsoft web site at http://msdn2.microsoft.com/en-us/library/aa479568.aspx. You can also specify the version information in the Property Pages dialog box. The information that you enter is persisted in the .wdproj file.

Since the web deployment project file (the .wdproj file) is an MSBuild file, you can extend it to support your own requirements. For example, if you open the file (using Notepad or another text editor), you'll find the empty targets shown in listing 8.11. You can override these targets as well as other targets defined in the Microsoft.WebDeployment.targets file to customize the build process.

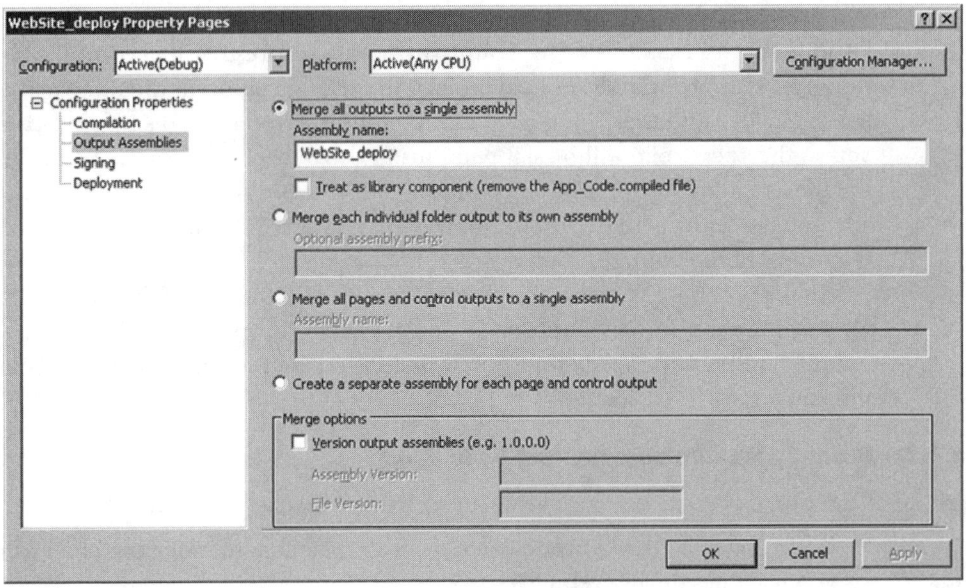

Figure 8.13   Assembly generation options available in a web deployment project

Listing 8.11   Empty targets defined in the .wdproj file for customization

```
<Target Name="BeforeBuild">
</Target>
<Target Name="BeforeMerge">
</Target>
<Target Name="AfterMerge">
</Target>
<Target Name="AfterBuild">
</Target>
```

If you specified the assembly version information in the Property Pages dialog box (see figure 8.13), the information will be stored persisted in the .wdproj file (see listing 8.12).

Listing 8.12   Assembly and file versions stored in corresponding .wdproj file

```
<ItemGroup Condition="'$(Configuration)|$(Platform)'
  == 'Debug|AnyCPU'">
  <AssemblyAttributes Include="AssemblyFileVersion">
    <Value>1.0.0.0</Value>
  </AssemblyAttributes>
  <AssemblyAttributes Include="AssemblyVersion">
    <Value>1.0.0.0</Value>
  </AssemblyAttributes>
</ItemGroup>
```

When you build the web deployment project using VS 2005, the build binaries are stamped with the version information indicated in the .wdproj file. When you build the web deployment project using Team Build, the generated assemblies are also marked with this version information. But you need to pay attention to the `Condition` attribute of the `ItemGroup` (see listing 8.12) and ensure that the Team Build configuration is set appropriately. For example, if the configuration in the .wdproj file is set to `Debug|AnyCPU` and the configuration in the build script is set to `Release|Mixed Platforms`, the `ItemGroup` will be skipped during the build operation in Team Build, leaving the assembly version numbers unassigned. You could simply delete the `Condition` attribute to ensure that the assembly numbers are assigned per your preference, regardless of the configuration.

At this point, we've created a process for marking the build binaries with a specific version number. But this approach doesn't solve the problem of autogenerating a unique build number each time a new build is created for your web site. We deal with this issue in the next section.

8.4.3   Strategy for autoincrementing build numbers

To recap, our goals when building an ASP.NET 2.0 web site are as follow:

1 To create a single output assembly in a repeatable manner (no change in assembly names during rebuild).

2 To enable the build team to maintain control of the assembly and file version information. Just like Windows applications, we want to keep the assembly version number relatively static and update the file version during each build. The build number contained in the file version number should be autoincremented for each build.

3 To label the source files with the current file version number for traceability purposes.

Our strategy for meeting these goals is as follows:

1 Use VS 2005 Web Deployment Projects to control the generation of output assemblies in a repeatable manner. As discussed in the previous section, WDP merges the numerous assemblies created by ASP.NET into a single assembly using the aspnet_merge.exe tool (if you select the Merge All Outputs to a Single Assembly option in the WDP project's property page). WDP also creates an MSBuild project file for performing the build operation.

2 To autoincrement the build number, use the `AssemblyInfo` task discussed earlier (refer to the discussions in sections 8.2 and 8.3). The `AssemblyInfo` task updates a reference AssemblyInfo.cs file. This file is copied to the App_Code directory in the build location just before the compilation step in the build process. At runtime, the `AspNetMerge` target, which is defined in the Microsoft.WebDeployment.targets file installed by WDP, stamps the version information on the generated assemblies. This information is obtained from the AssemblyInfo.cs file located in the App_Code directory. Refer to the next section for the modifications necessary in the build project file to implement this functionality.

3 Label the source code in TFVC with the current file version number.

8.4.4 Modifying the team project file

The changes needed are similar to those discussed in "Step 4—Modify the Team Build project file" under the Technical Approach section (section 8.3.1). In that section, we discussed the modifications necessary in the Team Build project file to support autoincrementing the build number for Windows applications. The changes are categorized as follows:

- Import the Microsoft.VersionNumber.targets file and override its custom properties to specify how the version numbers should be generated. In our case, we specify the nonvolatile portions of the assembly and file version numbers and indicate that only the build number contained in the file version should be autoincremented.

- Specify the location of the reference AssemblyInfo.cs file. The `AssemblyInfo` task updates the reference file with updated version information during the build process.

- Modify `BuildNumberOverrideTargetDependsOn` to call the `UpdateAssembly-InfoFiles` target. This target is defined in the Microsoft.VersionNumber.targets file and updates the version information in the reference AssemblyInfo.cs file.

- Create a custom target (named `CopyAssemblyInfoFile`) to copy the reference AssemblyInfo.cs file to the build location, just before the compilation step. Modify `CoreCompileDependsOn` to call this target.

For more information regarding the above changes, refer to "Step 4—Modify the Team Build project file" under the Technical Approach section in this chapter.

If you're specifying the version information in the Team Build project file (TFS-Build.proj file), remove the `AssemblyAttributes` item group from the web deployment project (.wdproj) file. Otherwise, the presence of these attributes will trigger the `GenerateAssemblyInfo` task (defined in the Microsoft.WebDeployment.targets file), which will create a separate AssemblyInfo.cs file containing the version numbers defined in the `AssemblyAttributes` section. The version attributes defined in the compiled AssemblyInfo.dll will be used by the aspnet_merge.exe tool when creating the output assembly. The outcome will be that the output assembly will be marked with the version numbers defined in the `AssemblyAttributes` section of the .wdproj file. But depending on the assembly generation options indicated in the property pages of the web deployment project, other assemblies (such as App_Code.dll) could be stamped with the version information specified in the Team Build project file (TFS-Build.proj). This will result in massive confusion. Therefore, remove the `Assembly-Attributes` section from the .wdproj file and specify the version information in the build project file.

8.5   Summary

In this chapter, we learned how to improve traceability between generated binaries and their sources using meaningful build numbers. We modified the build process to change the default build numbering scheme. We used a custom format and automatically incremented the build number for Windows as well as web applications. We saw that web applications need to be configured using an add-in so that they can be built using an MSBuild file.

In the next chapter, we look at selected topics related to operating and extending TFS. We also discover how the value of TFS can be augmented by leveraging other Microsoft products such as InfoPath 2007, Access 2007, SharePoint Server 2007 (MOSS 2007), and SQL Server 2005 Analysis Services.

Part 3

Administering and customizing TFS

In part 3 of the book, we learn about selected operational and extensibility features of TFS.

When administering TFS, you need to think about team project structure, current and projected load, capacity planning, security, high availability, disaster recovery, and so on. Your goal is to ensure that TFS is deployed as a good citizen in a data center and is managed like any other piece of critical IT infrastructure, using standard tools and processes.

When using TFS to implement your chosen software development process, you may need to extend TFS as well as interoperate with other complementary technologies. Additionally, you may find that there are out-of-band activities for which TFS offers just one piece of the solution—you may need a workflow system to tie all the pieces together.

In the following chapters, we learn about selected issues regarding TFS administration and customization. We discover the limitations as well as the possibilities.

Configuring and extending TFS

This chapter covers

- Organizing team projects
- Performance and high availability considerations
- Creating custom controls
- Creating key performance indicators

In this chapter, we look at a few issues that come up in real life. I assume that you have a general idea of TFS and an understanding of the TFS object model, and know how to install and administer the product. The topics discussed in this chapter provide concrete illustrations and insights regarding how you can extend TFS to suit your own requirements.

In previous chapters, we've discussed database management, version control, and build features, both for TFS 2005 and TFS 2008. In this chapter we discuss how to set up team projects, ensure scalability and high availability, promote ease-of-use via custom controls, and create high-level key performance indicators (KPIs). While discussing these topics, we drill down in relevant areas and talk about associated features, limitations, and workarounds.

This chapter doesn't provide introductory information regarding how to use TFS, program against its object model, create reports, and so on. I assume that you're familiar with TFS and know the basics. The goal of this chapter is to dive deep into selected problem areas, based on practical use cases and field experiences.

This chapter also explores how the value of TFS can be augmented by using complementary products such as Excel 2007, SharePoint Server 2007 (MOSS 2007), and SQL Server 2005 Analysis Services. Instead of using TFS as an island, you can derive greater value by interconnecting and interoperating TFS with complementary technologies. The value of the larger solution is greater than the sum of its parts. After all, TFS itself leverages key Microsoft platforms such as SQL Server 2005, SQL Server 2005 Reporting Services, Windows SharePoint Services 3.0, and so forth.

In this chapter, you'll learn about the following:

- *How to organize team projects*—Team projects establish coarse-grained administrative boundaries. Learn about the considerations, practices, and limitations associated with creating new team projects.
- *How to deploy TFS for performance and high availability*—Like any other enterprise asset, TFS needs to be deployed in a scalable, performant, and reliable manner. Learn how to use 64-bit machines, offload some work from the main server, and plan for disaster recovery.
- *How to create custom controls*—Custom controls offer the ability to customize work item forms and enhance the user experience. Learn how to create custom controls and host them in work item forms.
- *How to create KPIs for monitoring project health*—KPIs provide a high-level snapshot of project status. Learn how to create KPIs in SQL Server 2005 Analysis Services and how to surface them in various applications.

9.1   Company types and TFS configuration issues

How you deploy, configure, and operate TFS depends on the size of your development team as well as your organizational practices. Given the flexibility and extensibility of the product, you can use TFS in a variety of ways.

9.1.1   Small companies

If you have a small development team with no more than five members, consider using Team Foundation Server Workgroup Edition. Despite its name, TFS Workgroup Edition supports Active Directory domain users, in addition to Windows workgroup users. From a licensing perspective, TFS Workgroup Edition doesn't require user or device Client Access Licenses (CALs). For more information regarding the licensing model for TFS, visit http://go.microsoft.com/?linkid=8883276.

9.1.2   Large companies

If you're deploying TFS in a large organization, you'll probably want to install TFS in a dual-server configuration powered by appropriate hardware. For more information regarding TFS capacity planning, visit http://msdn2.microsoft.com/en-us/

teamsystem/aa718938.aspx for TFS 2005 and http://msdn.microsoft.com/en-us/
library/ms400691.aspx for TFS 2008. You should also configure the system to support
high availability and disaster recovery. Additional considerations include whether to
use 64-bit machines as well as virtual machines. Also, keep in mind that there's a practical upper limit regarding the number of team projects that can be installed in a single TFS instance.

9.1.3 Large companies with distributed TFS

You may need to install a network of distributed TFS instances due to a variety of reasons—you may have multiple operating geographies, a need to scale beyond the capacity
of a single TFS instance, multiple subsidiaries with their own IT departments, and so on.
In such cases, you may also need to generate cross-server reports (to do so, create a separate reporting database containing information from multiple TFS instances). Or you
may need to provide thin-client access to remote servers (to do so, use Team System Web
Access; download the TFS 2005 version from http://www.microsoft.com/downloads/
details.aspx?FamilyID=2105C9EE-565E-47B9-A5AC-9A8FF8A07862&displaylang=en
and the TFS 2008 version from http://www.microsoft.com/downloads/details.
aspx?FamilyId=C568FBA9-3A62-4781-83C6-FDFE79750207&displaylang=en). Or you
may need to create builds from source files located in multiple TFS machines (discussed
in chapter 7), and so on.

9.2 Organizing team projects

When setting up TFS, one of the basic issues that you'll need to think about is how to
organize your team projects. Should you create a separate team project for each application in your organization? How about for each version? If you work in a consulting
company, should you create a separate team project for every client project? How
about for each client? How many team projects should you put on a single TFS server?
Can you archive a team project or move it to a different machine, in case resources
become scarce in a single TFS box? In this section, we look at these typical questions
and try to gain an understanding of the underlying factors.

A team project establishes an administrative boundary for a set of code files, work
items, documents, test cases, and other artifacts. A team project can contain multiple
Visual Studio solutions and projects—don't confuse Visual Studio projects with team
projects. Conceptually, a team project is more of a management construct than a technical one. As such, it's intended to be coarse-grained.

Let's look at some of the elements that constitute a team project and review how
TFS handles them in the context of multiple team projects. We discuss how work
items, version control, reports, project portal, process model, and security considerations need to be evaluated when structuring team projects.

9.2.1 Work items

Although there's a single underlying database table for storing all work items belonging to all team projects (and a single `WorkItemStore` class that exposes all work items

stored in a particular TFS server), when using Team Explorer, work items are scoped to a single team project. (The exception is the My Work Items for All Team Projects work item query.) The scoping enables team members to manipulate work items within a particular team project. You can also copy a work item from one team project to another, although you can't select multiple work items and copy them together.

To copy a work item from one team project to another, right-click a work item in the Query Results pane and select Create Copy of Work Item from the context menu. Choose the target team project in the Copy Work Item dialog box (see figure 9.1). You can also link work items across projects. Click Add in the Links tab of the work item form; in the Add Link Dialog box, click Browse. This action brings up the Choose Related Work Item dialog box; you can choose various team projects from the Project drop-down (see figure 9.2).

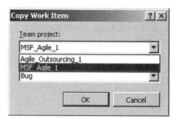

Figure 9.1   You can copy work items from one team project to another.

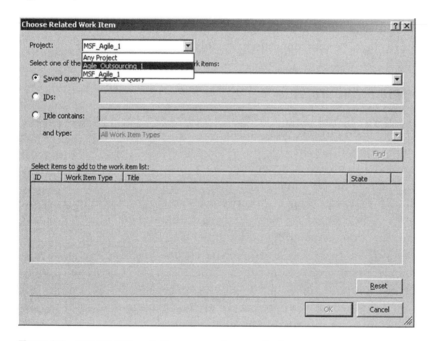

Figure 9.2   You can link work items across team projects.

9.2.2   *Version control*

TFS maintains a single version control tree with various team projects situated at peer levels. This is evident when you launch the Source Control Explorer in Team Foundation version control (TFVC). Assuming you have the necessary permissions, you can see the source files associated with all team projects (see figure 9.3). For sharing code, when creating a new team project, you can create a branch from the source tree of an existing team project. You can also branch across existing team projects at any time. Furthermore, you can map multiple team projects to a single workspace, facilitating code integration.

Figure 9.3   TFVC creates a single version control tree with team projects at peer levels.

9.2.3   Reports

The reports in a team project are scoped to the current team project. Let's review how this is actually implemented. Each report contains a report parameter named `Project`. The `DefaultValue` for the `Project` parameter is populated from the name of the team project folder in the report server. The `Default-Value` is set to the following expression:

```
=IIF(LEN(Parameters!ExplicitProject.Value) > 0,
Parameters!ExplicitProject.Value,
SPLIT(Globals!ReportFolder,
"/").GetValue(IIF(
split(Globals!ReportFolder, "/").Length >
1, 1, 0)))
```

The `Project` parameter is used in the underlying MDX queries to filter the report data and scope the query to a single team project. Consequently, when you view a report in Team Explorer or in the project portal, you see the data associated with a single team project. But the underlying data tier stores data for all team projects in a single relational data warehouse and in a single Analysis Services database. The Team System cube stores the aggregated measures and dimensions from all team projects. The team projects belong to a dimension named Team Project (see figure 9.4). There's nothing special about team projects as far as the cube is concerned. You can create custom reports to view server-level statistics, aggregating data from multiple team projects.

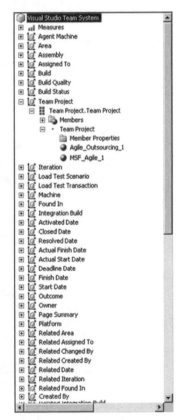

Figure 9.4   The Team System cube contains a dimension named Team Project.

9.2.4   Project portal

TFS creates a separate project portal for each team project. The project portal provides access to various reports, documents, lists, and so on. You can also set up shared announcements, tasks, events, and other lists for the team members. Distributed stakeholders can access near-real-time metrics using nothing but a web browser. But you can't share a project portal across team projects. If you're executing a collection of projects as part of a larger program, you can create a separate portal for the program, containing common artifacts as well as cross-project metrics. (You need to create the portal yourself; TFS won't do this for you.) For drill-down purposes, you can create links to the individual project portals from the program portal.

9.2.5   *Process model*

Team projects can be based on different process templates. TFS ships with two process models—MSF for Agile Software Development v4.2 (MSF Agile) and MSF for CMMI Process Improvement v4.2 (MSF CMMI). You can use additional third-party process models or create your own. But keep in mind that in addition to other factors, the complexity of the work item types associated with a process model determines the number of team projects that can be hosted in a single TFS server.

9.2.6   *Security*

TFS contains server-level groups as well as team project–level groups. To view the server-level groups, right-click the TFS server name, point to Team Foundation Server Settings in the context menu, and choose Security (see figure 9.5). The default server-level

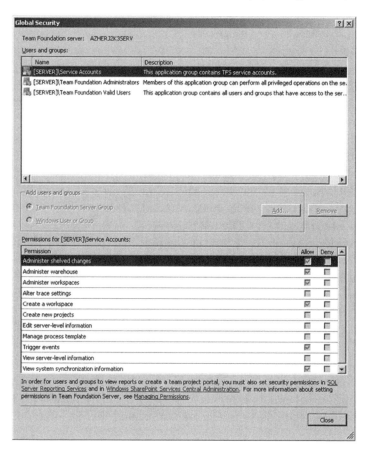

Figure 9.5   TFS creates three default server-level groups.

groups are Service Accounts, Team Foundation Administrators, and Team Foundation Valid Users. If you're using TFS Workgroup Edition, there's another group named Team Foundation Licensed Users. To view this group (assuming you're using TFS Workgroup Edition), right-click the TFS server name, point to Team Foundation Server Settings in the context menu, and choose Group Membership. To view the project-level groups, right-click a team project name, point to Team Project Settings in the context menu, and choose Security (see figure 9.6). The default project-level groups are Build Services, Contributors, Project Administrators, and Readers. Notice that two server-level groups—Team Foundation Administrators and Team Foundation Valid Users—are automatically included in the project-level group. For information about the permissions associated with these groups, visit http://msdn.microsoft.com/en-us/library/ms252587.aspx.

You need to be careful about the rights associated with the Team Foundation Valid Users group. This built-in group includes all TFS users, regardless of team projects. By default, the Team Foundation Valid Users group has View Project-level Information rights at the team project level. This means that any user of any team project can view

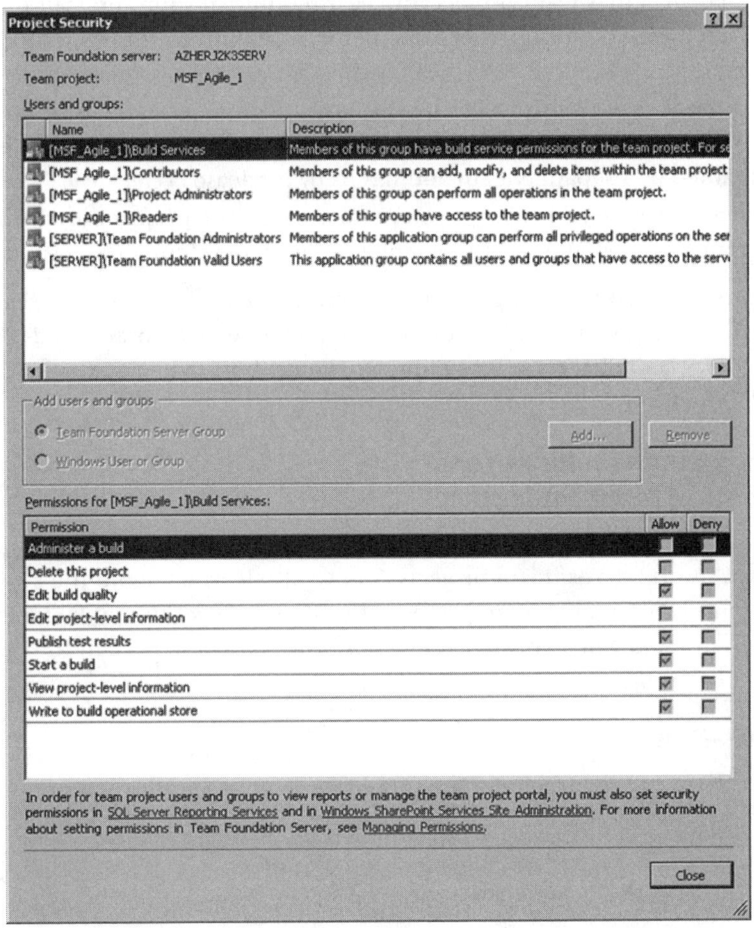

Figure 9.6
The project-level groups contain predefined server-level groups.

the list of all team projects located in a TFS server. He can also view the security groups and associated memberships of any team project, as well as see the build reports associated with any team project. For certain scenarios (such as multicustomer support), this behavior could be absolutely unacceptable. To prevent this behavior, remove the View Project-level Information right associated with the Team Foundation Valid Users group at the team project level. (To do so, right-click a team project name, point to Team Project Settings, click Security, and uncheck the View Project-level Information check box for the Team Foundation Valid Users group in the Project Security dialog box.)

9.2.7   General recommendations for organizing team projects

Given all that we have learned about team projects, we can distill our knowledge into a set of recommendations. Although many of the decisions that you'll have to make are situational, some general suggestions can be made regarding how to organize team projects:

- Don't create a new team project for every version of an application. Use the iteration categories to organize the work items along the time dimension.
- Don't create a new team project for every module in your application. Use the area categories to group the work items based upon the structure of your applications.
- Do create a new team project if you have a common framework code that's shared by multiple team projects. The common framework code is usually maintained by a separate team and has its own release cycle.
- Do create a new team project if you require a separate project portal (maybe for different stakeholders) or implement a different development methodology.

For more information on deciding whether to create a new team project versus whether to use an existing one, visit http://msdn.microsoft.com/en-us/library/ms242894.aspx and http://www.codeplex.com/BranchingGuidance/Wiki/View.aspx?title=Guidance%20for%20Structuring%20Team%20Projects.

9.3   Limitations and considerations when creating team projects

At this point, you should have a good understanding of how the subsystems within TFS work (or don't work) across team projects. You've also learned about the general recommendations for designing team projects. But there are additional factors that you need to keep in mind when constructing team projects. These pertain to system limitations and team project migrations.

9.3.1   System limitations

There are certain limiting factors that should be kept in mind when creating team projects. These are as follows:

- *Work item tracking metadata cache*—The size of the metadata cache determines both client and server resource consumptions. Having too many team projects in a single TFS server may impact performance, as well as cause the server to hit the IIS memory limits. One of the underlying problems in TFS is that regardless of membership, initially all users receive the metadata associated with all team projects. The recommendation from Microsoft is to have a maximum of 500 MSF Agile team projects or 250 MSF CMMI team projects per TFS server. For more information regarding the issues involved with the work item tracking metadata cache, visit http://msdn2.microsoft.com/en-us/library/aa974183(VS.80).aspx.

- *SQL Server column limit*—The work item table in the underlying TFS relational data warehouse contains all custom fields defined for all work item types in all team projects on a TFS server (see figure 9.7). Given the limit of 1,024 columns per table in SQL Server 2005, you need to make sure that you stay under this limit.

- *Lack of MS Project Server support*—There's no native integration with Project Server in TFS. (There's an open source version of the connector available; to learn more, visit http://www.codeplex.com/pstfsconnector.) Consequently, you can't get a cross-project view of resource utilization using the Microsoft Project client. Each team project is associated with a separate project plan. Therefore, it isn't possible to easily get a unified view of resource allocations across projects or perform resource-leveling beyond a single project, even if the same resource is working on multiple team projects.

If you start running into these problems, your first instinct may be to try to move some team projects to another machine. But this isn't as easy as you might initially think. In the next section, we discuss the issues involved in moving team projects from one TFS machine to another.

9.3.2 Moving team projects

There's no standard way to back up and restore an individual team project. There's also no standard way to move an individual team project from one TFS server to another. Consequently, if you start hitting the aforementioned limits or face performance degradation in a particular TFS instance (depending on hardware configuration and usage patterns), you won't be able to move some team projects to

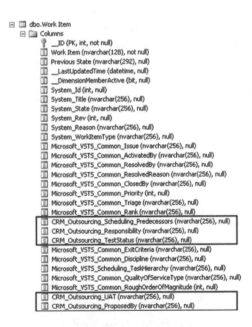

Figure 9.7 The Work Item table contains the custom fields defined in all team projects.

another TFS instance in order to reduce load (especially if the target machine is already populated with other team projects).

To transfer some team projects to a new TFS instance (one that doesn't have any existing team projects), back up the databases from the overloaded source TFS data-tier machine and restore the databases in the new target TFS data-tier machine. After restoring the databases, delete the unneeded team projects in the target machine (see "Deleting Team Projects," discussed later). Once you're sure that the migrated team projects have been accurately replicated in the target machine, delete them from the source machine.

For information on how to move a TFS instance from one machine to another, visit http://msdn2.microsoft.com/en-us/library/ms404869(VS.80).aspx for TFS 2005 and http://msdn2.microsoft.com/en-us/library/ms404869.aspx for TFS 2008. You can also use virtual machines to simplify TFS moves, provided you're using powerful hardware and find the performance, especially disk I/O, to be acceptable.

When copying TFS databases—backing up the databases from the source machine, restoring the databases in the target machine, and keeping both machines operational—you need to be aware of the problem associated with instance IDs. An instance ID uniquely identifies a TFS instance (it's a GUID stored in the database). When you move the databases from the source machine to the target machine, the source machine's instance ID also gets replicated in the target machine. Every client machine contains a file named ServerMap.xml (located in the %USERPROFILE%\Local Settings\Application Data\Microsoft\Team Foundation\1.0\Cache folder) that maps instance IDs to server URLs. Consequently, if there are two TFS instances running with the identical instance IDs, the client machines get confused about which machine to connect to, and could easily connect to the wrong one.

To solve this problem, use a utility named InstanceInfo.exe (located in the %ProgramFiles%\Microsoft Visual Studio 2008 Team Foundation Server\Tools folder) to stamp the target TFS instance with a new instance ID. The steps are outlined here: to clear the current instance ID, type the following (replacing *<<your new data tier>>* with the name of the target data-tier machine):

```
"%TFSInstallDir%\Tools\InstanceInfo.exe" stamp /setup /install
/rollback /d TFSWorkItemTracking,TFSBuild,TFSVersionControl,
TFSIntegration /s <<your new data tier>>
```

To generate a new instance ID, type the following (replacing *<<your new data tier>>* with the name of the target data-tier machine):

```
"%TFSInstallDir %\Tools\InstanceInfo.exe" stamp /d
TFSWorkItemTracking,TFSBuild,TFSVersionControl,TFSIntegration /s
<<your new data tier>>
```

When moving TFS tiers, also remember that a data-tier machine can talk to a single application-tier machine, and vice versa. This means that if you've moved some team projects to a separate data-tier machine (using the process described earlier), the new data-tier machine needs to be paired with a new application-tier machine. You can't use the old application-tier machine with both the old and the new data-tier machines.

When changing the data-tier machine, use the following command to notify the application-tier machine of the change:

```
TFSAdminUtil RenameDT <data_tier_machine_name>
```

When changing the application-tier machine, use the following command to inform the data-tier machine of the change:

```
TFSAdminUtil ActivateAT <application_tier_machine name>
```

DELETING TEAM PROJECTS

After the move, use the following command-line tool (located in the %Program-Files%\Microsoft Visual Studio 8\Common7\IDE folder in TFS 2005 and in the %ProgramFiles%\Microsoft Visual Studio 9.0\Common7\IDE folder in TFS 2008) to delete the unneeded team projects in the source and target TFS instances:

```
TFSDeleteProject /server:<tfs_server_name> <team_project_name>
```

Keep in mind that in TFS 2005, the TFSDeleteProject command doesn't delete the team project–related information from the data warehouse. It also doesn't physically delete the associated source files in TFVC. The source files in TFVC (the ones belonging to the deleted team project) are only marked as deleted. You can still view the deleted files along with their histories (and download the files to your local workspace) provided the Show Deleted Items in the Source Control Explorer option is selected. To see this option, on the Tools menu, click Options, expand the Source Control node, and click Visual Studio Team Foundation Server.

In TFS 2008, the TFSDeleteProject command permanently deletes all data including associated source files in TFVC. In TFS 2008, you can also use the tf destroy command to permanently remove source files (and folders) from TFVC as follows:

```
tf destroy <sever_file_spec>
```

This concludes our discussion of organizing and maintaining team projects. We now focus on another aspect of hosting TFS—how to ensure optimal performance and availability.

9.4 *Performance and high availability*

Performance and high availability are critical considerations when deploying TFS in an enterprise environment. As the codebase and number of users grow, you need to be able to scale TFS to meet increasing demands. Furthermore, you need to ensure that an important service such as TFS remains available and doesn't suffer from sudden disruptions.

9.4.1 *Load balancing*

TFS application-tier machines (assuming a dual-server installation) can't be load balanced using standard hardware load balancers or software solutions (such as network load-balancing clusters). There are two reasons for this. First of all, an application-tier machine maintains a number of system caches to optimize performance. For example, there's a Group Security Service cache that maintains group membership and authorization information, a Version Control cache that stores the changeset numbers, and another Version Control cache that stores the permission information. A second reason is the affinity between the data-tier and application-tier machines, as discussed previously. The data-tier machine is configured to communicate with a single application-tier machine. The name of the application-tier machine is stored in the tbl_registration_extended_attributes table in the TFSIntegration database (see fig-

Table - dbo.tbl...nded_attributes		
fk_registration...	name	value
1	ATMachineName	AZHERJ2K3SERV
2	ArtifactDisplayUrl	
1	ATNetBIOSName	AZHERJ2K3SERV
1	InstalledUICulture	1033
1	InstanceId	0BAC2C60-9748-4562-B18...
5	ArtifactDisplayUrl	
5	AttachmentServerUrl	/WorkItemTracking/v1.0/At...
6	ArtifactDisplayUrl	
7	ArtifactDisplayUrl	/Build
7	TeamBuild DB	TfsBuild
7	TeamBuild Server	AZHERJ2K3SERV
1	TfsIntegrationSchemaVersion	2
NULL	NULL	NULL

Figure 9.8   The name of the application-tier machine is stored in the data tier.

ure 9.8). Consequently, you can't load balance the application-tier machines using a bank of machines operating as a web farm; you need to stick to a single application-tier machine.

9.4.2   *Reducing load on the application-tier machine*

By default, the application-tier machine not only serves the TFS web service–based requests from the client machines, it also hosts the SharePoint-based team project portal and SQL Server Reporting Services components. Depending on your usage patterns, the presence of these two systems could place a burden on your application-tier machine and reduce performance. If your application-tier machine is under stress, consider offloading SharePoint and Reporting Services.

In addition to decreasing load on the TFS application-tier machine, another reason why you might need to move the SharePoint site has to do with the IT policies in your organization. Many organizations (especially larger ones) maintain a separate web farm and a separate back-end cluster to host the SharePoint sites. Having invested in such a scalable and fault-tolerant infrastructure, IT administrators are often not inclined to support a one-off SharePoint site sitting in a TFS box. For instructions on how to create project portals in a remote SharePoint machine, visit http://msdn2.microsoft.com/en-us/teamsystem/aa718901.aspx. TFS 2008 supports remote SharePoint instances, without going through complicated steps.

Note that currently there's no standard way in TFS 2005 to move existing project portals. The recommendation from Microsoft applies to creating new project portals in a remote SharePoint machine. Also, note that TFS 2005 is officially certified to work with Windows SharePoint Services 2.0 (WSS 2.0), not with SharePoint Portal Server 2003 (SPS). If you need to use SPS with TFS 2005, test thoroughly for potential compatibility issues before making a decision. If you need to use WSS 3.0 with TFS 2005, visit http://msdn2.microsoft.com/en-us/teamsystem/bb676233.aspx for detailed instructions. TFS 2008 adds built-in support for MOSS 2007 and WSS 3.0.

Using TFS 2008, you can also move Reporting Services to a remote server (running on any port). You can't do this if you're using TFS 2005. Offloading Reporting Services from the application-tier machine improves performance and scalability.

9.4.3 Reducing load on the data-tier machine

You can move the Analysis Services database to its own server in order to decrease the load on the data-tier machine. This reduces resource contention and is a best practice when designing scalable systems for business intelligence (BI). In order to perform the migration, you need to install TFS 2005 SP1 or TFS 2008. For instructions on how to move the Analysis Services database to another machine, visit http://msdn2.micro-soft.com/en-us/library/aa721760(VS.80).aspx for TFS 2005 SP1 installations and http://msdn.microsoft.com/en-us/library/aa721760.aspx for TFS 2008 installations.

9.4.4 64-bit processor support

To improve performance, consider using 64-bit machines. 64-bit processors improve performance by breaking the 4GB system memory limit imposed by 32-bit processors. The performance boost is significant for large memory-hungry applications. Since disk access is orders of magnitude slower than memory access, relational as well as Analysis Services databases perform better by caching data in memory. For more information regarding the increased capacities offered by 64-bit systems, visit http://support.microsoft.com/kb/294418. For information on the advantages offered by 64-bit platforms for running SQL Server 2005, visit http://www.microsoft.com/sql/edi-tions/64bit/overview.mspx.

To use TFS in a 64-bit environment, you need to adopt a dual-server configuration. The application tier (and the proxy server) needs to be installed on a 32-bit machine. If you try to install the application tier on a 64-bit machine, installation process will fail.

You can use TFS 2008 with 32-bit or 64-bit SharePoint installations. To use TFS 2008 with 64-bit SharePoint, download the 64-bit version of the TFS SharePoint Extensions (distributed as a power tool) from http://www.microsoft.com/downloads/details.aspx?FamilyID=00803636-1D16-4DF1-8A3D-EF1AD4F4BBAB&displaylang=en.

The data tier can be installed on 64-bit machines (using 64-bit versions of SQL Server). SQL Server for x64 Editions runs natively on 64-bit platforms. Team Foundation Build can also be installed in 64-bit machines, but will run under WOW64 (Windows on Windows) mode.

9.4.5 High availability and disaster recovery

As discussed, you can't use a web farm in the application tier for high availability purposes. The best you can do is maintain a "warm" standby machine. You can keep a second identical TFS application-tier machine on standby in case the primary machine fails. The standby server should be kept updated with respect to changes occurring in the primary TFS server—such as software updates, changes in security and group membership, changes to the reporting services encryption key, and deployed custom reports.

If the primary TFS server fails, bring the standby server online using the `TfsAdmin-Util ActivateAT` command. Also, change the DNS entries to point to the new machine. For more information on how to bring the standby server online, visit http://msdn2.microsoft.com/en-us/library/ms252501(VS.80).aspx for TFS 2005 and http://msdn.microsoft.com/en-us/library/ms252501.aspx for TFS 2008. A few third-party solutions are available to automate this process (for information regarding a solution from HP, visit http://h71019.www7.hp.com/ERC/downloads/4AA1-0019ENW.pdf).

To ensure high availability in the data tier, you can use SQL Server failover clustering. Clustering involves configuring a set of identical machines to access a common disk sub-system and switching over to another machine in case of a machine failure. But the shared disk introduces a single point of failure. To mitigate this risk, good clustering systems use RAID (redundant array of inexpensive disks)—or SAN (storage area network)—based solutions. For more information on how to configure TFS to use clustering, visit http://msdn2.microsoft.com/en-us/library/ms179530.aspx. Although you may need to go through some trouble to procure, set up, and maintain a cluster, the benefit you get is automatic failover.

The other option to ensure high availability in the TFS data tier is to use SQL Server mirroring. But when using mirroring with TFS, you don't get automatic failover capability. Despite this, you may find mirroring to be useful, since it's easier to set up and maintain than a cluster. For more information on setting up TFS data-tier mirroring, visit http://msdn2.microsoft.com/en-us/library/aa980644(VS.80).aspx for TFS 2005 and http://msdn.microsoft.com/en-us/library/aa980644.aspx for TFS 2008.

Finally, you can simply back up and restore at regular intervals for disaster recovery purposes. Due to the relatively long lead times involved, backup/restore is usually not a solution for high-availability purposes. When backing up TFS, you need to back up both the data-tier databases as well as the Reporting Services encryption key located in the application tier. Instructions for backup can be found in http://msdn.microsoft.com/en-us/library/ms253151.aspx. When restoring, you may choose to restore to the same machine or to a different machine. Instructions for restore can be found in http://msdn.microsoft.com/en-us/library/ms253082.aspx.

9.5   *Using custom controls in work item forms*

One of the most interesting features available in TFS 2005 Service Pack 1 and TFS 2008 is the ability to add custom controls to the work item form. This adds significant value—the functionalities that you can provide are limited primarily by your imagination. You could, for example, display a calendar control to select dates, create a time reporting form to capture hours worked, change the color of a control as deadlines approach, send the work item information via email, create a drop-down with custom sorting, show a progress bar based on percent completed, display custom or built-in reports—the possibilities are virtually limitless. Any data captured or computed using the custom control can be stored in a work item field or in a custom datastore.

In this section, we discuss how to create custom controls that can be hosted in the work item form.

9.5.1   *Creating custom controls*

The overall process for creating custom controls is as follows:

- Modify the process template and add information about the custom control—its name, location, field mapping, custom attributes, and so forth.
- Create a Windows control that inherits from `System.Windows.Forms.User-Control` as well as implements the `Microsoft.TeamFoundation.WorkItem Tracking.Controls.IWorkItemControl` interface.
- Create a configuration file containing assembly and type information regarding the custom control.
- Copy the assembly and configuration files to a predefined location where TFS can find the custom control at runtime.

In this section, we create two custom controls for demonstration purposes. The custom controls are displayed in the Details tab of the bug work item form (see figure 9.9). The Show Build Report custom control reads the build number (specified in the Found in Build field) and displays the corresponding build report. The Send Email custom control captures the data related to the current bug and sends it via email.

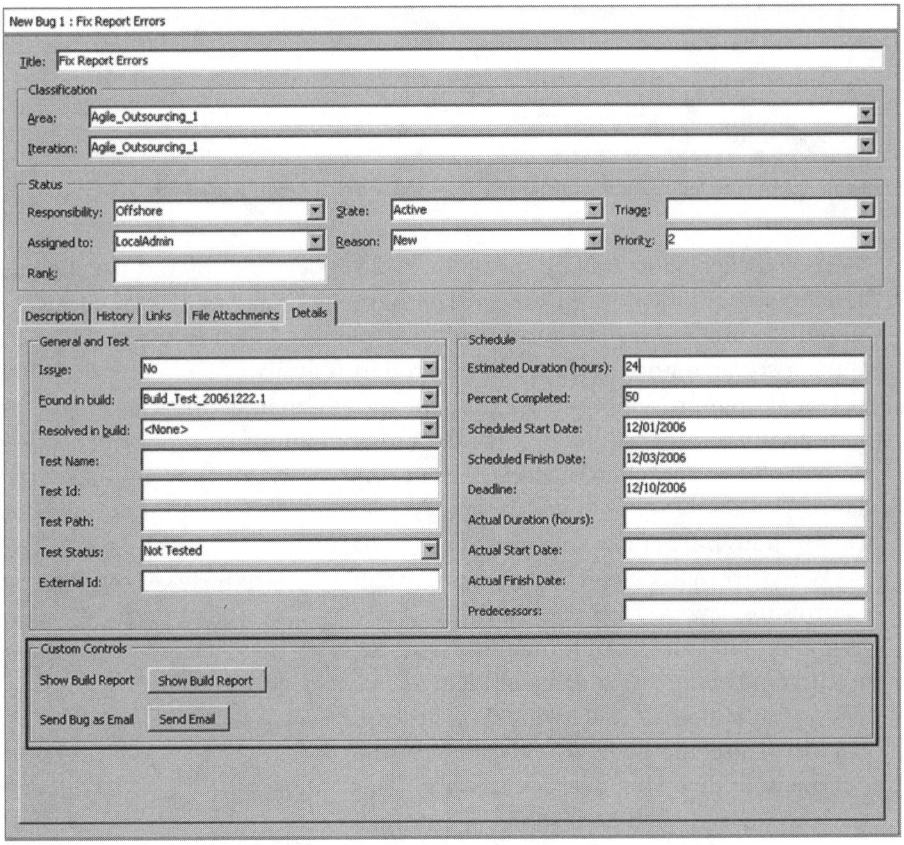

Figure 9.9   You can add custom controls to the work item form.

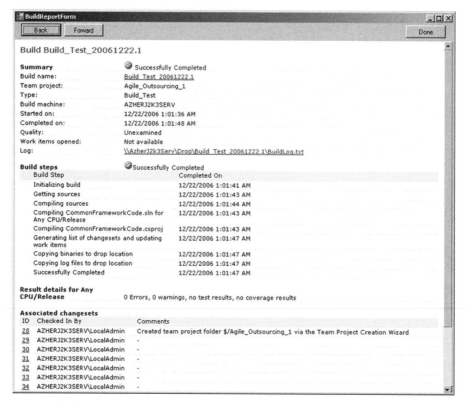

Figure 9.10   The build report is displayed when Show Build Report is clicked.

When you click Show Build Report, the build report is displayed (see figure 9.10). A developer could use this report to learn where the build binaries are located, copy the output assemblies, view the changesets that were included in the build, and get a list of the associated work items. The same report is available from the Team Build node in Team Explorer (double-click the build type and then double-click the target build), and the Builds report (double-click the target build in the report). The custom control enables you to quickly access the information right from the bug form without having to search for the build—a timesaver if you have a long list of builds, such as in a continuous integration scenario.

When you click Send Email, the custom control displays a form for specifying the recipient and subject information (see figure 9.11). The email contains all data associated with the bug, as well as attachments. You can customize the code to only include the information that you deem necessary. This enables you to conveniently send bug information to any party, on an ad hoc basis, at any stage of the work item's lifecycle.

Figure 9.11   You can send the work item information via an email using the Send Email custom control.

9.5.2 Technical review: creating custom controls

To learn about the technical issues involved, let's create a custom control from scratch. Armed with this knowledge, you'll be able to create custom controls to suit your own business goals and plug them into the work item form.

MODIFYING THE WORK ITEM TYPE

Begin by modifying a work item type to include information about the custom control. For more information on how to customize work item types, refer to http://msdn.microsoft.com/en-us/library/ms243849.aspx. In a nutshell, if you want to customize a work item type for use in new team projects, download the process template, modify the XML file representing the work item type, and upload the process template back to TFS. The download and upload operations can be performed from the Process Template Manager (see figure 9.12). To bring up the Process Template Manager dialog box, click the Team menu, point to Team Foundation Server Settings, and click Process Template Manager.

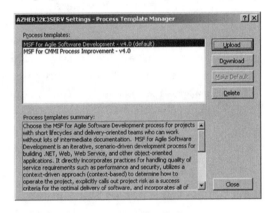

Figure 9.12 Use the Process Template Manager to download and upload process definitions for customization purposes.

To modify a work item type for an existing team project, use the `witexport` and `witimport` command-line utilities. To export a work item type, type the following:

```
witexport /f <your_filename> /t http://<TFS_server_name>:8080
/p <team_project_name> /n <work_item_type>
```

To upload a modified work item type, type the following:

```
witimport /f <your_filename> /t http://<TFS_server_name>:8080
/p <team_project_name>
```

Once you have access to the work item type definition file, insert the following line in the appropriate location under the "FORM" node:

```
<Control Type="<custom_control_name>" FieldName="<work_item_field_name>"
Label="<label_to_display_onscreen>" LabelPosition="Left"
CustomAttribute1="custom_attribute_1"
CustomAttribute2="custom_attribute_2"/>
```

You can add as many custom attributes as needed.

CONSTRUCTING THE CUSTOM CONTROL

Create a custom control as you normally would. Create a Windows Control Library project. Add references to the `Microsoft.TeamFoundation.WorkItemTracking.Client` and `Microsoft.TeamFoundation.WorkItemTracking.Controls` assemblies (see figure 9.13). On the design surface, drag and drop the necessary user interface controls from the toolbox.

Figure 9.13 Add the necessary reference files for creating a custom control.

Implement the `Microsoft.TeamFoundation.WorkItemTracking.Controls.IWork-ItemControl` interface (see figure 9.14). The code that you write to implement this interface will enable you to communicate with the work item host form as well as provide access to the work item object. The `Properties` collection contains the custom properties that you pass from the work item type definition file. The `WorkItemData-source` property gives you access to the current instance of the work item—you can retrieve the values of its fields as well as perform operations such as copy and validation. The `InvalidateDatasource` method is invoked by TFS (or your code) for rereading the data from the underlying datasource (or the work item object) and refreshing the control. TFS also invokes the `SetSite` method, which provides an `IServiceProvider` interface. By using the `GetService` method of the `IServiceProvider` interface, you can access the `DocumentService` service. The `Document-Service` service allows add-ins and VSIP packages to access the work item form, the query form, and the results screen.

Listings 9.1 and 9.2 show the code for a custom control that displays a build report based on the build number specified in the Found in Build field in the work item form. The general approach is to fetch the value of the `Microsoft.VSTS.Build.FoundIn` field from the work item object and then look up the build URI from the `BuildStore` object. This information is used to show the build report.

Figure 9.14 The `IWorkItemControl` interface contains the necessary members for communicating with the host work item form.

Listing 9.1 A custom control for displaying build reports

```
using System;
using System.Collections.Generic;
using System.Collections.Specialized;
using System.ComponentModel;
using System.Drawing;
using System.Data;
using System.Text;
using System.Windows.Forms;

using Microsoft.TeamFoundation.WorkItemTracking.Client;
using Microsoft.TeamFoundation.WorkItemTracking.Controls;

namespace BuildReportCustomControl
{
    public partial class BuildReportCustomControl :
        UserControl, IWorkItemControl
    {
        public BuildReportCustomControl()
        {
            InitializeComponent();
```

```csharp
}

#region IWorkItemControl implementation

// method implementations
void IWorkItemControl.Clear()
{
}

void IWorkItemControl.FlushToDatasource()
{
}

void IWorkItemControl.InvalidateDatasource()
{
}

private IServiceProvider _serviceProvider;
void IWorkItemControl.SetSite(
    IServiceProvider serviceProvider)
{
    _serviceProvider = serviceProvider;
}

// property implementations
private WorkItem _workItem;
object IWorkItemControl.WorkItemDatasource
{
    get
    {
        return _workItem;
    }
    set
    {
        _workItem = (WorkItem)value;
    }
}

private string _fieldName;
string IWorkItemControl.WorkItemFieldName
{
    get
    {
        return _fieldName;
    }
    set
    {
        _fieldName = value;
    }
}

private StringDictionary _properties;
StringDictionary IWorkItemControl.Properties
{
    get
    {
        return _properties;
    }
```

```
    set
    {
        _properties = value;
    }
}

private bool _readOnly;
bool IWorkItemControl.ReadOnly
{
    get
    {
        return _readOnly;
    }
    set
    {
        _readOnly = value;
    }
}

// event implementations
private EventHandler beforeUpdateDSEventHandler;
event EventHandler
    IWorkItemControl.BeforeUpdateDatasource
{
    add
    {
        beforeUpdateDSEventHandler =
            (EventHandler)Delegate.Combine(
            beforeUpdateDSEventHandler, value);
    }
    remove
    {
        beforeUpdateDSEventHandler =
            (EventHandler)Delegate.Remove(
            beforeUpdateDSEventHandler, value);
    }
}

private EventHandler afterUpdateDSEventHandler;
event EventHandler
    IWorkItemControl.AfterUpdateDatasource
{
    add
    {
        afterUpdateDSEventHandler =
            (EventHandler)Delegate.Combine(
            afterUpdateDSEventHandler, value);
    }
    remove
    {
        afterUpdateDSEventHandler =
            (EventHandler)Delegate.Remove(
            afterUpdateDSEventHandler, value);
    }
}

#endregion
```

```
/// this method is invoked when the Show Build Report
/// button is clicked
private void btnShowBuildReport_Click(object sender,
    EventArgs e)
{

    WorkItem wkItem = (WorkItem)(
        (IWorkItemControl)this).WorkItemDatasource;        Find FoundIn
    Field field = wkItem.Fields[                           number
        "Microsoft.VSTS.Build.FoundIn"];
    string buildNumber = field.Value.ToString();

    if (buildNumber != string.Empty)
    {
        BuildReportForm buildInfoForm = new             Display build
            BuildReportForm(buildNumber, wkItem.Project);  report form
        buildInfoForm.ShowDialog(this);
    }
    else
    {
        MessageBox.Show("Please Select a Build in the"+
            "Resolved in Build drop-down");
    }

    }
  }
}
```

At this point, we know how to display the build report form using the custom control. Let's look at the code for the build report form itself (see listing 9.2).

Listing 9.2   Code for the build report form

```
using System;
using System.Collections.Generic;
using System.ComponentModel;
using System.Data;
using System.Drawing;
using System.Text;
using System.Windows.Forms;

using System.Web.Services;
using Microsoft.TeamFoundation.Client;
using Microsoft.TeamFoundation.Build.Proxy;
using Microsoft.TeamFoundation.WorkItemTracking.Client;

namespace BuildReportCustomControl
{
    public partial class BuildReportForm : Form
    {
        public BuildReportForm()
        {
            InitializeComponent();
        }

        public BuildReportForm(string buildNumber,
            Project project) : this()
```

```
  {
     try
     {
        TeamFoundationServer tfs =
           project.Store.TeamFoundationServer;        Get ref to
        BuildStore buildStore = (BuildStore)           build store
           tfs.GetService(typeof(BuildStore));

        string buildUri = buildStore.GetBuildUri(
           project.Name, buildNumber);

        BuildData buildData =
           buildStore.GetBuildDetails(buildUri);

        string buildUrl;
        buildUrl = tfs.Uri.ToString()
           + "/Build/Build.aspx?artifactMoniker=" +      Determine and show
           buildData.BuildUri;                            build report URL

        buildReportBrowser.Navigate(buildUrl);
     }
     catch (Exception ex)
     {
        MessageBox.Show(ex.ToString());
     }
  }

  private void btnback_Click(object sender, EventArgs e)
  {
     buildReportBrowser.GoBack();
  }

  private void btnForward_Click(object sender,
     EventArgs e)
  {
     buildReportBrowser.GoForward();
  }
   }
}
```

DEPLOYING THE CUSTOM CONTROL

Deploying the custom control is simple. Instead of creating registry entries, simply create a configuration file containing the assembly name and the type name for the control. Create a file named *<your_custom_control_name>*.wicc; the contents are shown in listing 9.3. Copy the custom control assembly as well as the .wicc file to the Microsoft\Team Foundation\Work Item Tracking\Custom Controls folder under either the Environment.SpecialFolder.LocalApplicationData folder or the Environment.SpecialFolder.CommonApplicationData folder. Create the folder for the custom control if it doesn't already exist.

Once the assembly and .wicc files are deployed, bring up the modified work item form by creating a new work item or looking up an existing one. You'll see the custom controls displayed on the form in the designated location (see figure 9.9 shown earlier). Figure 9.9 also shows a second custom control for sending the work item information via an email; the source code for the custom control can be found in the book web site.

Listing 9.3 Contents of the custom control configuration file

```
<?xml version="1.0"?>
<CustomControl xmlns:xsi
   ="http://www.w3.org/2001/XMLSchema- instance"
   xmlns:xsd="http://www.w3.org/2001/XMLSchema">
   <Assembly>BuildReportCustomControl.dll</Assembly>
   <FullClassName>
      BuildReportCustomControl.BuildReportCustomControl
   </FullClassName>
</CustomControl>
```

This concludes our discussion of how to create and display custom controls. We now switch gears and talk about how to achieve another important real-life goal—displaying KPIs that present important information regarding the health of a project.

9.6   *Creating and using KPIs for TFS*

Key performance indicators (KPIs) represent critical metrics that quantify an organization's performance. KPIs have become increasingly prevalent in recent years, as part of an effort to improve the organizational decision-making process. KPIs are displayed in the executive dashboards of many organizations—providing a high-level, yet objective view of corporate activities vis-à-vis the defined goals. You can use KPIs to monitor project execution and team performance at an aggregate level.

Traditionally, KPIs have been created manually, based on analysis of project implementation data. The manual process often makes generating KPIs labor intensive and error prone. You can create KPIs automatically in TFS, leveraging the back-end SQL Server 2005 Analysis Services (SSAS) database. This approach not only eliminates the time-consuming manual process but also provides a near-real-time snapshot of your project's health.

In this section, we create a few representative KPIs for TFS using SSAS and surface them in Excel as well as MOSS 2007. You can apply these techniques to create your own KPIs and include them in your dashboards. We illustrate the process using a step-by-step approach.

9.6.1   *Step 1—Creating a business intelligence project*

Create a business intelligence project in Visual Studio. You can create the KPIs in one of two ways.

The first option is to create an Analysis Services project, add the necessary tables, create the appropriate data source views, design a cube with necessary measures and dimensions, and create the KPIs that you're interested in. For a tutorial on how to create an Analysis Services project, visit http://msdn.microsoft.com/en-us/library/ms170208 (SQL.90).aspx for SQL 2005 servers and http://msdn2.microsoft.com/en-us/library/ ms170208.aspx for SQL 2008. If you use this approach, you'll need to refresh the cube periodically in order to reflect the updated data stored in the underlying TFS relational data warehouse.

Alternatively, you can create an Import Analysis Services 9.0 Database project, import the TFSWarehouse database (see figure 9.15), and create custom calculated columns and KPIs per your requirements. Figure 9.16 shows the structure of the Team System cube after it's imported. If you modify the existing TFSWarehouse Analysis Services database to include your KPIs, then TFS will keep your KPIs updated by refreshing the cube periodically. Of course, you need to be especially careful when changing

Figure 9.15   You can import an Analysis Services database to view its underlying design.

the TFSWarehouse Analysis Services database, so as not to introduce errors inadvertently. The name of the target Analysis Services database is specified in the property pages of the project (see figure 9.17). The target database is updated when you actually deploy the project.

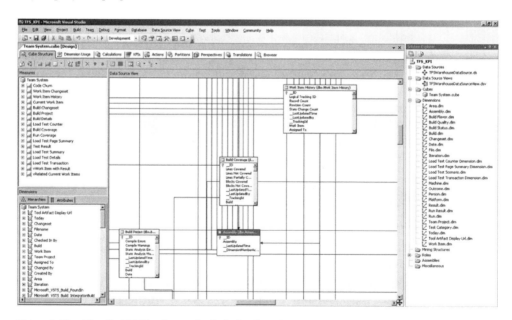

Figure 9.16   After the TFSWarehouse Analysis Services database is imported, you can study the design of the Team System cube and make appropriate changes.

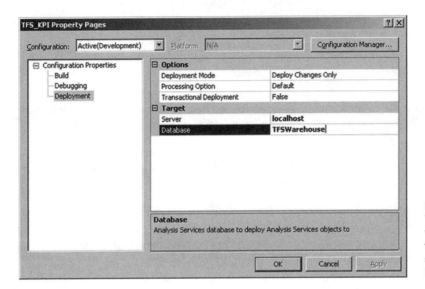

Figure 9.17
You can specify where to deploy the modified schema with KPIs.

9.6.2 Step 2—Creating calculated members

Browse the Team System cube and click the Calculations tab. Create the necessary calculated members to support the KPI calculations. For our sample KPIs, create the following calculated members:

- [Total_Reactivated_Bug_Count]—Total number of bugs that were made Active from Closed or Resolved states (see listing 9.4).

- [Total_Active_Bug_Count]—Total number of bugs that are currently in Active state (see listing 9.5).

- [Total_Bug_Count]—Total number of bugs in the system (see listing 9.6).

- [Total_Estimated_Task_Duration]—Total number of hours estimated for task completion (see listing 9.7). Since this field doesn't exist in MSF Agile, you need to create it as a custom field by modifying the task type in the process template.

- [Total_Actual_Task_Duration]—Total number of hours actually spent for task completion (see listing 9.8). Since this field also doesn't exist in MSF Agile, you need to create it as a custom field by modifying the task type in the process template.

Figure 9.18 shows the definition of the [Total_Reactivated_Bug_Count] calculated member.

Listing 9.4   Calculation for [Total_Reactivated_Bug_Count]

```
Sum (
    {
        ([Work Item].[System_WorkItemType].&[Bug],[Work
            Item].[Previous State].&[Resolved],[Work
            Item].[System_State].&[Active]),
```

```
        ([Work Item].[System_WorkItemType].&[Bug],[Work
        Item].[Previous State].&[Closed],[Work
        Item].[System_State].&[Active])
    },
    [Measures].[Cumulative Count]
    )
```

Listing 9.5 Calculation for [Total_Active_Bug_Count]

```
Sum
    (
        {([Work Item].[System_State].&[Active],[Work
          Item].[System_WorkItemType].&[Bug])
        },
        [Measures].[Cumulative Count]
    )
```

Listing 9.6 Calculation for [Total_Bug_Count]

```
Sum
    (
        [Work Item].[System_WorkItemType].&[Bug],
        [Measures].[Cumulative Count]
    )
```

Listing 9.7 Calculation for [Total_Estimated_Task_Duration]

```
Sum
    (
        [Work Item].[System_WorkItemType].&[Task],
        [Measures].[CRM_Outsourcing_Scheduling_EstimatedDuration]
    )
```

Listing 9.8 Calculation for [Total_Actual_Task_Duration]

```
Sum
    (
        [Work Item].[System_WorkItemType].&[Task],
        [Measures].[CRM_Outsourcing_Scheduling_ActualDuration]
    )
```

TIP   When you click the Calculations tab, you may get an error saying "Unexpected error occurred." To resolve this problem, make sure that the assemblies named msmdlocal.dll and msmgdsrv.dll are located in the %ProgramFiles%\Microsoft Visual Studio 8\Common7\IDE\PrivateAssemblies\folder. Also, make sure that they're identical to the ones located in the %ProgramFiles%\Common Files\System\Ole DB\ folder. If the assemblies aren't the same, copy the newer versions to the other location so that both folders have the same version.

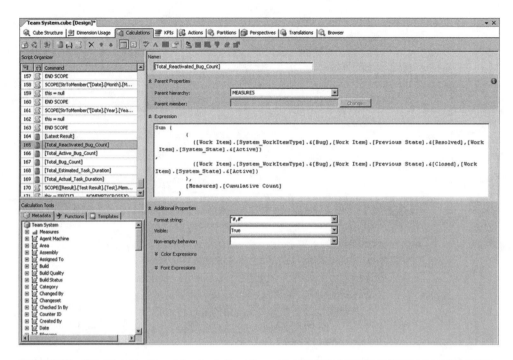

Figure 9.18 The [Total_Reactivated_Bug_Count] **calculated member allows you to determine how many bugs have regressed.**

9.6.3   Step 3—Constructing KPIs

Browse the Team System cube and click the KPIs tab. For information on how to create KPIs, visit http://msdn2.microsoft.com/en-us/library/ms174538.aspx. Create the following KPIs:

- Bug_Reactivation_Ratio—Represents the proportion of bugs that are reactivated, compared to the total number of bugs that are fixed (see listing 9.9). This KPI helps you understand issues such as whether there's a problem with inadequate unit testing at the developer level (prior to submission to the SQA team) or whether something is causing the system to regress.

- Bug_Active_Count_Ratio—Represents the proportion of bugs that are currently active, compared to the total number of reported bugs (see listing 9.10). This KPI gives you a feel for the current "bug debt."

- Task_Actual_vs_Estimated_Ratio—Represents the proportion of time taken to implement tasks compared to the estimated time (see listing 9.11). This KPI tells you how good your estimation process is.

Figure 9.19 shows the definition of the Bug_Reactivation_Ratio KPI. When defining a KPI, you can select a status indicator to graphically represent the value. Note that in the status expression, a return value of -1 means very bad, a value of 0 means good, and a value of 1 means very good. Values in between -1 and 1 can also be returned to indicate

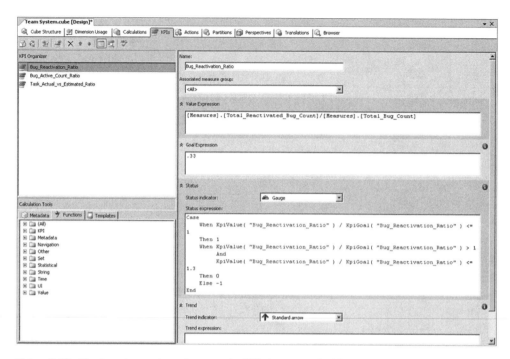

Figure 9.19   The `Bug_Reactivation_Ratio` **KPI gives you a feel for the effectiveness of the unit testing process within the development team.**

intermediate states. You can also specify the trend calculation (and a corresponding indicator) to display how your KPIs are doing compared to another time period.

Listing 9.9   Calculations for `Bug_Reactivation_Ratio` KPI

```
Value Expression:
[Measures].[Total_Reactivated_Bug_Count]
     /[Measures].[Total_Bug_Count]

Goal Expression:
.33

Status Expression:
Case
   When KpiValue( "Bug_Reactivation_Ratio" ) / KpiGoal(
      Bug_Reactivation_Ratio" ) <= 1
         Then 1
   When KpiValue( "Bug_Reactivation_Ratio" ) / KpiGoal(
      "Bug_Reactivation_Ratio" ) > 1
      And
      KpiValue( "Bug_Reactivation_Ratio" ) / KpiGoal(
      "Bug_Reactivation_Ratio" ) <= 1.3
         Then 0
   Else -1
End
```

Listing 9.10 Calculations for `Bug_Active_Count_Ratio` **KPI**

```
Value Expression:
[Measures].[Total_Active_Bug_Count]
    /[Measures].[Total_Bug_Count]

Goal Expression:
.4

Status Expression:
Case
   When KpiValue( "Bug_Active_Count_Ratio" ) / KpiGoal(
      "Bug_Active_Count_Ratio" ) <= 1
         Then 1
   When KpiValue( "Bug_Active_Count_Ratio" ) / KpiGoal(
      "Bug_Active_Count_Ratio" ) > 1
      And
      KpiValue( "Bug_Active_Count_Ratio" ) / KpiGoal(
      "Bug_Active_Count_Ratio" ) <= 1.3
         Then 0
   Else -1
End
```

Listing 9.11 Calculations for `Task_Actual_vs_Estimated_Ratio` **KPI**

```
Value Expression:
[Measures].[Total_Actual_Task_Duration]
    /[Measures].[Total_Estimated_Task_Duration]

Goal Expression:
   1

Status Expression:
   Case
   When KpiValue( "Task_Actual_vs_Estimated_Ratio" )
      / KpiGoal(
      "Task_Actual_vs_Estimated_Ratio" ) <= 1
         Then 1
   When KpiValue( "Task_Actual_vs_Estimated_Ratio" )
      / KpiGoal( "Task_Actual_vs_Estimated_Ratio" ) > 1
      And
      KpiValue( "Task_Actual_vs_Estimated_Ratio" )
      / KpiGoal( "Task_Actual_vs_Estimated_Ratio" ) <= 1.3
         Then 0
   Else -1
End
```

9.6.4 *Step 4—Viewing KPIs*

Click the Browser View icon in the KPI tab to view the KPIs that you've defined (see figure 9.20). The browser view evaluates the KPIs and helps you validate that your KPI calculations are working properly. Once you're satisfied that the KPIs are correct, you can surface them using Excel 2007, MOSS 2007, or custom applications.

Display Structure	Value	Goal	Status
Bug_Active_Count_Ratio	0.89	0.4	
Bug_Reactivation_Ratio	0.05	0.33	
Task_Actual_vs_Estimated_Ratio	1.5	1	

Figure 9.20   KPIs can be viewed in SQL Server 2005 and other products.

USING EXCEL

The TFS KPIs defined in SSAS can be accessed from Excel. Click the Data tab and create a new connection or use an existing connection (see figure 9.21) to connect to the Team System cube. Create a PivotTable to display the data. You'll find that the KPIs are

Figure 9.21   Excel 2007 allows you to easily connect to TFS Analysis Services databases.

Figure 9.22   The KPIs defined in an Analysis Services database are displayed in the Pivot Table pane.

available in the PivotTable Field List (see figure 9.22). You can select the value, goal, status, and trend information to be displayed in the spreadsheet (see figure 9.23).

Note that as you expand your row hierarchies, the corresponding KPI calculations are automatically recalculated. This means that at a granular row level, the KPI for a row could show one kind of status, and when that row is rolled up to an aggregated row, the corresponding KPI could show a different status (since the KPI information is

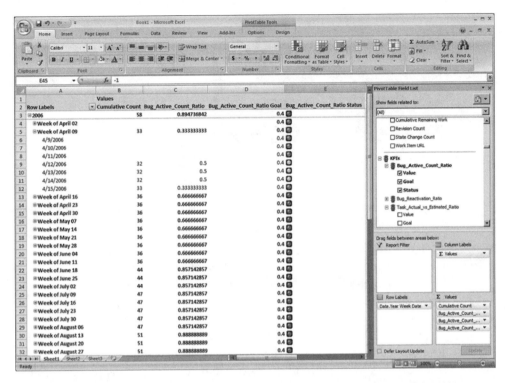

Figure 9.23   KPIs defined in SQL Server 2005 Analysis Services databases can be displayed in Excel 2007.

recalculated at each level). The automatic recalculation feature helps you to drill down and discover the underlying cause of a problem.

Using Excel Web Services, you can host the same spreadsheet in SharePoint and the stakeholders can view the information (including the KPI information) using only a web browser. This allows you to create rich analytical dashboards reflecting your project status and expose them to distributed stakeholders with minimal IT support. You need to maintain the MOSS 2007 server, of course, but your target audience doesn't need a connection to SSAS, since you're hosting the spreadsheet on the server side.

USING SHAREPOINT

MOSS 2007 Enterprise version provides built-in support for displaying KPIs defined in SSAS. Just like Excel Web Services, this allows you to surface the TFS KPIs directly in executive dashboards. If you don't need the full analytical capabilities available in Excel Web Services (such as drill-down, pivoting, and so on), use the MOSS 2007 KPI list; it provides a simpler view.

The goal is to make the project-related KPIs available to distributed stakeholders without requiring them to have access to TFS. The near-real-time metrics regarding the project health provide great value to senior management. This approach is better than manually creating the key metrics from raw data and embedding them in weekly

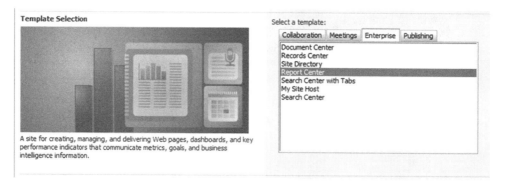

Figure 9.24   Use the Report Center site template to display TFS-related KPIs in MOSS 2007.

status reports. The manual process carries a high overhead, is prone to errors as well as misreporting, and doesn't provide near-real-time information.

To display the KPIs in MOSS 2007, create a Report Center site collection (see figures 9.24 and 9.25). The Report Center site template is available only in the Enterprise version.

In the newly created site collection, create a Data Connection Library. Populate the Data Connection Library by uploading an existing data connection (.odc) file. The .odc file should point to the SSAS database that contains the KPIs. You can create an .odc file in an Office 2007 application and then upload it to the Data Connection Library.

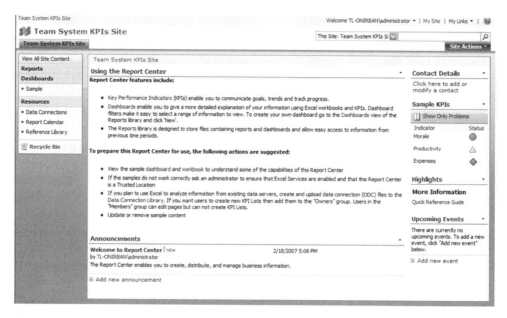

Figure 9.25   A Report Center site offers business intelligence capabilities.

Export a data connection (for example, the one used in the previous section, "Using Excel") from Excel 2007 to MOSS 2007. To export the data connection, select the Data menu in Excel 2007 and click Connections (see figure 9.26). In the Workbook Connections dialog box, select a connection, and then click Properties. In the Connection Properties dialog box, click Export Connection File (see figure 9.27) and save the connection to the data connection library in MOSS 2007. In the Web File Properties dialog box, choose Database as the connection type, and ReadOnly as the UDC Purpose.

Figure 9.26 The Connections menu displays the available connections.

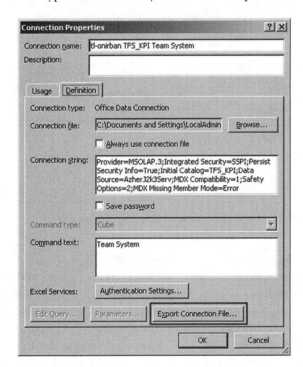

Figure 9.27 Click Export Connection File and export the data connection to MOSS 2007.

The new data connection is added to the Data Connection Library with its approval status as Pending (see figure 9.28). Change its approval status to Approved by clicking

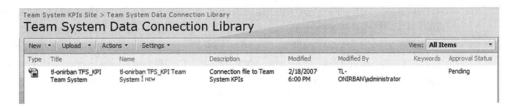

Figure 9.28 The data connection file exported from Excel is available in a data connection library in MOSS 2007, with its initial approval status as Pending.

the Approve/Reject option available in the drop-down menu associated with the name of the connection.

After the data connection is created, it needs to be marked as trusted. From the SharePoint Central Administration page, select a shared service and navigate to the corresponding Shared Services Administration page. In the Excel Services Settings section, click Trusted Data Connection Libraries, and then click Add Trusted Data Connection Library. In the Add Trusted Data Connection Library screen, add the URL of the previously created data connection library and create a trusted data connection library (see figure 9.29).

Figure 9.29   Create a trusted data connection library to store safe connections.

At this point, you have a trusted data connection library ready to be consumed from your site collection. The Report Center site template contains a new type of list called KPI List. Create a new KPI list for hosting the KPIs defined in TFS. To add the KPIs to the list, on the New menu, select Indicator Using Data in SQL Server 2005 Analysis Services. In the New Item screen, specify the path to the trusted data connection in the Data Connection text box. The available KPIs will be displayed in the KPI List list box (see figure 9.30). Select a KPI and click OK to add it to the KPI list. Repeat this process for each KPI. The KPI list will contain all the KPIs that you've added (see figure 9.31).

Once the KPIs from TFS are available in the KPI list, the next step is to add a web part to display the KPIs in the dashboard. MOSS 2007 introduces a new web part named Key Performance Indicators (see figure 9.32). In the design page of the dashboard, click Add a Web Part and add a Key Performance Indicator web part. In the Indicator List text box, type the URL of the KPI list created previously. Save your changes. The KPIs from TFS now appear in the dashboard (see figure 9.33).

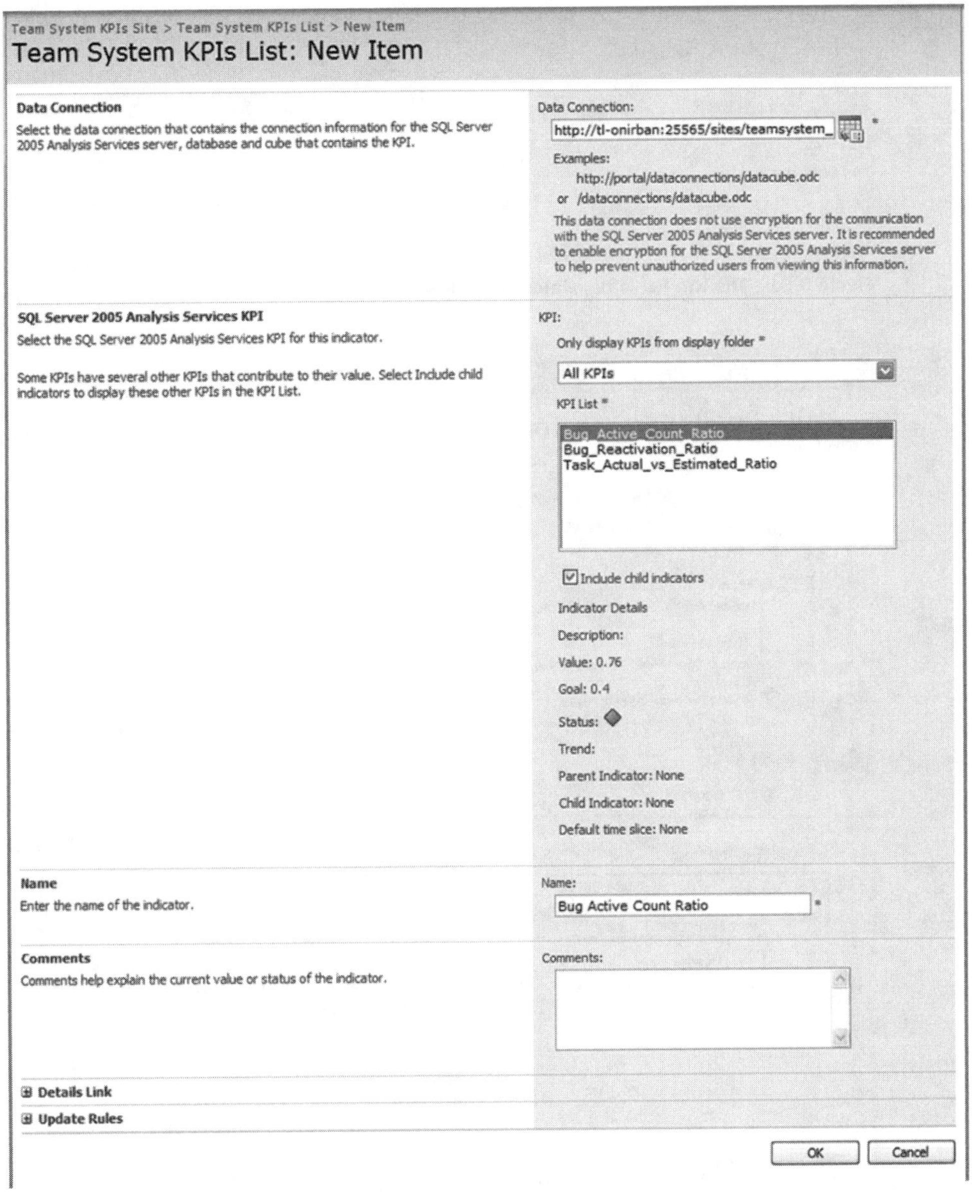

Figure 9.30 Create a KPI list to host the KPIs from TFS.

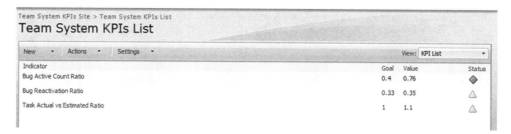

Figure 9.31 The KPI list is populated with KPIs from TFS.

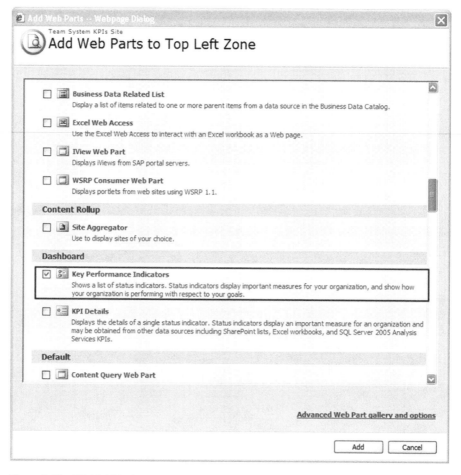

Figure 9.32 MOSS 2007 introduces a new web part for displaying KPIs.

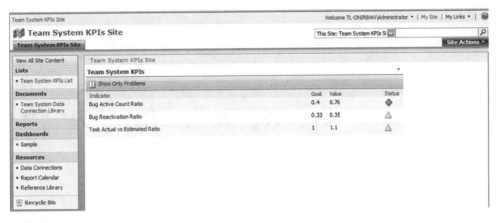

Figure 9.33 The dashboard in MOSS 2007 displays KPIs based on team project metrics, providing key insights into project health.

9.7 Summary

In this chapter, we saw that TFS was designed with extensibility in mind. Since there's no one-size-fits-all solution that can resolve the myriad challenges associated with developing software for many different kinds of businesses, it's essential for a horizontal platform such as TFS to have easy customization options. As we learned in this chapter, you can extend TFS to support custom controls as well as create KPIs to provide operational intelligence. The open architecture of TFS also facilitates easy integration with complementary applications, such as Excel, Project, Outlook, InfoPath, SharePoint Server, SQL Server 2005 Reporting Services, SQL Server 2005 Analysis Services, and so on. Some of these integrations are available out of the box, while other applications can be integrated via custom programming.

Integration with various third-party products (for example, requirements-gathering tools such as Borland CaliberRM) helps fill the gaps that exist in TFS. Other third-party products, such as Teamprise, make TFS accessible from non-Microsoft platforms. You can also modify the process templates to support development methodologies such as rational unified process (RUP) or Scrum, or create a custom process for your own organization.

In the next chapter, we discuss how to use TFS as part of a larger workflow. In any development organization, one of the key challenges is to set up an effective workflow so that routine issues get resolved in a predictable way. If you can automate the routine activities as part of a desired workflow, you can better ensure that issues don't fall through the cracks. Furthermore, instead of expending your energy chasing the routine matters, you can focus on the exceptions. An automated workflow-based system helps improve the productivity of the entire team.

Using workflow with TFS

Many human interactions are inherently asynchronous. When working with a team of people, you may not always receive instant feedback. Your colleagues may need to perform the requested tasks on their own schedules and convey the results back to you later. Workflow technologies help manage long-running interactions between humans as well as systems. A workflow solution provides an overarching framework for orchestrating a group of activities that may run in sequence or in parallel—in a predefined or dynamic path, based on rules and events. Modern workflow systems support serialization in durable storage, sequential and state-machine based processes, tracking and auditing features, dynamic modifications at runtime, and flexible hosting models. These systems offer a compelling solution for managing team interactions and business processes.

Although the benefits of separating business rules from other application logic have been obvious for a long time, until now, there hasn't been a widely available inexpensive framework to create and manage workflows. Most workflow systems in the market have been proprietary vertical applications. Microsoft's entry in this market, via Windows Workflow Foundation (WF), changes the game. WF is a part of

Microsoft .NET Framework 3.x. By pushing workflow and rules capabilities down to the infrastructure services layer, Microsoft enables you to use workflow technology in a wide variety of applications. Workflow is no longer a niche concept with a proprietary implementation—WF has made workflow technology available for the masses.

This chapter goes beyond TFS and discusses how you can orchestrate TFS to operate with complementary systems as part of a larger workflow. We discuss how you can use WF to support asynchronous interactions in conjunction with TFS. We start with the realization that there are many typical out-of-band activities in a real-life software development process that aren't supported in TFS (such as a structured code review process). In order to be effective, TFS needs to coexist within an ecosystem of interoperable tools and technologies that drive the development process. TFS isn't the be-all and end-all solution to all software development problems.

Regardless of which version of TFS you're using, you'll find that certain kinds of asynchronous team interactions are common and important in the development process. If your project happens to be based on a distributed delivery model—with multiple organizations and teams involved in requirement gathering, project management, development, quality assurance, deployment, hosting, and production support—I believe you'll quickly realize that while TFS can be an important piece of the solution, it's not suited to be the *only* solution. In such cases, you'll need to integrate TFS in a heterogeneous distributed environment with unpredictable response times (keep in mind potentially different time zones and jurisdictions). For example, you may want to integrate TFS with partner organizations who may have proprietary project management, version control, and issue-management systems. In such a scenario, you'll find WF to be a valuable tool along with TFS. Workflow technologies help coordinate activities across systems that weren't designed to work with one other.

In this chapter, you'll learn about the following:

- *Windows Workflow Foundation*—The architecture of Windows Workflow Foundation (WF) and what the main building blocks are.
- *How to integrate WF with TFS*—Streamline your operations by using WF to orchestrate development activities in concert with TFS. We look at how WF can be used to manage distributed builds in a scalable, maintainable, and fault-tolerant manner.

10.1 Company types and workflow issues

Automation and workflow needs vary depending on how many people are involved, how much the processes change over time or across business units, how closely located the stakeholders are, and a host of other factors. For small organizations, the default workflows available in MOSS 2007 may be sufficient. For large organizations, you may need to create a custom application integrating WF and TFS. For very complex workflows with significant authoring, customization, simulation, reporting, tracking, and management needs, you may look at orchestrating TFS activities using full-blown business process management (BPM) solutions.

BPM solutions offer enterprise-class platforms with rapid application development capabilities using flexible process modeling tools, reporting dashboards, business rules engines, role-based security, full auditability, dynamic modification of in-flight processes, multiplatform support, and so on. These systems also include sophisticated process monitoring infrastructure for identifying bottlenecks, running what-if analysis, optimizing performance, and so forth. If your development project spans multiple stovepipe systems, departments, and even enterprises, you'll benefit from end-to-end process management capabilities offered by BPM systems. (For more information on the BPM technology, visit http://www.bpminstitute.org.) You can use BPM engines to integrate single or multiple TFS systems in your enterprise.

10.1.1 Small companies

Although in a small company, you may be able to get by without using a workflow system for managing collaborative activities (you could use Microsoft Outlook or Microsoft Project to manage your tasks, for example), you'll encounter instances when using workflow technology increases your productivity and efficiency. A small company can't afford to have a large project management office. Given the scarcity of project management personnel, many process-related activities need to be self-managed. When multiple parties are involved and their work needs to be coordinated outside TFS—such as when collaboratively developing business requirements involving multiple stakeholders—you'll find that without a process framework, the efforts become haphazard. If a small company has contributors located in multiple locations (which is increasingly likely in this day and age), the manual collaboration process becomes even more difficult to manage.

10.1.2 Large companies

In a large company, the need for effective coordination between multiple stakeholders is significantly higher. Keeping track of multiple threads of activities and identifying the blocking issues requires nontrivial efforts. How do you know who's supposed to do what and what's actually been accomplished within the overall execution context? You could maintain a simple task list in Microsoft Outlook or Microsoft Project and update the status daily. But you'll quickly find that this approach is neither scalable nor sustainable for large teams. You'll spend too much manual effort every day to determine status of outstanding tasks, and depending on their individual status, to channel each of them to the appropriate person.

The goal should be to minimize manual involvement in routine tasks. To manage asynchronous multiparty interactions, you need to set up a process that has its own lifecycle and can take care of itself. While running, the process should be able to wait for a response—removing itself from memory to conserve resources—and then continue from the last execution point. The behavior should be configurable using triggers and rules. The process should know what to do next, based on external events and its current state. It should notify stakeholders when exceptions take place or if something doesn't get done for too long. Once the process is launched, you should be able to "fire and forget" and focus your attention to other tasks. You should only need to get involved on an exception basis. Once the infrastructure is set up, you should be able to start a workflow-enabled process and rely on the workflow engine to guide the process through the necessary steps and to its conclusion.

10.1.3 Large companies with distributed TFS

In a company with multiple TFS servers, you'll find workflow technology useful when coordinating activities across TFS machine boundaries. Since the machines could be distributed in multiple locations—possibly connected via WAN links—you'll face the inherent challenges associated with long-distance communications. Given the latency and unpredictability of WAN links, you'll need to deal with unexpected failures and unplanned wait times. A workflow framework makes the multisite coordination process more sustainable and scalable.

10.2 Built-in workflow capabilities in TFS

TFS has the built-in capability to handle workflows, as part of the Microsoft Solution Framework (MSF) process model. MSF comes with a number of predefined process models, namely MSF for Agile Software Development (MSF Agile) and MSF for CMMI Process Improvement (MSF CMMI). MSF can also be used to create additional process models; third-party process templates exist to support Scrum, XP, and so on.

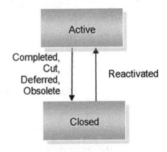

Figure 10.1   The states and transitions associated with the `Task` **work item in MSF Agile**

Each process model in MSF implements the notion of workflows by defining states and rules for state transitions. Each work item type definition contains an associated workflow that describes various state transitions and corresponding actions (see figure 10.1). When you create a new work item or change its state, the workflow logic is invoked automatically. The workflow logic determines what happens next.

The workflow capability in TFS is independent of WF. You can't create a workflow in WF and use it in the work item tracking system in TFS. To create a custom workflow for a particular work item type in TFS, you need to edit the corresponding type definition XML file in the process template.

Although many activities can be modeled as TFS work items, you'll encounter out-of-band issues that need to be managed outside TFS. People typically use multiple applications to manage the process of human collaboration. For example, Microsoft Outlook is used for asynchronous communications, Office Communicator for real-time interactions, and MOSS 2007 for group-oriented collaborations. In order to integrate these applications with TFS as part of a larger long-running activity, you need workflow support. When coordinating multiapplication, multiparty, and even multiorganizational interactions, you need an infrastructure that provides general workflow capabilities.

Furthermore, collaborative tasks such as requirements review, code review, examining check-in exceptions, collecting multisite source files, and creating distributed builds aren't necessarily best modeled as TFS tasks. The reasons are as follow:

- Not all team members may have access to Team Explorer because of licensing, security, and connectivity requirements.
- The workflow associated with a task in a team project may not be suitable for an administrative task. A typical TFS task is usually associated with a scenario (or a requirement). A TFS task contains the fields and transitions necessary to track its implementation within a process framework. Consequently, the default TFS task (for example, the task type defined in MSF Agile) isn't suitable for managing ad hoc out-of-band activities.
- You may need to asynchronously coordinate multiple applications to implement your development process. You can't invoke an external application from the workflow associated with a TFS task. You could trap the `WorkItemChanged-Event` event to detect state changes and invoke custom logic in a web service, but this approach doesn't solve the core problem of orchestrating asynchronous human or system interactions.
- Since work items in TFS can't be deleted, inserting administrative tasks in the database creates permanent junk entries. Unless you're careful, the administrative tasks could end up in the Team System cube and also appear in the reports—producing potentially misleading information.

Because of these reasons, I feel that you'll find it more effective to use a workflow technology such as WF to manage asynchronous out-of-band tasks. These tasks are tracked outside TFS, although they might invoke specific functionalities in TFS. Without a well-defined workflow framework, too many things fall through the cracks when coordinating interdependent actions of multiple team members or applications.

10.3   *An overview of Windows Workflow Foundation*

Workflow technologies enable you to construct application logic using a graphical flowchart–type approach. This approach makes the code more understandable and maintainable. You can visually inspect the logic and determine its general structure and context without delving into potentially undocumented and unintelligible code. In complex enterprise applications—where the cost of ownership is relatively high—using workflow technologies to model the business logic brings greater visibility, flexibility, and simplicity in program design. A system based on a workflow technology is self-documenting, compared to a system implemented using pure code. Additionally, you get built-in support for long-running asynchronous interactions (for example, infrastructure-level support for state passivation and activation). A good workflow platform reduces the amount of custom code that needs to be written for performing routine orchestration-related functions, thereby improving productivity and quality.

Despite the appeal of workflow-based systems, one issue to consider is application performance. The farther abstracted you are from machine code, the greater the performance penalty at runtime. Given the multiple layers of infrastructure code that surround your custom workflow code, you need to make sure that the performance is acceptable on a given piece of hardware under the expected load.

Given the steady improvements in processing power and decreasing computation costs, in general, it's now practical to run workflow systems for business applications. Asynchronous human or system response times are orders of magnitude higher than program execution times anyway. Nevertheless, you should inspect the workflow-related performance counters to understand how the system is performing and where any potential bottlenecks might be. For a discussion on how to implement high-performance applications using WF, visit http://msdn2.microsoft.com/en-us/library/Aa973808.aspx#workflowperfcharacteristics_topic2. For information regarding WF-based workflow performance counters, visit http://windowssdk.msdn.microsoft.com/en-us/library/ms732345.aspx.

WF ships with support for both sequential and state-machine–based workflows (see figure 10.2). A sequential workflow goes through a well-defined series of steps; it follows a predictable execution path. A state-machine workflow, on the other hand, doesn't follow a deterministic path between its start and end points; the workflow transitions from one state to another, depending on the current state and the triggering event conditions. Generally, you'll default to using the sequential workflow model. But if you can't come up with a deterministic process or have too many variations in your standard process, you may find it simpler to model the workflow as a state machine.

Applications created with WF run on Windows Vista, Windows 2008, Windows 2003, and Windows XP (with SP2) machines. For Windows 2003 and Windows XP, you need to download and install the .NET Framework 3.x runtime files. In addition to a workflow engine, WF contains a rules engine that can be used to model business rules. The rules may support workflow conditions or may be consumed directly from external systems.

Figure 10.2   A sample sequential workflow

10.3.1 *Layers in WF*

WF is based on a layered architecture (see figure 10.3). The top-level building blocks in a WF application are activities. WF ships with a number of predefined activities (see figure 10.4). You can also create custom activities by implementing an interface. From an architectural perspective, WF consists of the following layers:

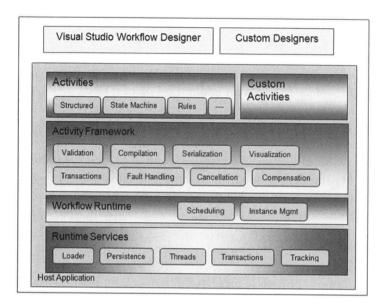

Figure 10.3   Windows Workflow Foundation is based on a layered architecture stack.

- *Hosting layer*—This layer provides the host process. Since workflows are nonexecutable assemblies, they can't run by themselves. The flexible hosting model allows you to run WF workflows in console applications, Windows applications, Windows services, web services, MOSS 2007, and in other custom applications.

- *Runtime layer*—This layer consists of two components: the runtime engine and the runtime services. The runtime engine launches the workflow, executes the activities, manages state, tracks progress, and so forth. The runtime services component provides the actual implementation of the services that are invoked by the runtime engine. These pluggable services include support for tracking, transactions, scheduling, threading, and so on. In addition to out-of-the-box services, you can create new custom services or create custom implementations of existing services.

- *Workflow model layer*—This layer consists of activities and associated rules. WF ships with a number of out-of-the-box activities for invoking conditional logic, looping, calling web services, handling events, and so on. There's also a general purpose activity for hosting custom code. You can write custom code in your workflow application either by using the generic code activity or by creating a new custom activity. WF also contains a

Figure 10.4   The predefined activities available in Windows Workflow Foundation

built-in rules engine that can be used to construct various conditions associated with activities. Activities in WF can also be composite—an activity can contain other child activities.

10.3.2 Creating WF applications

WF-based workflows can be created in a variety of ways, depending on the level of customization required and the technical skill level of the author. You can create workflows in Visual Studio (see figure 10.5). Using Visual Studio, you can leverage the full range of capabilities available in WF.

The workflow designer available in Visual Studio can be rehosted in custom applications, making it possible for nontechnical stakeholders (such as business analysts) to create or modify workflows without requiring Visual Studio. WF ships with a sample program that demonstrates how to host the workflow designer in a Windows Forms application. Third-party tools exist for hosting the workflow designer in ASP.NET/ AJAX applications. Business analysts can use SharePoint Designer 2007 to create simple workflows without writing any code.

A powerful feature of WF is the ability to make incremental changes dynamically to a running workflow. You can add or delete activities, create new rules, or change the properties of existing activities while a workflow is in progress. WF workflows can be

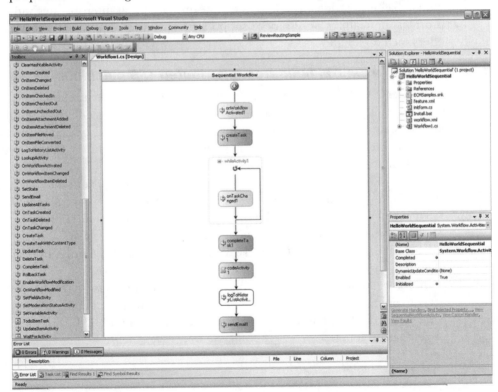

Figure 10.5   Visual Studio offers an integrated workflow authoring environment.

expressed in Extensible Application Markup Language (XAML), in pure code, or using a combination of XAML and code-beside files. The XAML approach enables workflow designers and developers to decouple their work. XAML support also makes the workflow definitions interoperable and exchangeable between compatible systems. No matter which authoring strategy you use, the workflows are compiled into .NET assemblies by the workflow compiler program (wfc.exe). Although WF doesn't support Business Process Exception Language–based workflows in version one, BPEL support is expected in a future version. (BPEL is a specification for creating web service–based interoperable business processes.)

WF is a core technology that's being embedded in several Microsoft products. In addition to MOSS 2007, other Microsoft products such as Microsoft Speech Server 2007, and future versions of Microsoft BizTalk Server, Microsoft Identity Integration Server, and Microsoft Dynamics will incorporate the WF technology. WF is an integral part of .NET Framework 3.x—along with sister technologies such as WPF (Windows Presentation Foundation) and WCF (Windows Communication Foundation).

Being a framework as opposed to an application, WF doesn't include high-level features such as built-in support for human workflows. For example, you can't assign tasks to users or groups, obtain a current To-Do list for a particular user, automatically notify users when tasks are assigned to them, and so on. To efficiently support human-based workflows, you also need a team portal that interoperates with WF and provides the features necessary to support effective human interactions. MOSS 2007 offers such capabilities.

10.4 *Creating a central build from distributed TFS machines*

In chapter 7, we looked at retrieving source files from multiple machines and creating a central build. We modified the build script to fetch source code from multiple TFS instances. Recall that in the build script, we modified the `TeamSystemUrl` property to download the source files from specified distributed TFS machines. In this section, we implement a solution for creating a central build using WF.

Using WF, we can make the build process more automated, fault-tolerant, and integrated. Figure 10.6 shows the process associated with creating a central build from two TFS machines. You can extend the example to include additional TFS servers.

This example serves as a proof-of-concept regarding how WF can be used to enhance the value of TFS. Using WF, you can extend and integrate the capabilities offered by TFS as part of a larger solution.

In this example, we assume that there are two team projects—a primary team project containing the main code and a reference team project containing the supporting code. The workflow steps associated with creating a central build from the two team projects are as follow:

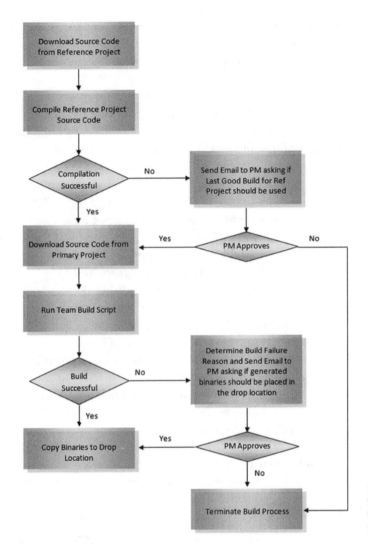

Figure 10.6 A workflow for creating a central build from multiple TFS source machines

1 Download the source files from the reference team project into the build machine. Create a temporary workspace in the build machine as needed in order to download the files from TFVC. If there are connectivity problems, attempt this process several times. If the download process fails even after multiple retries, email the project manager and ask if the build should be aborted or the last good build binaries (for the reference project) should be used.

2 Compile the code downloaded from the reference team project to see if there are any errors that prevent the code from compiling. Use the MSBuild command-line utility to build the reference solution file.

3 If compilation fails, send an email to the project manager asking whether the last good build binaries for the reference project should be used. If the project

manager doesn't approve, abort the overall build process. The workflow remains in a suspended state until a response is received from the project manager. Moreover, the workflow process is serialized in a database, conserving machine resources.

4 Download the source code from the primary team project to the build machine. Although we could download the primary source files using the build script (which downloads the source code files by default), we choose to download the source code programmatically, as it gives us more control regarding what to do in case the download fails. If the download process fails for some reason, email the project manager and ask whether the last good build binaries should be used.

5 Execute the build script and compile the primary source files. Use the `AdditionalReferencePath` property in the build script to refer to the location of the reference binaries, so that MSBuild finds the supporting assemblies when compiling the primary project. Set the `SkipGet`, `SkipClean`, and `SkipInitialize` properties to `true` in the build script so that Team Build doesn't try to download the source files again during execution of the build project.

6 If the build succeeds, copy the newly created binaries to the drop location. If the build fails, email the project manager and inform him of the underlying cause of the build failure. If the build failed because the primary project couldn't be compiled, ask the project manager if the last good build binaries (for both the primary team project as well as the reference team project) should be placed in the drop location. If the build failed because one or more build verification tests (BVTs) failed, the project manager needs to make a determination regarding how critical the failed BVTs are. She can decide to use the new binaries anyway or use the last good build binaries. You can modify the example to provide additional capabilities—such as automatically trying various combinations of new and old primary and reference assemblies in order to come up with a build that passes critical BVTs and contains as much new code as possible.

Given our conceptual understanding of the proposed distributed build process, let's now review how we can implement the process in code.

10.5 *Technical review: using WF to manage a distributed build process*

In this section, we create an application to manage the build process using WF. The logical steps were discussed in the previous section. Let's review the mechanics associated with creating the application. The goal is to leverage the workflow framework offered by WF and create an automated process that takes into account the practical issues involved in real-life asynchronous human and system interactions.

To create workflow applications in Visual Studio 2005, you need to install Visual Studio 2005 extensions for .NET Framework 3.x (Windows Workflow Foundation). Download the files from the Microsoft web site at http://www.microsoft.com/downloads/details.aspx?familyid=5D61409E-1FA3-48CF-8023-E8F38E709BA6&displaylang=en.

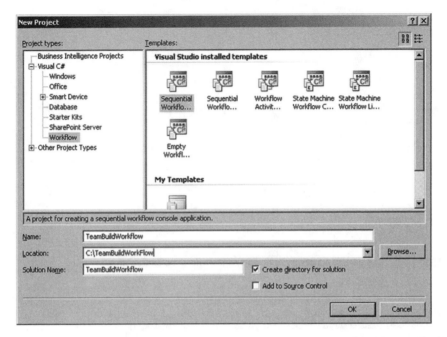

Figure 10.7   Visual Studio contains the necessary templates for creating workflow applications.

After installation, you'll find a new project type named Workflow when you create a new project in Visual Studio 2005 (see figure 10.7). Visual Studio 2008 includes the WF-related templates, eliminating the need for a separate download. Choose the Sequential Workflow Console Application template.

Drag and drop various activities from the toolbox to the design surface and write the necessary supporting code; the goal is to implement the logic depicted earlier in figure 10.6. The full source code is available online at http://www.manning.com/TeamFoundationServer2008inAction.

Let's walk through the steps involved in constructing the workflow. In this example, the workflow is hosted in a console application. You can modify the code to host the workflow in an application more suitable for your purpose.

10.5.1 *Step 1—Downloading source files from the reference project*

In this step, download the source files from the reference project. Use a `While` activity to try to download the code several times, in case there are connectivity problems. Recall that the source files are located in a separate TFS server, possibly connected via a WAN link. The `While` activity contains a `Code` activity that performs the actual work. The process is shown in figure 10.8. Listing 10.1 contains the various methods associated with downloading the source files.

After the `While` activity is completed, check whether the files were downloaded successfully. Use an `IfElse` activity to model the conditional logic. The next two steps deal with the activities associated with download failure and success.

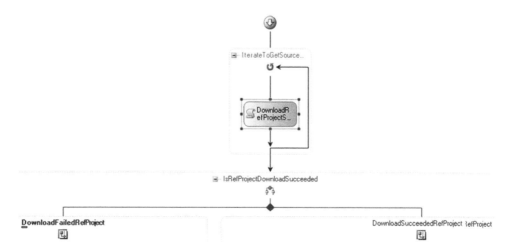

Figure 10.8   Use a `While` activity to download the reference source files.

Listing 10.1   Code for downloading source files from the reference project

```
/// <summary>
/// Handler for the CodeActivity
/// "DownloadRefProjectSource". This method downloads the
/// source files for the reference project from TFVC.
/// </summary>
private void DownloadRefProjectSource_ExecuteCode(
   object sender, EventArgs e)
{
   this.pDownloadSource(buildDataRefProject);
}
/// <summary>
/// Downloads source files based on information provided
/// via the buildData parameter
/// </summary>
private void pDownloadSource(BuildData buildData)
{
   try
   {
      TeamFoundationServer teamFoundationServer              Get reference
         = new TeamFoundationServer(buildData.TFSName);       to TFS server

      VersionControlServer versionControlServer =            Get reference to
         (VersionControlServer) teamFoundationServer.        version control
         GetService(typeof(VersionControlServer));           server

      // Check if the workspace for downloading source
      // files already exists. If it exists then delete it.
      Workspace[] workspaces
         = versionControlServer.QueryWorkspaces(
               buildData.SourceDownloadWorkspace,
               buildData.SourceDownloadWorkspaceOwner,
```

```
                          buildData.BuildMachine);

      if (workspaces != null && workspaces.Length != 0)
      {
         //first delete all source files in the directories
         //(not implemented here). Then delete the workspace
         //itself, as shown below.
         versionControlServer.DeleteWorkspace(
               buildData.SourceDownloadWorkspace,
               buildData.SourceDownloadWorkspaceOwner);
      }

      Workspace workspace =                            Create workspace
         versionControlServer.CreateWorkspace(         for downloading
         buildData.SourceDownloadWorkspace,            source files
         versionControlServer.AuthenticatedUser);

      workspace.Map("$/" + buildData.TeamProject,      Map
         buildData.SourceDownloadDirectory);           workspace

      workspace.Get();                            ⟵── Download source files from TFVC

      buildData.DownloadStatus = Status.Succeeded; ⟵⌐  Set source
   }                                                    download
   catch (Exception ex)                                 status to
   {                                                    Succeeded
      // Increment the source download iteration number.
      // The workflow tries to download five times
      // in case of failure.
      buildData.DownloadIterationNumber++;             Set download
                                                        status to Failed
      buildData.DownloadStatus = Status.Failed;   ⟵⌐
   }
}
```

10.5.2 *Step 2—Handling failed download of the reference project*

The goal of this step is to deal with failures when downloading source code from the reference project. In case the source files can't be downloaded, we first send an email to the project manager using the CallExternalMethod activity. The CallExternal-Method activity accepts an interface name and a method name that belongs to the interface. The specified method is invoked when the activity is executed. In our case, the method contains the code necessary to send emails.

The email informs the manager that the source files couldn't be downloaded and asks him what should be done next. The options are to use the last compiled binaries or to terminate the overall build process. If the manager doesn't respond within 24 hours, the build is aborted. We use a HandleExternalEvent activity to accept the manager's feedback and a Delay activity to handle the timeout condition. If a timeout occurs, the workflow is terminated via the Terminate activity. The HandleExternal-Event activity accepts an interface name and an event name that belongs to the interface. If the manager indicates that the previously generated binaries should be used, copy the files to the target location using a Code activity. The workflow model is shown in figure 10.9. You could also add a Retry activity to handle temporary server downtime (not shown here).

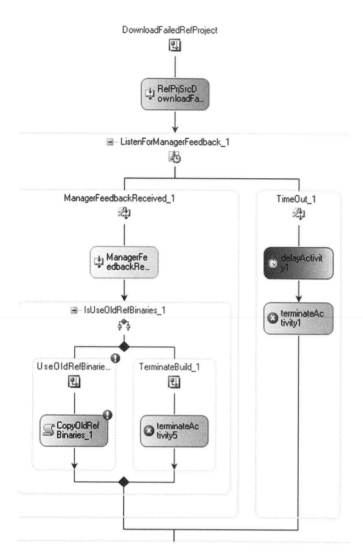

Figure 10.9   Logic for handing failed download of the reference source files

10.5.3   Step 3—Handling successful download of the reference project

Now we deal with source files that have been successfully downloaded from the reference project. First, compile the source files using MSBuild. This action is encapsulated in a Code activity (see listing 10.2).

If code compilation fails, email the project manager using a CallExternalMethod activity, just as we did in the previous step. If the manager decides to use the previously generated files, copy the last-known-good binaries to the target location using a Code activity. If the manager decides to abort the build process, terminate the workflow. As before, the workflow is also terminated if the manager doesn't respond within the specified timeframe. The workflow is depicted in figure 10.10.

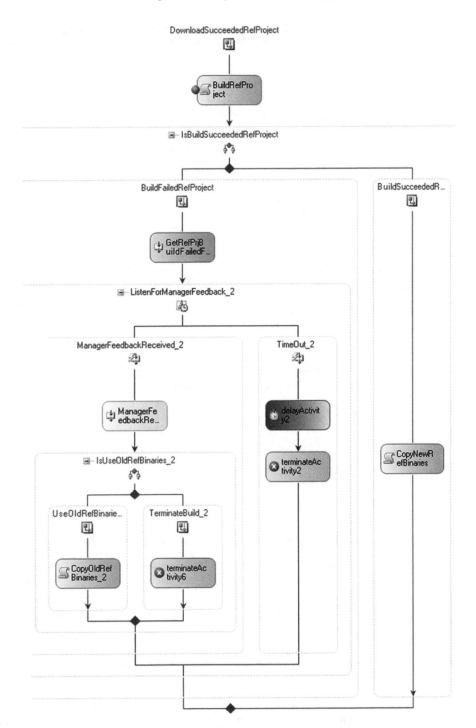

Figure 10.10 Logic for handing successful download of the reference source files

Listing 10.2   Compiling source files associated with the reference project

```
/// <summary>
/// Handler for the CodeActivity "BuildRefProject".
/// This method builds the reference project using MSBuild.exe
/// </summary>
private void BuildRefProject_ExecuteCode(object sender,
    EventArgs e)
    {
        // Create an instance of Process, which executes
        // the MSBuild.exe
        Process process = new Process();
        process.StartInfo.FileName = Constants.MSBuildPath;
        string args = Path.Combine(
                buildDataRefProject.SourceDownloadDirectory,
                Constants.RefPrjSolPath);
        process.StartInfo.Arguments = args;
        process.StartInfo.UseShellExecute = false;
        process.StartInfo.RedirectStandardOutput = true;

        process.Start();

        string buildOutput =
            process.StandardOutput.ReadToEnd().ToLower();

        // Determine if the build succeeded or failed.
        // Do this on the basis of existence of a specific string
        // ("build failed") in the return value.
        if (buildOutput.LastIndexOf("build failed") == -1)
        {
            buildDataRefProject.BuildStatus = Status.Succeeded;
        }
        else
        {
            buildDataRefProject.BuildStatus = Status.Failed;
        }

        process.WaitForExit();
    }
```

> **Retrieve output string generated by build process** (annotation pointing to the `string buildOutput = process.StandardOutput.ReadToEnd().ToLower();` lines)

10.5.4   Step 4—Downloading source files from the primary project

In this step, we download the source files from the primary project. The logic is similar to that of downloading source files from the reference project (see figure 10.11). Use a While activity to wrap a Code activity. The Code activity contains the code for downloading the source files (similar to listing 10.1). The While activity provides multiple retry attempts, in case of download problems.

10.5.5   Step 5—Handling failed download of the primary project

This step is similar to handing failures when downloading source files from the reference project (see figure 10.12). An email is sent to the manager, and based on his instructions, either the build is terminated or the previously generated files are placed in the drop location (along with the reference binaries). There are several possibilities in the workflow:

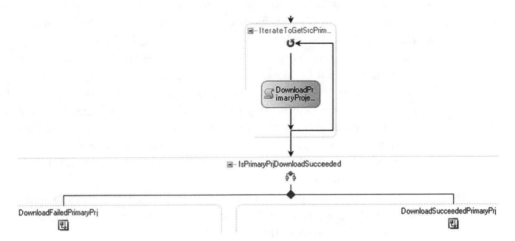

Figure 10.11 Use a `While` activity to download source files for the primary project.

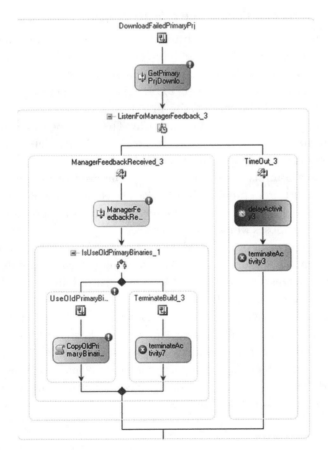

Figure 10.12 Logic for handing failed download of primary source files

- Use the old primary assemblies with old reference assemblies. This option essentially copies all old build files since the new code isn't used at all.
- Use old primary assemblies with new reference assemblies (assuming new reference assemblies were created in the previous steps). This option carries the risk of an inconsistent build, since the two sets of assemblies may be incompatible. But if there are compatibility problems, they'll probably be detected in the subsequent build verification step when running the BVTs. Nevertheless, if you use this approach, carefully test the output assemblies to ensure that there are no hidden but serious problems associated with mixing old and new bits. We don't implement this condition in the sample workflow, but you could easily extend the example to do so.
- Retry downloading the source files (not implemented in this example). If the server is down temporarily (perhaps due to maintenance), retrying after a specific interval could solve the problem.
- Terminate the build.

10.5.6 *Step 6—Handling successful download of the primary project*

We finally get to execute the Team Build script in this step. The workflow logic is shown in figure 10.13. The action is performed in a `Code` activity and is displayed in listing 10.3. Obtain a reference to the primary TFS machine and use the `Microsoft.TeamFoundation.Build.Proxy.BuildController` class to execute the build script in the build machine. The build script is shown in listing 10.4.

If the build fails for some reason, try to determine why. There can be two main reasons. A build may fail if the code fails to compile or if a BVT fails. We determine the underlying cause and report to the project manager via an email.

If the build fails due to a compilation problem, the options are to either terminate the build or use the previously generated build files. You could also re-download the source files in case there is a newer changeset in the server that fixes the problem (not shown here). The manager chooses which action to take.

If the build fails due to failure of one or more BVTs, the options are to either terminate the build or deploy the new build binaries. The manager's decision will depend upon the importance of the failed BVTs. If critical BVTs have passed, he might choose to go ahead and use the newly generated binaries anyway.

To determine the status of the BVTs, invoke the `GetTestResultsForBuild` method of the `Microsoft.TeamFoundation.Build.Proxy.BuildStore` class (see listing 10.3). The `GetTestResultsForBuild` method returns a collection of `TestResultData` objects. Each `TestResultData` object has a property named `RunPassed` that indicates whether the test passed. The `TestResultData` object has additional properties that provide more granular information about the tests.

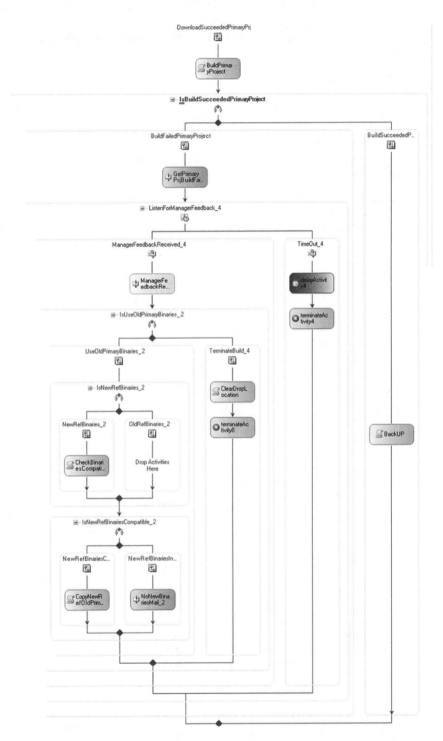

Figure 10.13 Logic for handing successful download of the primary source files

Listing 10.3   Code for running the Team Build script

```
/// <summary>
/// Handler method of BuildPrimaryProject. This method
/// builds the primary project. It uses
/// the StartBuild(Microsoft.TeamFoundation.Build.
/// Proxy.BuildParameters)
/// method of the Microsoft.TeamFoundation.Build.Proxy.BuildController
/// class. We also determine the success or failure of the build.
/// </summary>
private void BuildPrimaryProject_ExecuteCode(object sender,
   EventArgs e)
    {
        TeamFoundationServer teamFoundationServer = new
          TeamFoundationServer(
          buildDataPrimaryProject.TFSName);

        // Create the proxy objects
        Proxy.BuildController controller =
          (Proxy.BuildController) teamFoundationServer.
          GetService( typeof(Proxy.BuildController));
        Proxy.BuildStore store = (Proxy.BuildStore)
          teamFoundationServer.GetService(
          typeof(Proxy.BuildStore));
        Proxy.BuildParameters buildParams = new
          Proxy.BuildParameters();

        // Set build parameters
        buildParams.TeamFoundationServer =
            buildDataPrimaryProject.TFSName;
        buildParams.TeamProject =
            buildDataPrimaryProject.TeamProject;
        buildParams.BuildType =
            buildDataPrimaryProject.TeamBuildType;
        buildParams.BuildDirectory =
            buildDataPrimaryProject.BuildDirectory;
        buildParams.BuildMachine =
            buildDataPrimaryProject.BuildMachine;
        string buildUri = controller.StartBuild(buildParams);

        bool buildComplete = false;

        Proxy.BuildData bd;
        BuildConstants.BuildStatusIconID status;

        //in TFS 2008, the classes in
        //Microsoft.TeamFoundation.Build.Proxy have been deprecated.
        //To determine build status, you should use
        //IBuildDetail.Status property in the
        //Microsoft.TeamFoundation.Build.Client namespace.

        //wait until the build completes
        do

        //adjust the polling interval as appropriate
         System.Threading.Thread.Sleep(10000);
           //fetch build results
           bd = store.GetBuildDetails(buildUri);
```

Get reference
to TFS server

Start
build

Sleep for
a second

```
    status = (BuildConstants.
        BuildStatusIconID)bd.BuildStatusId;

    buildComplete = (status ==
        BuildConstants.BuildStatusIconID.BuildSucceeded
        || status ==
        BuildConstants.BuildStatusIconID.BuildFailed ||
        status == BuildConstants.BuildStatusIconID.
        BuildStopped) && (bd.FinishTime.Year > 1);

} while (!buildComplete);

buildDataPrimaryProject.DropLocation = bd.DropLocation;

//check if build succeeded
if (status ==
    BuildConstants.BuildStatusIconID.BuildSucceeded)
{
    buildDataPrimaryProject.BuildStatus =
        Status.Succeeded;
}
else
{
    buildDataPrimaryProject.BuildStatus = Status.Failed;

    //let's determine if build failure was caused by
    //compilation failure or BVT failure

    StringBuilder testResultString = new StringBuilder();

    int numOfFailedTests = 0;
    bool isTestRunFailed = false;

    Proxy.PlatformFlavorData[] platFalvData =
        store.GetPlatformFlavorsForBuild(buildUri);
    foreach (Proxy.PlatformFlavorData platFalvDatum in
        platFalvData)
    {
        Proxy.TestResultData[] testData
            = store.GetTestResultsForBuild(buildUri,
            platFalvDatum.PlatformName,
            platFalvDatum.FlavorName);

        foreach (Proxy.TestResultData testDatum
            in testData)
        {
            testResultString.AppendLine("Test Name: " +
                testDatum.Name);
            testResultString.AppendLine("Run Id: " +
                testDatum.RunId);
            testResultString.AppendLine("Run user: " +
                testDatum.RunUser);
            testResultString.AppendLine(
                "Overall test status: " + (
                testDatum.RunPassed ?
                "Succeeded" : "Failed"));
            testResultString.AppendLine(
                "Total number of tests: " +
                testDatum.TestsTotal);
            testResultString.AppendLine(
```

Indicate that build succeeded

Indicate that build failed

Holds test result info

```
                        "Number of successful test: " +
                        testDatum.TestsPassed);
                    testResultString.AppendLine(
                        "Number of failed test: " +
                        testDatum.TestsFailed);

                    numOfFailedTests += testDatum.TestsFailed;
                    if (!testDatum.RunPassed)
                    {
                        isTestRunFailed = true;
                    }
                }
            }

            if (isTestRunFailed)
            {
                this.PrimaryProjectBuildFailBody += "Build failed
                    due to test failure. Test Data: \n\n";

                this.PrimaryProjectBuildFailBody +=
                    testResultString.ToString();
            }
            else
            {
                this.PrimaryProjectBuildFailBody += "Build failed
                    due to compilation error";
            }
        }
    }
```

Build failed
due to BVT
failure

Build failed
due to
compilation
failure

At this point, we know how to launch the build process and evaluate the results. But to fully understand what's going on, we need to look at the build script as well. Listing 10.4 shows the Team Build project file (TFSBuild.proj).

Listing 10.4   Modified Team Build project file to build the primary project

```xml
<?xml version="1.0" encoding="utf-8"?>
<Project DefaultTargets="DesktopBuild"
  xmlns="http://schemas.microsoft.com/developer/msbuild/2003">

  <Import Project="$(MSBuildExtensionsPath)\Microsoft\
    VisualStudio\v9.0\TeamBuild\
    Microsoft.TeamFoundation.Build.targets" />
  <ProjectExtensions>
   <!-- DESCRIPTION
     The description is associated with a build type.
     Edit the value for making changes.
   -->
   <Description>
   </Description>
   <!-- BUILD MACHINE
    Name of the machine which will be used
    to build the solutions selected.
    Put your machine IP below.
   -->
   <BuildMachine>x.x.x.x</BuildMachine>
  </ProjectExtensions>
  <PropertyGroup>
```

```xml
<!-- TEAM PROJECT
  The team project which will be built using this build type.
-->
<TeamProject>MSF_Agile_1</TeamProject>
<!-- BUILD DIRECTORY
 The directory on the build machine that will
 be used to build the selected solutions. The directory
 must be a local path on the build
 machine (e.g. c:\build).
-->
<BuildDirectoryPath>c:\build2</BuildDirectoryPath>

<DropLocation>\\vsts\drop</DropLocation>
<!-- TESTING
  Set this flag to enable/disable running tests
  as a post build step.
-->
<RunTest>true</RunTest>
<WorkItemFieldValues>Symptom=build break;Steps To
  Reproduce=Start the build using Team Build
</WorkItemFieldValues>
<RunCodeAnalysis>Default</RunCodeAnalysis>

<!-- UPDATE ASSOCIATED WORK ITEMS
  Set this flag to enable/disable updating associated
  workitems on a successful build
-->
<UpdateAssociatedWorkItems>true</UpdateAssociatedWorkItems>
<!-- Title for the work item created on build failure -->
<WorkItemTitle>Build failure in build:</WorkItemTitle>
<!-- Description for the work
  item created on build failure -->
<DescriptionText>This work item was created by
  Team Build on a build failure.
</DescriptionText>
<!-- Text pointing to log file location on build failure -->
<BuildlogText>The build log file is at:</BuildlogText>
<!-- Text pointing to error/warnings file location on
build failure     -->
<ErrorWarningLogText>The errors/warnings log file is at:
</ErrorWarningLogText>
</PropertyGroup>
<ItemGroup>

  <SolutionToBuild Include="$(SolutionRoot)\MyTestConsoleApp\
    MyTestConsoleApp.sln" />
</ItemGroup>
<ItemGroup>
  <!-- CONFIGURATIONS
    The list of configurations to build. To add/delete
    configurations, edit this value. For example, to add a
    new configuration, add following lines -
    <ConfigurationToBuild Include="Debug|x86">
      <FlavorToBuild>Debug</FlavorToBuild>
      <PlatformToBuild>x86</PlatformToBuild>
    </ConfigurationToBuild>

    The Include attribute value should be unique for each
```

```
      ConfigurationToBuild node.
   -->
   <ConfigurationToBuild Include="Debug|Any CPU">
     <FlavorToBuild>Debug</FlavorToBuild>
     <PlatformToBuild>Any CPU</PlatformToBuild>
   </ConfigurationToBuild>
 </ItemGroup>

 <ItemGroup>
   <MetaDataFile Include="$(SolutionRoot)\MyTestConsoleApp\
   MyTestConsoleApp.vsmdi">
     <TestList>BVTConsoleApp</TestList>
   </MetaDataFile>
 </ItemGroup>

 <ItemGroup>
   <AdditionalReferencePath Include="C:\build1\BookValidation\
   WFTeamBuildClassLibrary\Binaries\Debug" />
 </ItemGroup>

 <PropertyGroup>
   <SourceDirectory>
   C:\temp2\MyTestConsoleApp\*
   </SourceDirectory>
   <DestinationDirectory>
    $(SolutionRoot)\MyTestConsoleApp
   </DestinationDirectory>
 </PropertyGroup>

<!-- Set the following properties so that the source code is not
   Downloaded. The source files were downloaded by workflow code
   earlier.
-->

 <PropertyGroup>
   <SkipGet>True</SkipGet>
   <SkipClean>True</SkipClean>
   <SkipInitializeWorkspace>True</SkipInitializeWorkspace>
 </PropertyGroup>

<!-- Override BeforeGet and copy downloaded source
   files to destination directory
   /S Copies directories and sub-directories
   /I If destination does not exist and we are copying
     more than one file, assumes that
     destination is a directory.
   /Y Overwrites existing files without prompting.
   /R Overwrites read-only files.
-->
 <Target Name="BeforeGet" >
   <Exec Command="XCOPY $(SourceDirectory)
       $(DestinationDirectory) /S /I /Y /R" />
 </Target>
</Project>
```

10.5.7 *Step 7—Handling outgoing and incoming emails*

In any human-oriented workflow system, you'll likely need to send and receive emails.
In our example, when creating a central build from distributed TFS machines, emails

are sent out at several points, requesting feedback from the project manager. Based on his replies, various execution paths are taken in the workflow.

But managing email communications from WF in an automated fashion is a non-trivial effort. Since we can't expect Outlook 2007 to be installed on the server, we use the IIS SMTP service to send and receive emails. As we'll see, sending emails is easy; it's the receiving part (and automatically processing the reply) that gets tricky.

Begin by creating two custom activities—a `SendMail` activity that inherits from `CallExternalMethodActivity` (see listing 10.5) and a `MailReceived` activity that inherits from `HandleExternalEventActivity` (see listing 10.6).

Listing 10.5   Source code for the `SendMail` activity

```
namespace TeamBuild.SmtpMailServices
{
    using System;
    using System.ComponentModel;
    using System.Workflow.Activities;
    using System.Workflow.ComponentModel;
    using System.Workflow.ComponentModel.Design;
    using System.Workflow.ComponentModel.Compiler;

    [ToolboxItemAttribute(typeof(ActivityToolboxItem))]
    public partial class SendMail : CallExternalMethodActivity
    {
        public static DependencyProperty MessageIdProperty =
            DependencyProperty.Register("MessageId",
            typeof(System.Guid), typeof(SendMail));

        public static DependencyProperty HostNameProperty =
            DependencyProperty.Register(
            "HostName", typeof(string), typeof(SendMail));

        public static DependencyProperty PortProperty =
            DependencyProperty.Register(
            "Port", typeof(int), typeof(SendMail));

        public static DependencyProperty FromProperty =
            DependencyProperty.Register(
            "From", typeof(string), typeof(SendMail));

        public static DependencyProperty ToProperty =
            DependencyProperty.Register(
            "To", typeof(string), typeof(SendMail));

        public static DependencyProperty SubjectProperty =
            DependencyProperty.Register(
            "Subject", typeof(string), typeof(SendMail));

        public static DependencyProperty BodyProperty =
            DependencyProperty.Register(
            "Body", typeof(string), typeof(SendMail));

        public SendMail()
        {
            base.InterfaceType = typeof(
                TeamBuild.SmtpMailServices.ISmtpMailService);
```

```
      base.MethodName = "SendMail";
   }

   [BrowsableAttribute(false)]
   [DesignerSerializationVisibilityAttribute(
      DesignerSerializationVisibility.Hidden)]
   public override System.Type InterfaceType
   {
      get
      {
         return base.InterfaceType;
      }
      set
      {
         throw new InvalidOperationException(
            @"Cannot set InterfaceType on a
            derived CallExternalMethodActivity.");
      }
   }

   [BrowsableAttribute(false)]
   [DesignerSerializationVisibilityAttribute(
      DesignerSerializationVisibility.Hidden)]
   public override string MethodName
   {
      get
      {
         return base.MethodName;
      }
      set
      {
         throw new InvalidOperationException(
            @"Cannot set MethodName on a
            derived CallExternalMethodActivity.");
      }
   }

   [ValidationOptionAttribute(ValidationOption.Required)]
   public System.Guid MessageId
   {
      get
      {
         return ((System.Guid)(this.GetValue(
            SendMail.MessageIdProperty)));
      }
      set
      {
         this.SetValue(SendMail.MessageIdProperty,
            value);
      }
   }

   [ValidationOptionAttribute(ValidationOption.Required)]
   public string HostName
   {
      get
      {
         return ((string)(this.GetValue(
```

```
          SendMail.HostNameProperty)));
    }
    set
    {
      this.SetValue(SendMail.HostNameProperty, value);
    }
}

[ValidationOptionAttribute(ValidationOption.Required)]
public int Port
{
   get
   {
      return ((int)(this.GetValue(
         SendMail.PortProperty)));
   }
   set
   {
      this.SetValue(SendMail.PortProperty, value);
   }
}

[ValidationOptionAttribute(ValidationOption.Required)]
public string From
{
   get
   {
      return ((string)(this.GetValue(
         SendMail.FromProperty)));
   }
   set
   {
      this.SetValue(SendMail.FromProperty, value);
   }
}

[ValidationOptionAttribute(ValidationOption.Required)]
public string To
{
   get
   {
      return ((string)(this.GetValue(
         SendMail.ToProperty)));
   }
   set
   {
      this.SetValue(SendMail.ToProperty, value);
   }
}

[ValidationOptionAttribute(ValidationOption.Required)]
public string Subject
{
   get
   {
      return ((string)(this.GetValue(
         SendMail.SubjectProperty)));
   }
```

```
            set
            {
                this.SetValue(SendMail.SubjectProperty, value);
            }
        }

        [ValidationOptionAttribute(ValidationOption.Required)]
        public string Body
        {
            get
            {
                return ((string)(this.GetValue(
                    SendMail.BodyProperty)));
            }
            set
            {
                this.SetValue(SendMail.BodyProperty, value);
            }
        }

        protected override void OnMethodInvoking(
            System.EventArgs e)
        {
            this.ParameterBindings["messageId"].Value
                = this.MessageId;
            this.ParameterBindings["hostName"].Value
                = this.HostName;
            this.ParameterBindings["port"].Value
                = this.Port;
            this.ParameterBindings["from"].Value
                = this.From;
            this.ParameterBindings["to"].Value = this.To;
            this.ParameterBindings["subject"].Value
                = this.Subject;
            this.ParameterBindings["body"].Value
                = this.Body;
        }
    }
}
```

At this point, we know how to create an activity for sending emails. Let's now review how to create an activity for receiving emails (see listing 10.6).

Listing 10.6   Source code for the `MailReceived` activity

```
namespace TeamBuild.SmtpMailServices
{
using System;
using System.ComponentModel;
using System.Workflow.Activities;
using System.Workflow.ComponentModel;
using System.Workflow.ComponentModel.Design;
using System.Workflow.ComponentModel.Compiler;

[ToolboxItemAttribute(typeof(ActivityToolboxItem))]
public partial class MailReceived : HandleExternalEventActivity
{
```

```csharp
public static DependencyProperty SenderProperty =
   DependencyProperty.Register(
   "Sender", typeof(object), typeof(MailReceived));

public static DependencyProperty EProperty =
   DependencyProperty.Register("E", typeof(
   TeamBuild.SmtpMailServices.SmtpMailEventArgs),
   typeof(MailReceived));

public MailReceived()
{
   base.InterfaceType =
      typeof(TeamBuild.SmtpMailServices.ISmtpMailService);
   base.EventName = "MailReceived";
}

[BrowsableAttribute(false)]
[DesignerSerializationVisibilityAttribute(
   DesignerSerializationVisibility.Hidden)]
public override System.Type InterfaceType
{
   get
   {
      return base.InterfaceType;
   }
   set
   {
      throw new InvalidOperationException(
         @"Cannot set InterfaceType on a derived
         HandleExternalEventActivity.");
   }
}

[BrowsableAttribute(false)]
[DesignerSerializationVisibilityAttribute(
   DesignerSerializationVisibility.Hidden)]
public override string EventName
{
   get
   {
      return base.EventName;
   }
   set
   {
      throw new InvalidOperationException(
         @"Cannot set EventName on a derived
         HandleExternalEventActivity.");
   }
}
[ValidationOptionAttribute(ValidationOption.Required)]
public object Sender
{
   get
   {
      return ((object)(this.GetValue(
         MailReceived.SenderProperty)));
   }
   set
```

```
      {
         this.SetValue(MailReceived.SenderProperty, value);
      }
   }

   [ValidationOptionAttribute(ValidationOption.Required)]
   public TeamBuild.SmtpMailServices.SmtpMailEventArgs E
   {
      get
      {
         return (
            (TeamBuild.SmtpMailServices.SmtpMailEventArgs)
            (this.GetValue(MailReceived.EProperty)));
      }
      set
      {
         this.SetValue(MailReceived.EProperty, value);
      }
   }

   protected override void OnInvoked(System.EventArgs e)
   {
      this.Sender = this.ParameterBindings["sender"].Value;
      this.E = ((
         TeamBuild.SmtpMailServices.SmtpMailEventArgs)(e));
   }
}
}
```

The `SendMail` and `MailReceived` custom activities interact with a class named `Smtp-MailServices` via the `ISmtpMailService` interface. The `SmtpMailServices` class contains the implementation code to send emails and respond to incoming emails. The source code for the class is shown in listings 10.7 and 10.8.

Note that the `SendMail` method uses the `SmtpClient` class to send outgoing emails. After sending an email, the `SendMail` method sets up a callback method named `pRaiseMailReceivedEvent`. This method inspects a Microsoft Message Queue (MSMQ) queue to determine whether a correlated message reply has arrived. If it finds a correlated message, indicating a reply to an outgoing email, it raises an event, which is ultimately trapped in the `Listen` activity in the build workflow.

Listing 10.7 Source code for `SmtpMailServices` (private methods omitted)

```
// .. using statements omitted for brevity

namespace TeamBuild.SmtpMailServices
{
   public class SmtpMailService : ISmtpMailService
   {

      #region ISmtpMailService Members

      public event EventHandler<SmtpMailEventArgs> MailReceived;

      public ArrayList sendMessageMarkList = new ArrayList();

      /// <summary>
```

```
/// This method sends the mail message.
/// </summary>
public void SendMail(Guid messageId, string hostName,
    int port, string from, string to,
    string subject, string body)
{
    SmtpClient client = new SmtpClient(hostName);
    client.Port = port;

    MailAddress fromAddr = new MailAddress(from);
    MailAddress toAddr = new MailAddress(to);

    MailMessage message =
        new MailMessage(fromAddr, toAddr);
    message.Body = body;

    // Add some marker data to the mail, which will be
    // used to recognize the corresponding reply mail
    // Add messageId to the subject.
    subject += ": " + "<messageId "
        + messageId.ToString() + " messageId>";
    message.Subject = subject;

    client.Send(message);

    //Create SmtpMailEventArgs parameter DTO object
    //The DTO object will be stored in a list so that
    //when a response comes, it can be correlated with
    //the message that was sent.
    SmtpMailEventArgParameterDTO smtpParameterDTO =
        new SmtpMailEventArgParameterDTO();
    smtpParameterDTO.WorkFlowId
        = WorkflowEnvironment.WorkflowInstanceId;
    smtpParameterDTO.MessageId = messageId;
    smtpParameterDTO.ReplyStatus = ManagerFeedback.Old;

    sendMessageMarkList.Add(smtpParameterDTO);

    if (!messageId.Equals(Guid.Empty))
    {
        pWaitForMailReceivedEvent();
    }
}
#endregion ISmtpMailService Members
```

- **Create SMTP client object and assign to port**
- **Create sender/receiver mail address objects**
- **Create mail message**
- **Send mail message**
- **Store DTO in a list**
- **Wait for response message**

In listing 10.7, we saw the public methods of the SmtpMailServices class (we omitted the private methods for brevity). Listing 10.8 shows the private methods of the SmtpMailServices class.

Listing 10.8 Source code for SmtpMailServices (private methods only)

```
/// <summary>
/// Sets up a message queue and waits for response
/// messages
/// </summary>
private void pWaitForMailReceivedEvent()
{
```

```
      try
      {
         MessageQueue messageQueue = null;

         messageQueue =                                    │ Initialize queue
            new MessageQueue(Constants.MSMQPath);

         if (!MessageQueue.Exists(Constants.MSMQPath))     │ Create queue if
            MessageQueue.Create(Constants.MSMQPath);       │ it doesn't exist

         messageQueue.Formatter =                          │ Define formatter
            new XmlMessageFormatter(                        │ for message
            new Type[] { typeof(MailDTO) });

         messageQueue.ReceiveCompleted +=                  │ Register event handler
            new ReceiveCompletedEventHandler(              │ for ReceiveCompleted
            messageQueue_ReceiveCompleted);

         messageQueue.BeginReceive();      <── Wait for messages to arrive
      }
      catch (Exception ex)
      {
         System.Diagnostics.Trace.Write(ex.Message);
      }
   }

   /// <summary>
   /// Handles the ReceiveCompleted event
   /// </summary>
   void messageQueue_ReceiveCompleted(object sender,
      ReceiveCompletedEventArgs e)
   {

      MessageQueue messageQueue = sender as MessageQueue;
      try
      {                                                     │ Flag for matching
         bool isReplyMatch = false;                   <──── │ reply message

         Message message = messageQueue.EndReceive(         │ Terminate async
            e.AsyncResult);                                 │ message reception

         MailDTO mail = message.Body as MailDTO;       <──   Extract
                                                            │ message
         SmtpMailEventArgParameterDTO mMessage = null;     │

         if (mail != null)
         {
            string mailIdSubject = mail.Subject;

            //correlate the response message with the
            //message that was sent out
            foreach (SmtpMailEventArgParameterDTO
               mailmessage in sendMessageMarkList)
            {
               if (mailIdSubject.Contains(
                  mailmessage.MessageId.ToString()))
               {
                  isReplyMatch = true;

                  EventHandler<SmtpMailEventArgs>
```

```
                    feedbackReceived
                    = this.MailReceived;

                if (feedbackReceived != null)
                {
                    string pmReply                      Retrieve feedback
                       = this.pParseBody(               from mail body
                       mail.Body).ToLower();

                    if (pmReply == "new")
                    {
                        mailmessage.ReplyStatus
                           = ManagerFeedback.New;
                    }

                    SmtpMailEventArgs args
                       = new SmtpMailEventArgs(
                       mailmessage.WorkFlowId,
                       mailmessage.MessageId,
                       mailmessage.ReplyStatus);      Raise message
                                                       received event
                    feedbackReceived(null, args);   ◄─

                }
                mMessage = mailmessage;

            }
        }

    }
    if (isReplyMatch)
    {
        sendMessageMarkList.Remove(mMessage);
    }
    else                                       Start receiving
    {                                          messages again
        messageQueue.BeginReceive();        ◄─
    }
}
catch (Exception ex)
{
    System.Diagnostics.Trace.Write(ex.Message);
    messageQueue.BeginReceive();
}
}
/// <summary>
/// This method parses the mail body
/// to get the PM's feedback.
/// </summary>
private string pParseBody(string mailBody)
{
    string reply = string.Empty;

    try
    {
        Regex regPattern = new Regex(
           "<reply (?<pmReply>[^ >]+) reply>");
        Match match = regPattern.Match(mailBody);
```

```
            if (match.Success)
                reply = match.Groups["pmReply"].Value;
        }
        catch (Exception ex)
        {
        }

        return reply;
    }
  }
}
```

There's one more thing that you need to set up in order to handle incoming emails. As you saw in listing 10.8, the program periodically inspects an MSMQ queue to see if a correlated message has arrived. The question is, how does an incoming email get inserted in the queue in the first place? The answer is that we write a piece of code, which detects the event associated with the arrival of an incoming email and inserts the new email in the MSMQ queue. Listing 10.9 shows the associated code.

Listing 10.9   SMTP event sink that listens to incoming emails

```
using System;
using System.Configuration;
using System.Collections.Generic;
using System.Messaging;
using System.Runtime.InteropServices;
using System.Text;
using System.IO;
using CDO;

using TeamBuild.DTO;

namespace TeamBuild.SmtpMailServiceEventSinks
{
    /// <summary>
    /// This class acts as an event sink for the
    /// SMTP service. It detects incoming emails and
    /// forwards them via messages in a MSMQ queue.
    /// </summary>
    [ComVisible(true)]
    [Guid("3B6D20BD-517F-4af5-BC0A-663A199F3E8D")]
    public class SmtpEventSink : ISMTPOnArrival
    {
        public void OnArrival(CDO.Message Msg,
            ref CdoEventStatus EventStatus)
        {
            // Check if the mail is from PM's address
            if (Msg.From.Contains(Constants.PMMail))
            {
                // Create a MailDTO instance, which
                // will be sent to the MSMQ. This object
                // encapsulates of the mail data.
                MailDTO mailDTO = new MailDTO();
                mailDTO.From = Msg.From;
                mailDTO.To = Msg.To;
```

```
        mailDTO.Subject = Msg.Subject;
        mailDTO.Body = Msg.TextBody;

        MessageQueue queue =                        Create queue
            new MessageQueue(Constants.MSMQPath);

        queue.Send(mailDTO, mailDTO.From);    ◁    Insert mail
    }                                              message
  }                                                into queue
}
}
```

At this point, we've successfully created a SMTP event sink to receive incoming emails. Next we learn how to deploy it in the server.

DEPLOYING THE SMTP EVENT SINK

Refer to http://msdn2.microsoft.com/en-us/library/ms998610.aspx to learn about the steps necessary for deploying the event sink on the production server. In summary, the steps are as follow:

1 Copy the assembly to the production server and register it with the RegAsm utility. Type the following in the command prompt:

```
RegAsm.exe <your_assembly_name> /codebase
```

2 Use the smtpreg.vbs script (which can be found at http://msdn2.microsoft.com/en-us/library/ms528023.aspx) to register the event sink object. Type the following in the command prompt:

```
cscript smtpreg.vbs /add 1 OnArrival <name_of_managed_sink>
<fully_qualified_name_of_exported_COM_object> EHLO
```

Congratulations! We've successfully completed the application for creating a distributed build. It was a long process, involving multiple technologies such as TFS, WF, MSMQ, and IIS, but the robustness of the application will serve us well in the real world.

In the next two sections, we look at two built-in capabilities of WF—persistence and tracking. Using these capabilities, you can make the application more scalable and transparent.

10.6 *Enabling workflow persistence*

One of the advantages of using WF is the framework's ability to remove idle workflows from memory and store them in an external database. (You could of course write a custom persistence service and store the dehydrated workflow in other durable media.) Since our TFS build workflow waits for the project manager's feedback at various points, there's no reason to leave idle workflows in memory, consuming system resources. A further benefit of storing the workflow in a database is fault tolerance. If the host machine crashes, you can retrieve the passivated workflow from the database and continue running it from the last persistence point in another machine.

Storing in-progress workflows in an external database also provides scalability. In a large organization, you may have a build farm—multiple identically configured machines dedicated to building a single or multiple applications. In case of projects practicing continuous integration, having a bank of build machines becomes even more important, since the frequency of builds is much higher. Once a particular build workflow is serialized in a database by a given host, the build machine can move on to process other build requests. If a second build machine becomes free at a later time, it can pick up the persisted workflow from the database and run the workflow from where it was stopped.

TIP   Before you can persist a workflow, you need to create a suitable database structure for storing the workflow instances. Use the WF persistence-related scripts supplied by Microsoft (located in the "%WinDir%\Microsoft.NET\Framework\v3.0\Windows Workflow Foundation\SQL\EN" folder). Execute the scripts named SqlPersistence-Service_Schema.sql and SqlPersistence-Service_ Logic.sql. The table named In-stanceState stores the persisted workflow instances.

WF provides a class named `SqlWorkflowPersistenceService` to manage persistence of workflows in databases (see figure 10.14). The class contains public methods and properties to obtain a list of all persisted workflows, load workflows whose timers have expired, specify how frequently the database should be polled for expired workflows, and so on. The class also contains several protected methods that are invoked by the workflow runtime. Behind the scenes, the `SqlWorkflowPersistenceService` class calls a stored procedure named `InsertInstanceState` to serialize the workflow. Persisted workflows are deleted when the workflow completes or is aborted.

One of the constructors of the `SqlWorkflowPersistenceService` class allows you to specify whether the workflow should be automatically unloaded when it becomes idle:

Figure 10.14 `SqlWorkflowPersistenceService` **provides built-in support for serializing in-progress workflows in a SQL Server database.**

```
public SqlWorkflowPersistenceService(string connectionString, bool
    unloadOnIdle, System.TimeSpan instanceOwnershipDuration,
System.TimeSpan loadingInterval)
```

The following parameters are available in the constructor:

- `connectionString`—Connection string for accessing the persistence database.
- `unloadOnIdle`—If set to `true`, the workflow is automatically persisted when it enters an idle state (such as a `Delay` or `HandleExternalEvent` activity). If set to `false`, you can unload the workflow using the `Unload` method of the `System.Workflow.Runtime.WorkflowInstance` class.

- instanceOwnershipDuration—Indicates how long the ownership lock will be maintained once the workflow is loaded in memory. When a workflow is persisted in the database, it's unlocked. Any host can load and execute the workflow at this point. Once the workflow is loaded into memory, it's placed in a locked state in the database to prevent multiple execution of the same workflow instance. But at the end of the period specified by the instanceOwnership-Duration parameter, the workflow instance is unlocked and can be loaded by other hosts. This parameter doesn't need to be specified if the persistence database is associated with a single workflow runtime. Use another constructor for SqlWorkflowPersistence Service if you have a single workflow runtime.

- loadingInterval—Indicates how frequently the database is polled for workflow instances with expired timers. The SQLWorkflowPersistenceService class uses a stored procedure named RetrieveExpired-TimerIds to fetch the expired workflow instances. It's important to keep in mind that this parameter value affects workflow instances with expired timers only (for example, a persisted workflow instance that's idling in a Delay activity). Also keep in mind that incoming message deliveries aren't affected if a workflow is persisted. For example, if a workflow is persisted when idling in a Listen activity, the workflow is immediately loaded in memory when a message arrives, regardless of the value specified in the loadingInterval parameter.

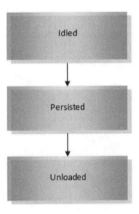

Figure 10.15 Events raised by the SqlWorkflow-PersistenceService class when persisting a workflow

The modified host application for enabling persistence is shown in listing 10.10. The events fired by the SQLWorkflowPersistenceService class during workflow persistence are shown the figure 10.15.

Listing 10.10 Modified host application for persisting idle build workflows

```
using System;
using System.Collections.Generic;
using System.Text;
using System.Threading;
using System.Workflow.Runtime;
using System.Workflow.Runtime.Hosting;

namespace HostingWorkflowRuntime
{
    class Program
    {
        static string connectionString = "Initial
            Catalog=TrackingStore;" +
            "Data Source=localhost; Integrated Security=SSPI;";

        static void Main(string[] args)
```

```
{
    using(WorkflowRuntime workflowRuntime = new
        WorkflowRuntime())
    {

        //add service to persist workflow in DB
        workflowRuntime.AddService(new
        SharedConnectionWorkflowCommitWorkBatchService(
        connectionString));
        workflowRuntime.AddService(new
            SqlWorkflowPersistenceService(
            connectionString, true, TimeSpan.FromSeconds(10
            ), TimeSpan.FromSeconds(10
            )));

        AutoResetEvent waitHandle
            = new AutoResetEvent(false);
        workflowRuntime.WorkflowCompleted += delegate(
            object sender,
            WorkflowCompletedEventArgs e)
            {waitHandle.Set();};
        workflowRuntime.WorkflowTerminated += delegate(
            object sender,
            WorkflowTerminatedEventArgs e)
        {
            Console.WriteLine(e.Exception.Message);
            waitHandle.Set();
        };

        workflowRuntime.WorkflowLoaded += new
            EventHandler<WorkflowEventArgs>
            (workflowRuntime_WorkflowLoaded);
        workflowRuntime.WorkflowIdled += new
            EventHandler<WorkflowEventArgs>
            (workflowRuntime_WorkflowIdled);
        workflowRuntime.WorkflowPersisted += new
            EventHandler<WorkflowEventArgs>
            (workflowRuntime_WorkflowPersisted);
            workflowRuntime.WorkflowUnloaded += new
            EventHandler<WorkflowEventArgs>
            (workflowRuntime_WorkflowUnloaded);

        WorkflowInstance instance =
            workflowRuntime.CreateWorkflow(
            typeof(
            HostingWorkflowRuntime.SimpleWorkflow));

        instance.Start();

        waitHandle.WaitOne();

        Console.WriteLine(
            @"Workflow Completed -
            press ENTER to continue");
```

```
            Console.Read();
        }
    }

    static void workflowRuntime_WorkflowIdled(object sender,
        WorkflowEventArgs e)
    {
        Console.WriteLine("Workflow {0} idled",
            e.WorkflowInstance.InstanceId);
        ThreadPool.QueueUserWorkItem(pUnloadInstance,
            e.WorkflowInstance);
    }
    static void workflowRuntime_WorkflowUnloaded(
        object sender, WorkflowEventArgs e)
    {
        Console.WriteLine("Workflow {0} unloaded",
            e.WorkflowInstance.InstanceId);
    }
    static void workflowRuntime_WorkflowPersisted(
        object sender, WorkflowEventArgs e)
    {
        Console.WriteLine("Workflow {0} persisted",
            e.WorkflowInstance.InstanceId);
    }
    static void workflowRuntime_WorkflowLoaded(
        object sender, WorkflowEventArgs e)
    {
        Console.WriteLine("Workflow {0} loaded",
            e.WorkflowInstance.InstanceId);
    }

    static void pUnloadInstance(object workflowInstance)
    {
        WorkflowInstance instance =
            (WorkflowInstance)workflowInstance;

        try
        {
            Console.WriteLine(@"UnloadInstance:
            attempting to unload \'{0}\'",
            instance.InstanceId);
            instance.Unload();
        }
        catch (Exception ex)
        {
            Console.WriteLine(@"UnloadInstance:
                failed \r\n{0}", ex);
        }
    }
  }
}
```

10.7   *Enabling workflow tracking*

Transparency of execution is a key to success when executing any complex process. When executing a long-running workflow process, you need to know which steps have been completed and what's going on currently. Instead of requiring developers to write custom instrumentation code, WF provides an out-of-the-box service for recording workflow, activity, and user events in a SQL Server database. The `SqlTrackingService` class provides the tracking functionality (see figure 10.16). We leverage this capability to gain visibility into the current state of the build process. We can see which build steps have been completed and which step is being executed currently. Both ASP.NET as well as Windows Forms applications can be used to display the tracking information.

Figure 10.16   The `SqlTrackingService` class provides out-of-the-box capability to store events in a SQL Server database.

TIP   When using both `SqlWorkflowPersistenceService` and `SqlTracking-Service` services (as we do in our build application example), use the same database for performance reasons. Also, add the `SharedConnectionWork-flowCommitWorkBatchService` service to avoid the overhead associated with multiple database connections and Distributed Transaction Coordinator (DTC) transactions.

Adding tracking capability to a workflow application is simple. Add the `SQLTracking-Service` class to the workflow runtime as follows:

```
workflowRuntime.AddService(new SqlTrackingService(connectionString));
```

The constructor for the class takes a connection string pointing to the tracking database. The events that get recorded in the database are specified using a `Tracking-Profile` class. Listing 10.11 shows a representative tracking profile serialized to an XML file.

TIP   To create the necessary database structure for tracking WF events, execute the tracking-related scripts supplied by Microsoft (located in the %WinDir%\Microsoft.NET\Framework\v3.0\Windows Workflow Foundation\SQL\EN folder). Execute the scripts named Tracking_Schema.sql and Tracking_Logic.sql.

Listing 10.11   A representative tracking profile showing the logged events

```
<?xml version="1.0" encoding="utf-16" standalone="yes"?>
<TrackingProfile xmlns="http://www.microsoft.com/
   WFTrackingProfile" version="3.0.0">
```

```
<TrackPoints>
 <WorkflowTrackPoint>
  <MatchingLocation>
   <WorkflowTrackingLocation>
    <TrackingWorkflowEvents>
     <TrackingWorkflowEvent>
      Created
     </TrackingWorkflowEvent>
     <TrackingWorkflowEvent>
      Completed
     </TrackingWorkflowEvent>
     <TrackingWorkflowEvent>
      Idle
     </TrackingWorkflowEvent>
     <TrackingWorkflowEvent>
      Suspended
     </TrackingWorkflowEvent>
     <TrackingWorkflowEvent>
      Resumed
     </TrackingWorkflowEvent>
     <TrackingWorkflowEvent>
      Persisted
     </TrackingWorkflowEvent>
     <TrackingWorkflowEvent>
      Unloaded
     </TrackingWorkflowEvent>
     <TrackingWorkflowEvent>
      Loaded
     </TrackingWorkflowEvent>
     <TrackingWorkflowEvent>
      Exception
     </TrackingWorkflowEvent>
     <TrackingWorkflowEvent>
      Terminated
     </TrackingWorkflowEvent>
     <TrackingWorkflowEvent>
      Aborted
     </TrackingWorkflowEvent>
     <TrackingWorkflowEvent>
      Changed
     </TrackingWorkflowEvent>
     <TrackingWorkflowEvent>
      Started
     </TrackingWorkflowEvent>
    </TrackingWorkflowEvents>
   </WorkflowTrackingLocation>
  </MatchingLocation>
 </WorkflowTrackPoint>
 <ActivityTrackPoint>
  <MatchingLocations>
   <ActivityTrackingLocation>
    <Activity>
     <Type>System.Workflow.ComponentModel.Activity,
      System.Workflow.ComponentModel, Version=3.0.0.0,
      Culture=neutral, PublicKeyToken=31bf3856ad364e35
     </Type>
```

```
            <MatchDerivedTypes>true</MatchDerivedTypes>
          </Activity>
          <ExecutionStatusEvents>
            <ExecutionStatus>Initialized</ExecutionStatus>
            <ExecutionStatus>Executing</ExecutionStatus>
            <ExecutionStatus>Canceling</ExecutionStatus>
            <ExecutionStatus>Closed</ExecutionStatus>
            <ExecutionStatus>Compensating</ExecutionStatus>
            <ExecutionStatus>Faulting</ExecutionStatus>
          </ExecutionStatusEvents>
        </ActivityTrackingLocation>
      </MatchingLocations>
    </ActivityTrackPoint>
  </TrackPoints>
</TrackingProfile>
```

Once the events are recorded in the database, you can query them using the `SqlTrackingQuery` class (see figure 10.17). Listing 10.12 shows the associated code. Microsoft also provides a sample application that graphically displays the workflow execution status. For more information about the Workflow Monitor application, visit the Microsoft web site at http://msdn2.microsoft.com/en-us/library/ms741706.aspx.

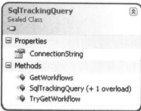

Figure 10.17   The `SqlTrackingQuery` class provides the capability to query recorded events.

Listing 10.12   Code for querying recorded events using `SqlTrackingQuery`

```
static void pGetInstanceTrackingEvents(Guid instanceId)
    {
        Console.WriteLine("\r\nInstance Tracking Events :");
        SqlTrackingQuery sqlTrackingQuery = new
            SqlTrackingQuery(connectionString);
        SqlTrackingWorkflowInstance sqlTrackingWorkflowInstance;
        sqlTrackingQuery.TryGetWorkflow(instanceId, out
            sqlTrackingWorkflowInstance);

        try
        {
            foreach (WorkflowTrackingRecord
              workflowTrackingRecord in
              sqlTrackingWorkflowInstance.WorkflowEvents)
            {
              Console.WriteLine("EventDescription : {0}
                DateTime : {1}",
                workflowTrackingRecord.TrackingWorkflowEvent,
                workflowTrackingRecord.EventDateTime);
            }
        }
        catch (Exception)
        {
            Console.WriteLine("Instance Tracking Events Not Found");
        }
    }
```

TIP You can extend the sample workflow to include activities for deploying the build binaries in test, staging, and production environments. The deployment process requires interactions with multiple parties (such as between testers, project managers, product managers, and release engineers) and is a great candidate for automation using a structured workflow process.

10.8 Summary

In this chapter, we saw how to use workflow technology to better manage document review, code review, and distributed build processes. We saw that the WF engine can be hosted in various applications. We created a custom application to support the build process using workflow technology. We also learned how to use the built-in persistence and tracking capabilities available in WF to provide scalability, fault-tolerance, and transparency.

WF can be used to extend the capabilities of TFS in novel and productive ways. As discussed, TFS has a mini workflow system built into the work item tracking module—one that provides flexible state transition, security, and user assignment capabilities. But when it comes to integrating TFS with external applications or coordinating cross-TFS activities, you'll find WF to be a valuable tool. WF helps you manage long-running collaborative tasks between team members, as well as interactions with external systems (such as third-party version control, issue tracking, and project management systems). WF also empowers you to orchestrate self-managing rule-based processes that span machine, network, and organizational boundaries—a need that you're likely to face as you manage an increasingly global workforce.

This concludes our discussion of using workflow with TFS and brings us to the end of the book. It's been a long journey. We've seen how to effectively use TFS to solve real-life problems typically encountered in development organizations. We've learned to extend TFS when out-of-the-box features aren't adequate.

We all know that enterprise software development isn't easy. The best of teams struggle with scope, schedule, quality, communications, bureaucracy, and so on. Collectively, as software professionals, we're still learning how best to cope with changing technologies, shifting geographies, and evolving priorities. No matter how you choose to deal with your unique set of challenges, I believe that effective use of TFS can help bridge the gap between your aspirations and reality. TFS works.

index